From Dogma to History

From Dogma to History

*How our understanding of the
early Church developed*

William H. C. Frend

scm press

British Library Cataloguing in Publication data

A catalogue record for this book is available
from the British Library

0 334 02908 2

First published in 2003 by SCM Press
9–17 St Albans Place, London N1 0NX

www.scm-canterburypress.co.uk

SCM Press is a division of
SCM-Canterbury Press Ltd

Printed and bound in Great Britain by
Biddles Ltd, Guildford and King's Lynn

Contents

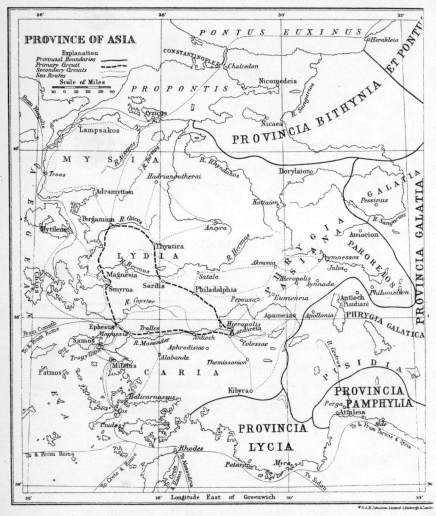

Graeco-Roman Asia Minor as known by Ramsay, 1900,

from *The Letters to the Seven Churches of Asia*
(Hodder and Stoughton, 1909)

Abbreviations

To my wife
(1927–2002)

Introduction

This is a book about six scholars whose work collectively transformed the study of the early Church from the history of the development of doctrinal orthodoxy to the history of Christianity in all its many forms and ideals during the first six centuries AD. Theirs was a movement 'from dogma to history', to reverse an aphorism attributed to Cardinal Manning, to the effect that 'history must give way to doctrine'.

My work on the early Church has been decisively influenced by these scholars. I have attempted to build on their foundations, to integrate the study of the mission and thought of the early Christian churches into the social and political movements of the day, and to add archaeological evidence to that derived from literary sources. It corresponds to my earliest experiences, leading to a love of late-Roman archaeology, prompted by the gift of some Roman pottery by the guardian of the Roman villa at Bignor at the end of a childhood visit.

I have taken Adolf von Harnack (1851–1930) as the founder of a then new approach to early Church history. He was a scholar who cut through some of the niceties of Lutheran ecclesiastical law to a faith based on a minimum of credal statement and an acceptance, as he put it, of the fatherhood of God and the brotherhood of man revealed in the New Testament. He was among the first to study the early Church, principally the Church in the first three centuries, on a foundation of an acute and accurate study of manuscript traditions. He was also a public figure, the Director of the Kaiser Wilhelm Library, Rector of the Humboldt University and a trusted adviser of the Kaiser. He believed that a scholar should also be a 'doer' in the service of his country.

Von Harnack was not an archaeologist, and, indeed, made mistakes in handling archaeological evidence. A combination of these studies still had to await Hans Lietzmann, Harnack's student and successor as Professor of Church History at Berlin, whose seminar I attended in 1937–8. Lietzmann introduced me to the comparative study of Christian dissenting movements, Montanism and Donatism, both biblically inspired and drawing their main strength from a single province. At the end of my stay he provided me with an introduction to Louis Poinssot, Inspector-General of Antiquities in Tunisia. Leaving Berlin on 15 March 1938 immediately after the *Anschluss*, I was to help him in classifying early Christian inscriptions in Tunisia.

Poinssot introduced me to the wealth of discoveries already made and waiting to be made in Tunisia. After a month in his office he gave me a letter to André Berthier, a scholar trained in the École des Chartes and the energetic curator of the Musée Gustave Mercier in Constantine (Algeria). I could not have come at a better time. Berthier was working with his friend, Maurice Martin, *propriétaire* of a farm at Châteaudun du Rummel, and Fernand Logeart, the Administrator of the Commune Mixte of Ain M'lila on a project aimed at surveying and carrying out excavations on a large number of Roman–Berber sites in central Algeria north of the Aurès mountains. Churches and chapels along with olive presses and granaries were the principal remains to be investigated. From my reading of Optatus of Milevis' work against the Donatists and Augustine's anti-Donatist books it was clear that a number of the sites were likely to have Donatist remains. And so it turned out. Southern Numidia was revealed as an area packed with villages in which there could be up to half a dozen chapels each with their martyr's reliquary. A few inscriptions carrying the Donatist watchword 'Deo laudes' or commemorating the deaths of martyrs completed the picture.[1] It was a gift for my Oxford thesis on 'The Donatist Church down to AD 430'.

In addition, I was enabled in June 1939 to carry out excavations for the museum at the site of Kherbet Bahrarous, 12 miles south of Saint Arnaud, a rare privilege for an Englishman.[2] With my team of Berber workmen – outstandingly loyal – I gained the impression that all was set fair for continued French rule in Algeria. The independence movement under Ferhat Abbas was almost negligible. Nationalist aspirations were better represented by Ben Djelloul, who aimed at widening the scope of French citizenship and gaining more control for the Commissions Financières, advisory bodies for regulating the economies and local taxation in the three *départements* into which Algeria was divided. I often think that had the Projet Violette prepared under the Blum government in 1937 been carried out there would have been a good chance for France to have forged a viable association with Algeria, which would have enabled the settlers to retain their properties.

Berthier and his colleagues were building on the work of Stéphane Gsell (d. 1932), and were the heirs to the latter's archaeological surveys of the same area carried out in 1893–4. When I was working in the public library in Tunis in the spring of 1938, the librarian, M. Esquer, presented me with a sheaf of notes, mainly references to Tertullian's works, that had formed part of Gsell's *Nachlass* (literary remains), evidence that he had intended to continue his eight-volume *Histoire ancienne de l'Afrique du Nord* into the Christian period. They were given to me as though I should carry on Gsell's work, and Gsell not surprisingly forms the third chapter of this book. Together, these scholars provided evidence for the reality of a social and economic background for the church that opposed Augustine and the African Catholic Church. The Donatist Church was, in fact, the majority church in North Africa throughout most of the fourth century.

Sir William Ramsay's pioneer work in Asia Minor, particularly Phrygia, had much in common with Gsell's activities in Algeria. Both established archaeological maps of inland areas removed from the Classical influences of the coastal towns. Both found themselves involved in plotting the development of different types of Christian mission, in North Africa, the Donatists, in Asia Minor, the Montanists and Novatians. Both were Classicists who

applied historical standards to the evidence without clerical fear or
favour. In Ramsay's case this was particularly apparent in his
handling of the inscription from Kalendres (Hieropolis) commemorating the merchant-bishop Avircius, dating to *c.*190.
Against sceptical German critics (including Harnack) he defended
the Christian character of the memorial as the earliest undoubted
Christian inscription. Though a firm Presbyterian, in 1888 he
presented the surviving fragments to the Lateran Museum. His
New Testament studies, not least of St Paul's stay in Ephesus, also
based on research on the ground, remain valuable today.

His approach had a strong influence on my research. In 1951, I
had been elected to the S. A. Cook Bye Fellowship in religious
studies for two years at Gonville and Caius College, Cambridge, to
start in October 1952. *The Donatist Church* was now published and
had been well received, so that in 1953 I was elected to an Assistant
Lectureship in the Divinity Faculty. In lieu of a second year on the
Bye Fellowship I was offered travel expenses for a period of overseas
travel, and in that year I chose to follow Ramsay's footsteps in Asia
Minor. The British School at Ankara, Ramsay's lasting legacy,
provided me with a plan for using my time to best advantage. At
Afyon a stumble over what proved to be a Graeco-Roman funerary
inscription in the bus station led to my identification of a valuable
third-century inscription in the museum. Together, the curator
and I worked through some 40 lines of mixed Latin and Greek,
recording a lawsuit by peasants from two villages before the
procurator, Threptus, in 236. The quarrel concerned respective
responsibilities for the upkeep of a road in the immediate neigh-
bourhood. Peasants had brought in the stone from Sulmenli
(ancient Soa) where it had remained untouched until my arrival.[3]
Travelling via Konia (Iconium) I was able to spend two days on the
Maden Shehir, the site of the Thousand and One Churches,
explored by Ramsay and Gertrude Bell in 1907. On the way up to
the plateau in which the ruins, still visible, stood, I found a rock
carving and altar dedicated to Gaia, the Phrygian Greek goddess of
earth and hence of agriculture.[4] The great man had left something
for his successors to find.

Mgr Louis Duchesne was an altogether different character. He was a Breton, the son of firm but liberally-minded Catholic parents and was educated in the Catholic school near his native parish of Saint-Servan. His irrevocable decision to enter the priesthood in 1867 meant that his life, after a short period of Infallibilist enthusiasm at the time of the First Vatican Council in 1870, would be a prey to stress. He was to find it increasingly difficult to reconcile his instinct as a historian of Christian antiquity with his calling as a priest. While his personal piety survived he became more and more critical of the Church's senior hierarchy, including successive popes, Leo XIII (1878–1903) and Pius X (1903–14). There is little doubt that the Italian translation of volume 2 of the *Early History of the Church* would have been received with less hostility if Duchesne had not been branded as 'the father of Modernism' and even as a 'heretic'. As it was, all three volumes were placed on the Index in 1912, and the fourth, covering the sixth century, was never completed. He was protected from a worse fate at the hands of the Church through being Director of the École française de Rome and an Academician, but despite his great scholarship he died a sad and disappointed man. More recently his reputation in his own country has been restored by the efforts of members at the École française de Rome. There have been a full-length, if at times uncritical, biography by Brigitte Wache, 757 pages in all, a series of essays by specialists in various aspects of his life and work, and a full edition of his voluminous correspondence with J. B. de Rossi, 594 letters written between 1874 and 1891 With these studies a historian has the means of arriving at a more balanced estimate of him. What I owe to him personally is the scrupulous method of study which resulted in the *Early History of the Church* and his ever fair-minded balance between history and the development of doctrine leading up to the Council of Chalcedon.

His *Early History of the Church* shared with B. J. Kidd's three-volume *History of the Church to A.D. 461* and Wolff's (inadequate) translation of Lietzmann's *History of the Church* the main source of teaching in my early years in the Faculty of Divinity. They formed a well-balanced group. Kidd's somewhat didactic style covered a wealth of learning drawn from an immense knowledge of the Fathers, to guide one's students and oneself through the details of the development of Christian orthodoxy. With Duchesne, though the heretics might eventually get short shrift, their case was presented fairly, and the defects of the orthodox, including popes, such as Liberius (352–66), exposed. With Lietzmann, Duchesne was an exponent of church history as history without transcendent, providential overtones, an approach from which I have never sought to deviate.

Norman Baynes shared the supervision of my D.Phil. thesis with Hugh Last, Camden Professor of Ancient History at Balliol College, Oxford. Last was a scholar of the highest calibre and among other achievements a notable epigraphist. Baynes was a Byzantinist of magisterial standing, and he was also a confidant and friend.

It is not easy today to recall the fraught days of the Phoney War (1939–40). All one can say is that for anyone attempting to complete a thesis in a limited time they were difficult and discouraging. As a volunteer on the Cadet Reserve I was called up on 12 September 1939 only to be confronted by letters from Baynes and Last requesting I be stood down in order to complete a thesis on which two years' work had been spent. As 'there were already more than enough junior officers' drawn from the Reserve this request was granted. I returned to Oxford to get down to the task of writing up and illustrating the work I had done in Berlin, North Africa and Paris since my election to the Craven Fellowship in 1937.

The ensuing six months were depressing, especially February– March 1940, when we seemed to be intending to take on the Soviets as well as Germany in a defence of the Finns (who joined Germany soon after the latter invaded Russia in 1941!). Moreover, as one who had seen something of the tactics and results of German propaganda in 1938, I felt that our case was not being put effectively. There was too little positive statement of war aims or how we conceived post-Hitler Europe.[5] It was a trying time.

Baynes kept in touch, encouraging me to keep at my task. I did. I finished on time; passed a viva with the skin of my teeth and took my degree on the day Paris fell, 14 June 1940.

After the war, Baynes was a strong influence in hauling me back to my original subject of the early Church. During my two stays in Germany I had become fluent in German, and this had stood me in good stead during the war. When a job I was offered by the British Council as Professor of English Life and Letters at Salonica University broke down because of revolutionary conditions in Salonica (December 1946), I joined the three-nation (England, France, USA) Editorial Board, editing the captured German Foreign Ministry documents. Later in 1949, a difficulty arose between the Foreign Office Librarian E. J. Passant and myself. Baynes persuaded me not to resign, but to accept the offer of a move to Whaddon Hall where the main work of selecting documents for publication took place. Selection, however, had run far ahead of publication – one of the probable causes of the disagreement with the librarian – and considerable free time, combined with pleasant surroundings, enabled me to write up my thesis as the book, *The Donatist Church: A Movement of Protest in Roman North Africa*. It was published by the Oxford University Press in 1952. Even so, it was not easy to abandon German historical studies, and only after failure to achieve a university post in that field and renewed persuasion from both Last and Baynes did I return to the early Church. A year at Nottingham University (1951–2) was succeeded by the S. A. Cook Bye Fellowship at Caius (1952–4) and entry on an academic career in that field.

Why do I stop with my last contact with Norman Baynes in 1955? It is that thereafter I was on my own, to pursue the career which great scholars of the previous generation had inspired. There are others I could have included, such as Paul Monceaux the 'Africanist' and Christian scholar who gave me of his time when I was in Paris in 1938 and 1939,[6] or Ernesto Buonaiuti, friend of Duchesne and writer of one of the best books on Christianity in Roman Africa, or William Calder, Ramsay's successor in the field of archaeology in Asia Minor. To all these I am grateful. But from

1955 it was up to me to build on the foundations already laid. Last
had suggested to me a new subject, the persecutions of the early
Church in the Roman empire, a subject that combined Classical
and Ecclesiastical studies. *Martyrdom and Persecution in the Early
Church* was published in 1965. Beyond that it is for others to judge
whether or not I have been a faithful steward.

W. H. C. Frend,
Gonville and Caius College, Cambridge
November 2002

I

Adolf von Harnack (1851–1930)*

As in every other branch of learning, the study of the early history of Christianity has undergone massive changes during the last century. This has been due not only to the vast accumulation of knowledge through new discoveries, but to new approaches to the subject, together with the rise of archaeology as a principal factor in providing fresh information. The study of the early Church has as a result moved steadily from dogma to history, from attempts to interpret divine revelation through the development of doctrinal orthodoxy down the ages, to research into the historical development of an earthly institution of great complexity and of great significance in the history of mankind over the past two thousand years.

Many scholars have shared in this process. One need only mention Hans Lietzmann and Hans von Campenhausen, Paul Monceaux, Stéphane Gsell and Henri-Irenée Marrou, William Ramsay and William Calder, to name a few of those who have done most to forge a new understanding of the early history of the Church. But one name stands out, that of Adolf von Harnack. Without his genius allied to intense application to study, coupled with administrative ability and an unbreakable conviction of the value of his subject as a historical study, the labours of his younger contemporaries and successors would have been harder. They would have lacked the example of the master and the firm foundation he had laid for the construction of a historian's view of early Christianity.

By any measure von Harnack (he was ennobled by the Kaiser in March 1914) is one of the 'greats' of European historical scholar-

*Chapter 1 reprinted from the *Journal of Eccesiastical History*, vol. 52.1., is acknowledged with thanks to the Cambridge University Press.

ship.[1] The 1611 entries in Friedrich Smend's bibliography of
Harnack's work,[2] include, among countless articles and scholarly
reviews and addresses, works of permanent importance, such as
the three-volume *Lehrbuch der Dogmengeschichte*,[3] the *Geschichte
der altchristlichen Literatur bis Eusebius*, the *Mission und Ausbreitung
des Christentums in der ersten drei Jarhunderten*, the monograph on
Marcion and the enormously influential *Das Wesen des Christentums* which went through 15 editions between 1901 and 1950.[4]
And all the time, Harnack was becoming a public figure. In 1903
he became president of the Evangelical-Social Congress, a tribute
to his blend of Lutheran conservatism and quest for social justice
for the less fortunate. In May 1906 he became director-general
of the Royal Library and, in 1911, president of the emperor's
Royal Institute of Sciences designed to encompass all major fields
of national, academic and economic life. After the war he was
offered, but refused, appointment as ambassador in Washington
(1921). He died at Heidelberg after a short illness on 10 June 1930
while attending a conference of the Kaiser Wilhelm Institute of
Sciences.[5]

Adolf Harnack was born in the Baltic German university town
of Dorpat (now Tartu in Estonia) on 7 May 1851. His father,
Theodosius Harnack, was Professor of Homiletics and Historical
Theology, returning thither from Erlangen where he had held a
similar chair between 1856 and 1866. He was a firm Lutheran with
Pietistic leanings (which his son never shared),[6] and his wife
similarly. Though his mother died at Erlangen in November 1858,
when Harnack was only seven, her memory had an abiding
influence on him, and as late as 1902 he dedicated his *Mission und
Ausbreitung* to her. While Harnack's twin, Axel, and two younger
brothers were all to flourish in the professions, he made up his
mind before he entered Dorpat University in 1869 that he wished
to be a theologian. In an enthusiastic letter to a friend from
Erlangen he wrote:

You will have heard that I am going to study theology. I do not
know whether you are one of those who look down on every-

thing called religion and theology with disdain or indifference. And yet, no matter how one looks at Christianity, and possibly regards it as a mistake, is it not of real value to pursue the history of this mistake and discover which world-shaking events and transformations this mistake had caused? . . . The longer I live . . . the more I discover daily that all problems and conflicts finally go back to the religious dimension . . . and why the Christian point of view can never quite be discarded. That is why I am an enthusiastic theologian.[7]

But a theologian with a difference, for Harnack was to be first and foremost a historian trained in the discipline of classical philology. Natural and philosophical theology would leave him cold, but Church history he valued as part of the integral study of mankind.

His time at Dorpat from 1869 to 1872 gained him a gold medal for a study of Marcion, his first essay, like his last major work, devoted to the second-century non-orthodox follower of Paul. In 1872 he left Dorpat for the Lutheran university of Leipzig, equipped by his teacher Moritz von Engelhardt (d. 1881) with a knowledge of rigorous source criticism as the foundation of the scholarly study of early Church history. Engelhardt was to be a permanent influence, despite his early death, pointing to the universality of Christianity and its ability to make the ethical ideals of the non-Christian world its own. For Harnack also, Christianity was the religion of mankind. For the moment, however, Gnosticism and its problems attracted him, and his first major work, his dissertation, was entitled 'Source Criticism and the History of Gnosticism'. The seven years he spent at Leipzig, climbing steadily from the positions of research student, *Privat-dozent*, to professor extraordinary, were his formative years. The period from 1872 to 1875 was a time of enormously hard work, when Harnack accumulated that knowledge of the Greek and Latin Fathers for which he was to be celebrated. He had more than a photographic memory, being able to recall and repeat a page of Greek text after a first reading. Rigorous daily organisation of his work enabled him to write first his doctoral thesis (in five months in 1874) on source criticism and the history of Gnosticism and then his Latin *Habilitationschrift*, again on a Gnostic theme, 'The Monarchianism of the Gnostic Apelles'. At his viva he asserted (in opposition to Strauss and Renan) that it was not possible to write 'The Life of Jesus' and that 'the only approach to Scripture was the grammatical-historical one'.[8] In the autumn of 1875 he began his university teaching career which was to last until 1921, when at the age of 70 he retired from his chair at the Humboldt University in Berlin.

The study of Church history was in the doldrums. Harnack's tutor, Engelhardt, remained at Dorpat. In Germany itself the Tübingen School and F. C. Baur (d. 1860) still brought back memories, and Harnack regarded himself as their descendant, but the name of Albrecht Ritschl (1822–89) almost alone represented the historical approach to the subject. Harnack met Ritschl at Göttingen in 1877 and was profoundly influenced by him,[9] not least in the arrangement and outlook of his first *magnum opus*, the *Lehrbuch der Dogmengeschichte*.

Meantime, the years 1875–9 were to be intensely busy and exacting. In 1876 he collaborated with a fellow Balt, Oskar von Gebhardt, and the historian of Judaism, Emil Schürer, in founding the *Theologische Literaturzeitung*, a vehicle to this day for scholarly Lutheran theology.[10] But through these years he was concentrating on an edition of the Apostolic Fathers, journeying to Paris and Italy to compare texts and with Gebhardt discovering in a monastery in Calabria the Codex Rossanensis, a fifth-century miniature manuscript of the Gospels of Matthew and Mark.[11] The results of his labours drew the praise of J. B. Lightfoot who sent him a copy of his own work on the Apostolic Fathers, and began thus a long-standing if intermittent contact between Harnack and British Church historians.[12]

His own ideas were maturing. The lengthy correspondence of these years shows him asking himself how he could become a disciple of Christ; what could a historian learn about his life? Was it necessary to believe the classical formulations of the doctrines of the Logos, the Trinity and every statement in the Creeds? Was

Christ really pre-existent? Christianity should not inflict new riddles on us. Christ who 'knew the Father' (cf. Matthew 11.27) had revealed him to his followers in clarity and simplicity. That was worthy of 'the highest belief'. There was no need for mystery.[13]

Meanwhile, his career at Leipzig prospered. His lectures were being hailed as heralding a new age. One student, Martin Rade, later Professor of Theology at Marburg, wrote home, 'When people such as Harnack give themselves to our subject, the outlook for theology cannot be so bad.'[14] Others commented on his 'completely new way of teaching Church history'.[15] His reward was to be promoted professor extraordinary, and offered a chair at Breslau university (1876) which he turned down, wanting to work in a Prussian state university. But first there was a call from Giessen in Hesse. A student petition to the minister of education of Saxony that Harnack should be retained at Leipzig failed, the minister replying with the time-honoured excuse that there was no money to pay him.[16] So, with 90 contributions already to his credit in five years of energetic work, Harnack left to take up his first chair in October 1879.

Giessen (1879–86) was an important step in other than academic ways.[17] In December 1879 Harnack married Amalie Thiersch. Amalie was a Catholic, but soon adapted herself to her husband's religious and social outlook; in 1929 they celebrated their Golden Wedding. The marriage was not spared its unhappiness, for in 1888 their son was diagnosed as blind and retarded mentally; he was to live on in an institution until 1921. The same year, Harnack's twin brother Axel died and the Technische Hochschule at Dresden was deprived of a brilliant professor. In these years too, Harnack gradually became estranged from his father, who deplored his son's doubts concerning the pre-existence of Christ (God would not have manifested himself to the Jews alone, Harnack had argued) and the orthodoxy of his views on Christ's Person. 'When Christ told his disciples that "they knew him" [John 14.7] he did not mean that they recognised him in Two Natures.' Theodosius Harnack was appalled, reproaching his son for 'trendiness' and 'modernism'. He should listen to the teaching of the Church instead of his own vanity. The older man felt impelled to write because of what he believed was 'the dechristianisation of the masses', a situation that could only be made worse by his son's teaching, and when in 1889 he died the breach had not been fully healed.[18]

Meantime, Harnack had been characteristically active. He found 15 students in the theological faculty. When he left for Marburg in July 1886, hundreds had attended his lectures between 1881 and 1883 on 'Monasticism: Its Ideals and Its History', and on 'Martin Luther and His Importance for the History of Science and Culture', as well as his own courses on early Christian history. He was able to stamp his outlook on the *Theologische Literaturzeitung,* with its emphasis on historical theological scholarship. His main achievement in these years lay in two directions. First, in 1882, he founded, again with Oskar von Gebhardt, the *Texte und Untersuchungen zur Geschichte der altchristlichen Literatur.* This series of studies that has lasted until the present day enabled scholars to examine patristic texts in depth and arrive at conclusions about their significance, and if possible their authorship. It also provided young scholars, such as the papyrologist Carl Schmidt, with the opportunity to write at length on their subject of research. The first volume, published in 1882, was mainly devoted to articles by Harnack on the manuscript traditions of the writings of the Greek Apologists and the publication by Gebhardt of the Codex Rossanensis; the second, published in 1883, included a discussion of the text of the anti-Manichaean *Acta Archelai,* and an alleged *Commentary on the Gospels* by Theophilus of Antioch. In 1892 Carl Schmidt published what proved to be the *editio princeps of* the Gnostic *Pistis Sophia* and the *Book of Jeu* from the Codex Brucianus. It covered 692 pages and effectively superseded Amélineau's considerable study of the same work published the previous year.[19] The same massive issue of *Texte und Untersuchungen* also contained a textual examination of the Catholic Epistles by Bernhard Weiss, contributions by Harnack on the Greek translation of Tertullian's *Apologeticus* and an essay on what could be ascertained concerning medical knowledge from early Christian texts. Reference to injuries to martyrs provided Harnack with a platform on which to mount a biting attack on religious intolerance 'throwing mankind back to the lowest cultural level and allowing the dark shadows of the abyss long conquered to reemerge'.[20] All in all the *Texte* series was a great achievement. It proved an inspiration to German patristic scholars, laying the foundation for a continuous flow of rigorous studies of texts as well as an entry into the labyrinth of anonymous works attributed arbitrarily to the Church Fathers of the third and fourth centuries.

Apart from the *Texte Und Untersuchungen* and 50 articles, the main product of the Giessen years was the *Lehrbuch der Dogmengeschichte*, the first volume of which was finished in the summer of 1885, and published in December of that year. In many ways it was as much Ritschl as Harnack.[21] Seven years before, Ritschl had written to him that 'the history of doctrine is the backbone of Church history' and that he should hold fast to his project of writing one.[22] The work proved to be a strenuous undertaking; this is made clear to the reader today in the immensely long introductory chapters of prolegomena and presuppositions before the author reaches the first great event in the history of the Church, the breach with Judaism. 'Do not forget just how difficult these questions are', wrote Harnack in the preface to the second edition in 1887, replying to critics of these early chapters. The strain indeed proved too much for him for he spent some time in hospital before he could send Ritschl the first published copy of the first volume on 19 December 1885, accompanied by an effusive letter of thanks, for inspiration, and for enabling him to reap the fruit of nearly 20 years' study.

The *Lehrbuch der Dogmengeschichte* treats the development of Christian doctrine as a historical and critical study, and the fundamental problems in discovering how dogma (or dogmas) had arisen.[23] It was among the first such works that tried to answer this question and follow the evolution of Church doctrine from the beginning to the Reformation. As he reminds his readers in the introduction, 83 years had passed since his grandfather, Gustav

Ewers, had edited a manual on the early history of dogma.[24] Not much had been written by Harnack's predecessors since that time. But this was a historical study, and, as Harnack points out, an ethical task[25] with little scope for divine revelation or for the working of the Holy Spirit in the decisions of the ecumenical councils, nor indeed any preference for orthodoxy over heresy.

Harnack believed that Church dogma in its conception and development was 'a work of the Greek spirit on the soil of the Gospel'.[26] It grew out of the religious attitudes and philosophies of the Greeks and Romans, principally Platonism, applied to the different and foreign structure of the Gospels. To a degree this development was inevitable once the Church had outgrown its Jewish origins and the eschatological and apocalyptic hopes in which it had been born. In the first two centuries the Catholics had been content to spiritualise and conserve the Old Testament aided by concepts derived from contemporary Greek philosophy. Their Gnostic opponents, in contrast, under the leadership of able thinkers such as Basilides, Valentinus and Heracleon, aimed at doing away with the Old Testament and 'in a swift advance, attempted to capture Christianity for Hellenic culture' and Hellenic culture for Christianity.[27] Their systems represented in Harnack's time-honoured judgement 'the acute secularising or Hellenising of Christianity . . . They were, in short, the theologians of the first century'.[28] Marcion, however, was not a Gnostic, but a theologian who 'succeeded in placing the greatness and uniqueness of redemption through Christ in the clearest light, and in beholding this redemption in the person of Christ, but chiefly in his death upon the cross'.[29] Marcion, the climax of Harnack's first volume, was a teacher of the Gospel and an authentic interpreter of Paul.

The Hellenic spirit, however, triumphed. The Alexandrians were of inestimable importance in transforming the heathen empire into a Christian one and Greek philosophy into ecclesiastical philosophy.[30] But they also transformed ecclesiastical tradition into a philosophy of religion, raising questions concerning the nature of the Trinity and the Person of Christ which the ecumenical councils strove to solve. Only with Augustine in the west did Christianity return to its roots, the relations of the human soul to God, guided by the gospel. 'God and the soul I want to know. Nothing more? Nothing whatever.'[31] Harnack would have agreed with the writer of the *Soliloquies*. The gospel which assured the Christian forgiveness of sins and eternal life was the means to that end.

The *Lehrbuch der Dogmengeschichte* set the learned and official worlds, as well as ordinary Christians in Germany, for or against Harnack. His father wrote that his son's doubts about the reality of the resurrection undermined his claim to be a Christian theologian.[32] Harvard, however, offered him a chair (in 1885), which he declined. Harnack wanted to stay in Germany, and in a Prussian university if possible. In 1886 he moved from Giessen to Marburg, still in Hesse, but soon opened negotiations with the Prussian ministry of education for a move to Berlin.

The *Lehrbuch der Dogmengeschichte* had been Harnack's personal credo, evangelical certainty that the gospel was eternal life in the midst of time but freed from the constraints of Lutheran (or any other) orthodoxy. As he wrote to Friedrich Loofs, the future author of a ground-breaking study of Nestorius, on 30 December 1885, he thanked God that he was able through his profession to say unreservedly what he thought about decisive questions (of religious history). One had to be iconoclastic. He felt like Luther at Worms. Above all, he wanted his students to think for themselves and not accept orthodoxies blindly, though basing themselves on the message of the gospel in its entirety.[33]

Harnack's short two-year stay at Marburg (July 1886–September 1888) was not fruitless. Contact was established with Wilhelm Herrmann, with whom he was later to collaborate on works relating to the social gospel. A second volume of the *Lehrbuch der Dogmengeschichte* traced the development of the Church's teaching through the councils of the fourth century to the period of Augustine. Augustine occupied many of his lectures to audiences of up to 150 students: he was to return to the *Confessions* in 1912 and 1913. The third volume (published in 1889) completed the work with a study of Luther, in which the author argued that too much of the dogmatic baggage of the past had been retained, and that more work was needed before the Reformation was complete. By this time Harnack was safely ensconced in Berlin. While at Marburg, however, he had a chance to visit and meet Louis Duchesne in Paris, and though he got on well with this already distinguished scholar, he found the atmosphere of the French capital unfriendly, and in contrast to frequent visits to Italy never returned there.[34]

Marburg was a staging post. As early as 1884 Harnack had come to the notice of Althoff, the far-sighted but choleric Ministerial-direktor (permanent secretary) of the Prussian ministry of education. A vacancy for the chair of Church history was in the offing at the Humboldt University in Berlin, for which Harnack seemed ideally suited. The Lutheran church authorities, however, thought differently. The *Überkirchenrat* (supreme synod) of Prussia sought to veto Harnack's appointment on the grounds of his unorthodoxy, which included his denial of the physical resurrection of Jesus and the sacramental character of baptism and its initiation by Jesus, coupled with a 'certain lack of warmth towards the spiritual aspects of the Church'. Also, for good measure, that he was critical of miracles and doubted traditional views as to the authorship of the Fourth Gospel, Paul's letter to the Ephesians, and 1 Peter.[35]

Negotiations dragged on for ten months from the winter of 1887, until the new Kaiser, Wilhelm II, intervened. On 18 September 1888 he signed a decree nominating Harnack to the now-vacant chair. From this point onwards the Church sought to side-line Harnack, never inviting him to examine theological students on behalf of the consistory or to become a member of the synod.

For his part, Harnack wasted no time in making his views known to his new masters. In a memorandum directed to Althoff on 27 September 1888 he emphasised the importance of early Church history in the education of theologians. 'The centre of gravity of Church historical study lies in the history of the Church and of dogma in the first six centuries', he wrote. It was important for students to know how Catholic doctrine emerged and developed. Historical research rather than exegesis or dogmatics

> will break the power of traditions that are now burdening the consciences of men. Cardinal Manning once made the frivolous remark, 'One must overcome history with dogma'. We say just the opposite. Dogma must be purified by history. As Protestants we are confident that by doing this we do not break down but build up.

He wanted to see authoritarian dogmatic thinking replaced by historical thinking. The gospel was once more to be seen clearly in distinction from Roman ecclesiasticism.[36]

For the next 18 years, until his nomination as director of the Royal Library in May 1906, Harnack was able to give his full attention to his university work as well as his growing family and circle of friends.[37] In 1890 he was elected a member of the Prussian Academy of Sciences which placed him among the foremost German scholars of his day. He was the first 'theologian' to receive this honour since Schleiermacher and Neander, and he was welcomed by Theodor Mommsen, now increasingly interested in the history of the early Church. Harnack continued a lively correspondence with him until his death in November 1903.[38] Correspondence flowed between the two scholars, Harnack with his famous closely scripted postcards, Mommsen in conventional letters.

This was the most productive period of Harnack's career as an academic. One of his first actions after his election was to get together in February 1891 a small committee including Mommsen and his friends Karl Holl, Friedrich Loofs and von Gebhardt to oversee a project aimed at publishing the works of the Greek Fathers in the first three centuries with full scholarly *apparatus criticus*. Fifty volumes were planned. The first volume of the resulting *Die griechischen christlichen Schriftsteller der ersten drei Jahrhunderten* was published in 1897, with the text of Hippolytus' *Commentary on Daniel*, and the series continues until today, though the range of authors treated has been extended to include fourth- and fifth-century writers, such as Theodoret, Socrates and Sozomen.

This was an achievement of the first order, on a par with the publication of *Texte und Untersuchungen*. It was followed by three equally magisterial works, *Das Apostolische Glaubensbekenntnis* (1892), which involved him in another controversy with the Church on the usefulness of the Apostles Creed in worship, the *Geschichte der altchristlichen Literatur bis Eusebius* (1893) and the *Chronologie der altchristliche Literatur bis Eusebius* (1897–1904) in which practically everything that was known about every early Christian work except some of the Apocryphal Gospels was described, dated and placed in the context of its time.

After writing 'as a diversion' the history of the academy in time for its jubilee in 1900,[39] Harnack turned to another enterprise. Maps, charts and the expansion of the early Church had always been among his interests, and in 1902 he published the *Mission und Ausbreitung des Christentums in der ersten drei Jahrhunderten*.[40] As the author justly claimed,[41] this was a pioneering work, one in which the part played by the Jewish Dispersion in the early expansion of the Church was stressed, and the third century identified as the period in which the Church became the religion of a very considerable number of the Mediterranean peoples and rivalled the authority of the Roman gods. If it had not been Constantine, then claimed the author, another emperor would have declared himself in favour of Christianity.[42] By 312 the battle had already been won against the immortal gods; the state religion of the empire (Harnack disliked state religion) had been defeated; and its replacement by Christianity was a matter of course.

However, of lasting importance though the *Mission* was, it reveals a chink in Harnack's armour. When dealing with north Africa and its bishoprics known to AD 325 he admits that he had not read Toulotte's *Géographie de l'Afrique chrétienne*,[43] and his handling of both north Africa and Britain shows a certain provincialism as well as a lack of understanding of the results of archaeological research. 'All we do know is that Britain was rapidly

christianised in the course of the fourth century'[44] was an un-
characteristic guess which has proved to be wrong; and at the same
time he failed to mention the church at Silchester that had been
discovered and excavated in 1892.[45] More serious were his mistakes regarding Christianity in north Africa. Twice he claims that
the Church failed to root itself among the Berbers,[46] and states his
belief that these were 'tribesmen inhabiting hills and steppes'
without towns, and as 'unions of natives' were directly controlled
by the provincial governors.[47] Such conditions 'rendered any
Christianising process out of the question'. Since 1890, however,
young French scholars from the École française de Rome, Auguste
Audollent, Henri Graillot and Stéphane Gsell, had been exploring
the abundant Romano-Berber remains in southern Numidia
(north of the Aurès mountains in central Algeria); they had found
a territory peopled by settled villagers, but in every village there
were the traces of a Christian church.[48] While these villagers were
pagan worshippers of Saturn down to the middle of the third
century, beyond that time there had been a steady movement
towards Christianity until, probably by the Council of Nicaea in
325, the overwhelming majority of the Berber *coloni* (not trans-
humant tribes living on steppes) were Christian. These results,
published in the *Mélanges de l'École française de Rome* of 1893 and
1894, do not seem to have been consulted by Harnack.

Similar neglect of archaeological evidence provided by William
Ramsay's discoveries in inland Asia Minor, and of the British
archaeological scholarship that these represented, resulted in one
of the few serious scholarly mistakes in Harnack's career. The
story of Ramsay's discovery among ruins near the ancient city of
Otrous (Kelendres) in Phrygia of the memorial of a certain
Alexander, son of Antonius who died in 216 has been described
most recently by the writer of this chapter.[49] The first lines of the
inscription read, 'I, a citizen of a distinguished city, made this tomb
while I was still alive', and, later on, claimed that he 'had been a
disciple (*mathétes*) of the shepherd'. Suspecting something odd
about the inscription, Ramsay researched when he returned to
England and found that the extant lines of the inscription coincided

with lines in the *Vita Abercii* written *c*.375 in honour of the anti-
Montanist Avircius Marcellus, bishop of Hieropolis *c*.190.[50] Two
years later, in 1883, Ramsay found three fragments of Avircius'
memorial embedded in the walls of a bathhouse in the same area.
Though the memorial was in the form of a pagan altar, the word-
ing of the inscription should have left little doubt as to the beliefs
of the dedicant. As in the Antonius inscription he was 'a citizen of
a distinguished city'. There were the words 'fish', 'Paul with Faith'
who had accompanied Avircius on journeys from Nisibis to Rome
during which he had found 'all gathered together', and had been
'provided by a pure virgin with bread and wine' for him and his
friends to partake. There was also mention of Rome as 'a queen,
golden sandalled'; the inscription finally included Avircius'
instructions on how 2,000 gold pieces were to be paid to the city's
treasury by anyone who disturbed his tomb.[51]

Instead of using his skills as a textual critic to follow and perhaps
to complete Ramsay's analysis, Harnack allowed one of his research students, Gerhard Ficker, to present to the Berlin Academy
a pedantic if closely argued paper 'proving' that the inscription
was probably in honour of a priest of Cybele, and that Avircius
may have been a disciple of Attis. Not a single phrase could be
reckoned Christian. Harnack set the stamp of his approval on
these theories by reading the paper at the session of the Academy
on 11 January 1894.[52] There was a howl of indignant protest.
Catholic scholars in France and Germany united in angry deri-
sion.[53]

Harnack's immediate reputation was saved by the fortuitous
discovery at Salona (Dalmatia) of a temple in honour of Magna
Mater which included a dolphin and a fish among creatures representing the goddess. In an article in *Texte und Untersuchungen* of
1895, Harnack was able to argue for a heathen-Christian syn-
cretism in evidence on the inscription. The reference to Pistis
(faith) suggested Gnosticism (*Pistis Sophia*!) while the fish suggested a relationship with Magna Mater or Cybele. Anyhow, it was
not orthodox Catholic.[54]

The controversy was allowed to die down. In *Mission* Harnack pays tribute to Ramsay's 'thoroughgoing investigations of the whole country' (Phrygia)[55] but makes no mention of the Avircius inscription nor to Ramsay's possibly Montanist (*Christianoi Christianois*) inscriptions. The consistent evaluation of archaeological material for the spread of the Church and its dissenting rivals would have to await the studies of Harnack's successor at Berlin, Hans Lietzmann.

The last decade of the century witnessed further conflict between Harnack and the Lutheran Church.[56] Already impatient of 'ecclesiasticism', Harnack now suggested a revision of the Creed in defence of a pastor who had been disciplined. He saw no reason why the baptismal service should include a recitation of the Apostles' Creed, whose individual statements, such as 'born of the virgin Mary' were at best unprovable. There should be a short confession based on a surer understanding of the Gospels, to include affirmations of belief in Father, Son and Holy Spirit (resembling the requirements of the present Anglican baptismal liturgy). Again there were denunciations in the Church press. Was Harnack the new 'Light of the World'? demanded the *Konsistorialblatt* of Kassel.[57] Harnack was tempted by the renewed offer of a chair at Harvard (made in 1892) where he was promised complete freedom to say and write as he thought. Again, he declined the honour. He wrote that he hoped that no Prussian should be obliged to quit his country because of lack of scholarly freedom.[58]

Harnack's thoughts reflecting his personal religion were to find expression in a remarkable series of 16 lectures he gave in 1899–1900 to vast audiences of students (some 600 in all) drawn from all faculties at the Humboldt, entitled *Das Wesen des Christentums*. They were delivered extempore but taken down in shorthand by an enthusiastic hearer, and translated into English by November 1900, as *What Is Christianity?* Much of what he was to say was already implicit in the *Lehrbuch der Dogmengeschichte*. 'The Fatherhood of God and the brotherhood of man', the popular description of the lectures' ideals, was not far off the mark. In his first lecture he told his audience that Christianity was 'some-

thing simple and sublime. It means one thing and one thing only;
Eternal life in the midst of time, by the strength and under the eyes
of God.'[59] It was Christ's 'peculiar greatness that led men to God;
so that henceforth they may live their own life with Him'.[60] It was
the historian's duty to determine what was essential and of permanent value in the Gospels, to free the essential from contemporary
husks. Miracles of nature did not happen. God worked through
nature not against it. He did not interrupt its course. But that
the lame walked and the blind saw again could not be dismissed as
illusions.[61] Could not God at times compel nature? We were not
yoked to inexorable necessity. The Gospels offered a plain picture
of Jesus' teaching; they described Jesus' life in the service of his
vocation and the impression he made on his disciples, which they
transmitted.[62] They had no relation to the Greek spirit, though
Greeks in Palestine were numerous. The essential message was
God himself in his power.[63] It was left to Paul to adapt and interpret this message to the Greek-speaking world. For Jesus 'the
Gospel had to do with the Father only and not the Son'. For his
hearers it proclaimed 'brotherly fellowship' joining the love of
God with the love of neighbour.[64] As in the *Lehrbuch der Dogmengeschichte*, Harnack blamed the Logos doctrine by which Greek
philosophers identified Christ with the Logos for mixing meta-
physics with historical fact and 'withdrawing minds from the
simplicity of the Gospel'.[65] It thereby introduced into Christianity
through the Creeds the element of compulsion 'that condemned
any religious experience that had not been sanctioned by sound
doctrine and approved by the priests'.[66] Protestantism, despite its
tendency to become 'a sorry double of Catholicism',[67] was still able
'to promote the liberty for which Luther fought in his best days'.[68]
The power of the gospel and the forces and principles of the
Reformation had not been outrun.

It was a significant personal statement, and little wonder that
the book went through 15 editions. For Harnack Christianity was
the religion, not just a way leading the soul to its Maker. In a speech
after his election as Rector of Berlin University in 1900, he
declared himself against faculties of religious studies of which

Christianity would form only one part.[69] He denounced ideas emerging from research into the mystery cults in the eastern provinces of the Roman empire, that Christianity derived anything significant from them. A little later he was to criticise scholars such as Arthur Andrews and Karl Kautsky who claimed that Christ may never have existed but was created as a myth of his times and perpetuated by Paul and the early Church.[70] He clashed with Alfred Loisy (1857–1940), who criticised the historical accuracy of the New Testament, but accepted the tradition of the Church and its sacraments as essential to the Christian life. His own somewhat provocative views were summed up in a letter to Loofs in 1901: 'the supernatural does not enter my thoughts, but I learn increasingly how great and all-embracing is God-installed Nature'. Christ was man's guide towards God; Augustine, St Francis and Goethe were pointers on the way.[71]

The rectorate of the university was the first of many senior administrative appointments that came his way between 1900 and 1914, but these did not prevent him from adding 455 items to his bibliography in that time. These included classics like *Militia Christi* (1905), Harnack's study of the Christian attitude to war and military service in the first three centuries, and *Luke the Physician* (1907). Luke's career and writings he appreciated from a strictly historical standpoint, believing that Acts was the product of personal contact with Paul, but written in all probability at Ephesus, *c*.80.[72] 'Q', in contrast, he believed was based 'exclusively on traditions in Palestine or Jerusalem', and hence a very early tradition. [73] Meantime he was being consulted by the government on syllabuses for higher education, enabling him to claim that a university without a theological faculty was not complete.[74] He wanted to be a 'doer' as well a teacher and his long-standing concern for social justice was signalled by his election in 1903 as president of the Evangelical Social Conference. The following year he published with Wilhelm Herrmann *Essays in the Social Gospel*, emphasising the moral consciousness that pervaded the teaching of the Gospels. At the same time, he would have nothing to do with the Social Democrats, whom he regarded as rabble-rousers, though some of their causes, such as the rights of workers and of women, he and his wife made their own.

In May 1906 came a greater challenge, his appointment through Althoff as director of the Royal Library. At the time this was not flourishing, but Harnack (though confining his working hours in the library to noon to 2 p.m. daily) made the difference. Rare works, such as the ninth-century manuscript of the Prüm Book of the Gospels, were secured, the library transferred to new and better quarters, and progress was made towards introducing lending facilities.[75] There were ever-increasing contacts with the court, friendship with Prince Bülow, the creation in October 1911 of a new Kaiser-Wilhelm-Gesellschaft embracing the humanities and sciences with Harnack as president and, in March 1914, Harnack's elevation to the nobility. Among the first initiatives of the *Gesellschaft* were the creation of the Chemical Institute in 1912 and sponsorship of a major archaeological expedition to Samarra. It was to survive the war, not least thanks to Harnack's efforts.

If during these years conflicts with the Lutheran Church were never distant they were balanced by growing contact between Harnack and British scholars and churchmen, as well as travels to the United States, Scandinavia, Holland and his old home in (modern) Estonia, but not France. Though at one time he had translated Edwin Hatch's *Influence of Greek Ideas and Usages on the Christian Church*, there could not be much in common with Hatch himself or with his associates, the canons of Christ Church. The canons were often men of deep piety as well as learning, the authors of hymns as well as works of scholarship. Hatch's own 'Breathe on me breath of God' impressed Harnack deeply,[76] but he was primarily a historian. Harnack's major works, however, had long been translated into English and appreciated. It is not surprising that, already involved in the German Peace Movement, he should have undertaken a lecture tour in England in 1911 and welcomed British representatives to Berlin. He was hailed as an 'Ambassador of Friendship and Goodwill'.[77]

It was too late. Rivalries between Britain and Germany over a whole field of interests were too deep, even without the German invasion of Belgium, to avert conflict. Harnack, however, saw the Balkans as the most serious threat to peace in Europe. In February 1913 he addressed the Prussian Academy of Sciences on the differences between the 'Spirit of the Eastern Churches as Opposed to the Western'.[78] He began by pointing out how the annexation of Bosnia-Herzegovina by Austria-Hungary (1908) and the Italian declaration that Albania (1912) must be removed from Slavic-Greek influence had brought into the open an age-old conflict. This was the struggle between east and west for control of the Balkans. He saw the end of the Turkish empire there as the signal for the redrawing of the frontier between Latin and Greek that had existed since the fourth century, leaving the former Turkish provinces on the Greek side and those occupied by Italy and Austria on the Latin. The unspoken question was (and still is) whether or not that frontier could be settled peaceably.

It could not, and on the afternoon of 4 August 1914, Harnack was engaged in drafting a speech for the Kaiser announcing a state of war between Germany and Russia and France, when news of Britain's declaration of war on Germany reached him.[79] He never forgave 'racially akin' Britain for what he regarded as an unprincipled act of aggression. In a letter written from Berlin on 10 September 1914, replying to an address by 11 English theologians, dated 27 August 1914, he rebutted passionately the accusation that Germany had broken a guarantee of Belgian neutrality and allowed aggression against Serbia. Britain had entered a coalition with Russia (*asiatischen Unkultur*), France and even Japan 'the Yellow Peril', against Germany Envy, not least of Germany's fleet, had motivated Britain's actions; he regretted, but accepted, the breach of relations.[80]

Through the war, Harnack maintained a strongly patriotic position. He rejoiced in the German successes of 1914.[81] Two years later he was arguing that Russia, which had no part in western civilisation, must be driven back to her 'natural frontiers' (?the Urals).[82] Only near the end, when Germany's defeat was certain, did he regret the lack of flexibility and the supremacy of the 'annexationists' that as late as June 1918 prevented Germany from securing a compromise peace.[83] Amidst the collapse of the Kaiser's regime and the civil conflicts of 1918–19, he stuck to the ideals of 'Freedom, Equality and Brotherhood' for which he believed Germany had fought the war.

The last decade of Harnack's life were marked by three events: the controversy with Karl Barth, Harnack's ecumenical hopes and the completion of his great study on Marcion. Barth had been Harnack's pupil, but now, in the more pessimistic climate of the post-war period, turned Harnack's historical approach to Church history on its head. Harnack had worked from the 'known', that is, humanity, to the 'unknown', that is, God, only approachable through Jesus Christ. Barth took the opposite route in search of reality from the revelation of God, manifested through the Gospels and the Pauline epistles to man. The conflict between the two approaches came into the open at a student conference at Aarau in Switzerland on 17 April 1920.[84] There, Harnack had asserted that with a controlled historical method of approach applied to the religious consciousness of Christians, those claims could be proved to be true. Barth denied this. Knowledge of the Person of Christ was not possible. Was not the wisdom of the world foolishness before God? The previous year Barth had published his *Die Römerbrief* ('Commentary on Romans') in which he had emphasised the utter dependence of man on God's grace; hence all cultural achievements including historical thought were tainted by sin. These views he had reiterated in his lecture that morning, on 'Biblical Questions, Insights and Vistas'. Harnack was astounded. Faith could not be awakened without a historical approach. He thought Barth's approach 'totally incomprehensible'.[85] Three years later, in 1923, he challenged 'the despisers of scientific theology', a challenge which Barth took up in *Fifteen Answers to Professor Adolf von Harnack*. Harnack stood for a 'science of understanding'; lengthy correspondence in the next three years left them both maintaining their original positions.[86]

More fruitful were Harnack's contributions to the cause of ecumenical Christianity. Harnack was a patriot who deeply regretted Germany's loss of part of Silesia and Memel as a result of plebiscites in 1920–1 and joined with international groups to protest against the terms of the Versailles treaty.[87] But he also worked for Christian unity across the whole spectrum of Protestant Churches on an international scale: this included friendly relations with the Roman Catholics.[88] Health did not allow him to attend the inter-faith Stockholm Life and Work Conference of 1925, but he wrote saying that the conference's aims summed up his own life and work. There might be differences between the Lutheran emphasis on the salvation of individual souls and the Anglican emphasis on practical work in the world and the spread of cultural values against a wide backcloth, but these could be overcome.[89] Two years later he did attend the World Conference of Faith and Order at Lausanne. There, he made a strong appeal for a less Creed-bound understanding of Christianity:

> The Conference must decide whether it shall demand the continuance of the dogmatic affirmation that Christ had two Natures, or restate the faith in Father, Son and Holy Spirit, and also in the God-man, Christ, but so far as the churches are concerned to make no binding rules about any further explanation.[90]

The conference listened but would not go as far as Harnack proposed. They agreed with him, however, when he spoke of the Christian religion as the greatest force for human reconciliation, but the creeds and dogma remained.

Through the war and in its aftermath, Harnack had continued to work on scholarly projects, in particular, on Augustine and Marcion. Both had always been with him, Augustine, whom he believed (wrongly) to be an emancipator from ecclesiasticism, Marcion as a reformer.[91] On 27 June 1920, a year before he retired from his chair, he completed the great work *Marcion das Evangelium von fremden Gott* ('Marcion: The Gospel of the Alien God').

He had gone back to his first work, the unpublished thesis on Marcion's doctrine and Tertullian's refutation of it, that he had

submitted for a prize in December 1870 as a 19-year-old student at
Dorpat. Marcion he regarded as a key figure in the early Church, a
heretic who provided Catholic orthodoxy with some of its basic
principles. Unlike his opponent Justin Martyr, he was a creative
force in religion, a teacher in the succession of the great prophets
and Paul's truest disciple, who like Paul wished to know of no
other God but the Crucified One. This God had nothing to do
with the Cosmos or its functions. 'Christ had made all things
new.'[92] The Old Testament with its Creator-god Marcion rejected. He had preached instead an entirely new gospel drawing
largely on the Pauline epistles and especially Galatians. His
enemies, like Paul's, had been those who sought to throw the
gospel back to Judaism.

Throughout his life Harnack had never accepted the Old
Testament as canonical Scripture, but he agreed that Marcion's
rejection of it was premature and an error.[93] It had been too early
for the Church to cast itself loose from its Jewish roots. Harnack
assembled every scrap of evidence relating to Marcion and his
church, even to an attempted reconstruction of Marcion's gospel.
He included the Deir-Ali (Lebaba) inscription dated to 318,
recording a 'synagogue of the Marcionites', whose presbyter was
named Paulus – one of Harnack's rare ventures into archaeology,
and an indication that Licinius in contrast to Constantine gave
toleration to heretical Christian congregations.[94]

Harnack in fact never stopped working. In 1926 he published
another study on Paul, *Die Briefsammlung des Apostels Paulus*. In
the last year of his life he was raising critical questions about the
authenticity of the Manichaean documents from Medinet Madi
that Carl Schmidt wanted the state library to purchase,[95] and,
finally, was writing a new discussion paper concerning *1 Clement*
4–5, relating to the deaths of Peter and Paul in Rome during the
Neronian persecution.[96] He died on 10 June 1930 while at a conference at Heidelberg.

Harnack was a Renaissance man translated into the early twentieth century. Liberal Protestantism coupled with his *Nebenruf* of
public service typified much that was best in pre-First World War

Germany. He was primarily an inspiring teacher-scholar, opening the way for a succession of German early Church historians to follow him. Karl Holl, whom he had had appointed as his associate professor at the University of Berlin, Hans von Soden and Hans Lietzmann, are a few who continued his work in the period between the wars, together with Hans-Georg Opitz, their successor, needlessly sacrificed on the Russian front in 1941. The abiding influences in his life were his parents, Goethe, whom he termed 'our contemporary from the 18th century', and whom he regarded as the embodiment of the humanism of the western Christian civilization,[97] and Ritschl. He was continually widening the scope of his interests, and one may feel that the ambassadorship at Washington offered to him in the autumn of 1921 would have been a fitting crown to his career. As it was, he continued to teach and write, on everything from New Testament criticism to Luther, until his colleagues despaired that he would leave them anything more to work on. Without his precise historical approach and monumental output the study of early Church history might not have progressed much beyond the scope of doctrinal history; it might have been reduced to the status of a 'special subject' on the borders of historical science, 'a dull subject for second rate men', as one Oxford professor described it in the 1930s.[98]

Seven years after von Harnack's death, the writer of this chapter would see a pen-portrait of him on the wall presiding over the seminar on Protestant theology taken by Hans Lietzmann in the Humboldt University. It was a guarantee, as one of his last pupils, Dietrich Bonhoeffer, said, 'that the history of the early Church would be studied by all who had the privilege of attending, with unerring striving for truth and clarity. All that mattered was the honesty of the answer. Thus, we learned from him that truth is born of freedom.'[99]

2

Hans Lietzmann (1875–1942)

Professor Hans Lietzmann's patristic seminar at the Humboldt University, Berlin, was a lively affair. It was based at the Centre for Protestant Theology at 2 Dorotheenstrasse hard by the Bahnhof Friederichstrasse. I made my way to it most days from December 1937 to March 1938 from my host's apartment in Levetzowstrasse, Moabit. Lietzmann aimed at building up a succession of young scholars who could maintain the tradition of patristic scholarship which Harnack and he had built up in Berlin. The standard in consequence was extremely high. My colleagues seemed to be adept in Greek, Latin and Hebrew, and know the contents of the successive issues of *Kleine Texte für Vorlesungen und Übungen* which Lietzmann had originated and still edited. While I had been at Oxford F. L. Cross's seminar on St Augustine, at Pusey House, had been demanding, but this was dwarfed by the knowledge and application required of its German counterparts.

Lietzmann's Assistant was Hans-Georg Opitz a large, rotund individual in his middle thirties, who was already a distinguished scholar, collaborator with Lietzmann in compiling a revised edition of Huck's *Synopsis of the First Three Gospels* and an expert on Eusebius of Caesarea and Athanasius. His untimely death on the central Russian front in July 1941 was an irreversible blow to patristic scholarship in Germany, as well as significant evidence for the failure of the Nazis to make the best use of their country's manpower. In Britain, Opitz would have been at Bletchley Park or perhaps at the Ministry of Economic Warfare but hardly a junior officer on the harshest sector of the Russian front. Fortunately, other members of the group survived the war. Johannes

Straub, Wilhelm Schneemelcher and Kurt Aland all achieved distinguished academic positions. But incipient genius was tempered by the presence of more ordinary mortals, a Würtemburger whose accent was so thick that Lietzmann had difficulty in following his paper, an artless German girl from the Ukraine and the extremely able Frl. Gitta Wodke, the only strongly but paradoxically antisemite in our class, who had already in 1935 published an article in the *Zeitschrift für Neutestamentliche Wissenschaft* on the paintings in the synagogue at Dura Europos.[1] Neither war nor communist aftermath could destroy entirely the seed being sown in the seminar during these fraught years. Lietzmann's legacy lives on.

Hans Lietzmann was born in Düsseldorf on 2 March 1875.[2] His father was a middle-ranking official in the Prussian Taxation Department. Unlike von Harnack, his parents had little influence on his ideas or career, his mother dying in childbirth and his father on 6 February 1885, just before his tenth birthday. He was brought up by his mother's sister whom Lietzmann always treated as his mother. They moved to Wittenberg in 1885 where he spent the remainder of his boyhood. These were hard years, especially financially. His 'mother' was obliged to eke out her wretched widow's pension by working for a public washing company (Der Wittenberger Waschegeschäft). Young Hans went to school at the Wittenberger Gymnasium where he gave evidence of an exceptionally enquiring mind, that led him towards natural sciences and, in particular, astronomy; this last interest with the equipment of a small telescope he never lost. Two teachers of genius, however, the school's Director Heinrich Grubauer and Hermann Hoffmann the teacher of Religious Studies influenced him profoundly, and this with his own strong Lutheran outlook drew him towards theology. He found he could apply his critical instincts towards the study of the Bible. Like Harnack, a basic loyalty to the Lutheran Church combined with a spirit of enquiry were to guide him throughout his life.

After a short and not too profitable year at Jena (1893–4) Lietzmann moved to Bonn,[3] where he immediately contacted

Eduard Grafe, the New Testament professor, and enrolled in his seminar in the summer of 1894. The seminar at that time was devoted to a study of the early Christian Eucharist, but was attacked by the Protestant conservative press as 'undermining belief' through the influence of 'unbelieving professors'. Lietzmann took his professor's side with a passion that earned him the reputation of being a 'strammer Parteimann' (a robust partisan). He was always to be on the 'Left' (like Harnack) in Church affairs with friendships that extended across the board from Friedrich Nippold, co-founder of the Evangelische Bund to Roman Catholic scholars in Germany and Belgium. He ended his theological studies in November 1896 when he gained his Licenciate in Theology, a step which he attributed to Grafe's New Testament teaching and his example as a man of religion. The years at Bonn left an indelible mark on his scholarship.

The second string to Lietzmann's bow at Bonn came in the form of a seven-term- (semester)-long membership of the Seminar for Classical Philology presided over by Professor Hermann Usener (d. 1905). Here, too, he found friendship as well as instruction, and when Usener's sight began to fail he became his amanuensis, reading and transcribing texts that the professor needed for his scholarly work.[4]

The year 1896 also saw Lietzmann's first published work, his examination of the New Testament concept of the Son of Man. He argued that the term used by Jesus of himself must have a meaning in Jesus' language, which was Aramaic. Looking for parallels in Jewish literature, including *Enoch*, he concluded that Son of Man was not a messianic title. Its interpretation as such was the result of interpretation by early Greek-speaking Christians who derived its messianic meaning from the Septuagint version of Daniel 7.13. There, in an apocalyptic passage, the seer uses the term 'anthropos' (man) to describe the one who had been 'given everlasting dominion' over 'all peoples, nations and languages'. In the second century this usage was to be found in Marcion's New Testament compiled in western Asia Minor. Thanks to Grafe the thesis was published by the distinguished house of J. C. B. Mohr, then of

Freiburg and Leipzig, in May 1896. Lietzmann was just twenty-one.

His promotion to the Licenciate on 28 November was not without opposition to his 'radical views', but in the previous month he had passed his First Theological Exam conducted by the church authorities in Koblenz. He could start on either an academic or a parochial career. After some hesitation he chose the former.

At this point luck intervened. His 'mother' was reading the paper and saw an announcement that the Göttingen Gesellschaft der Wissenschaften was offering as a prize competition the collection of fragments of the writings of Apollinaris of Laodicea (fl. 370–90).[5] After consultation with Usener, Lietzmann determined to enter. Secondly, though Lietzmann was still only a research student with no academic position, Hans von Soden, the New Testament scholar and historian, gave him the chance as a temporary assistant to travel to Paris for a fortnight to collate manuscripts of the Apocalypse as part of the project of collecting manuscripts for a new edition of the New Testament. Taking advantage of the early Church Fathers' use of series of biblical texts (*catena*) in their commentaries he was able to unite both studies to the advantage of his work on Apollinaris. Needless to say, a paper on patristic catena followed (1897) with a plan for a general catalogue of catena. This brought his ideas to the notice of eminent German patristic scholars of the day, including Harnack, Bonwetsch and Bousset. Lietzmann undertook a second trip to Paris on von Soden's behalf, but the collaboration between the two did not last. However, the result was fruitful. For the rest of his life he was an enthusiastic biblical textual critic, and in the 1920s organised yearly conferences on different aspects of New Testament scholarship, in German university cities. But for the time being his eyes were fixed on Apollinaris, and rightly so. In Paris he had carried out research on 50 different Apollinarian manuscripts. He saw Apollinaris as the father of the Monophysite Movement two centuries later. His enthusiasm was rewarded. On 6 May 1899 he received the prize at a special session of the Göttingen Akademie der Wissenschaften. He could look forward now to

a promising future. In 1904 the prize work was published as
Apollinaris und seine Schule: Texte und Untersuchungen, warmly
praised by senior scholars.[6]

Before submitting his study of Apollinaris, there had been yet
another hurdle to surmount. This was the Staatsexamen, compris-
ing papers on Religion, Hebrew, Greek and Latin, texts designed
to warrant his competence to teach at university standard. (One
cannot help contrasting the German demands with those on
budding Oxbridge dons of the time!) He passed.

A year's somewhat unsatisfactory obligatory teaching in a
Staatliche Gymnasium in Jena followed, presided over by a Herr
Direktor whom Lietzmann characterised as a disorganised ignora-
mus. He left with a determination that more must be done to
improve religious education, but it was not until 1927 that he had
time to publish a handbook on the subject.[7] After further excite-
ments and apparent changes in fortune, he was admitted to the
Theological Faculty at Bonn on 3 February 1900, as its youngest
member, but it was another two years before he received his
Habilitation with the salary and title of Privatdozent.

Lietzmann was to continue at Bonn until the winter term of
1905. He was now becoming well known in academic circles. His
correspondents in 1905 included Harnack, Wendland, Delehaye,
Loofs, Eduard Schwartz and Reitzenstein, a panorama of German
(and Belgian) patristic scholarship. Since 1896 he had been
employed as a reviewer in *Theologische Rundschau* and he was not
always merciful to his authors. A writer (C. G. Goetz) on Cyprian
of Carthage was told that he lacked a sense of history and had made
not the slightest effort to understand the period in which Cyprian
lived or the latter's development.[8] Another, writing on Julian of
Eclanum, was criticised roundly for not having the knowledge
necessary to assess Julian's scholarly achievement.[9] Enemies as
well as friends resulted, while Lietzmann started on the organisation of his first great claim to fame, the *Kleine Texte*. These were a
remarkable series of edited texts to be used at seminars, covering a
great many varied branches of biblical and early Christian themes,
including (in 1911) translations of Babylonian-Assyrian texts on

creation and the Flood, the text of the *Didache*, the Muratorian Fragment and other liturgical texts. His colleagues, including Harnack and Ernst Klostermann, contributed others, such as the New Testament Apocrypha and *Ptolemy's letter to Flora* (Gnostic), by Harnack. Like Harnack, Lietzmann was determined to put his knowledge and experience at the disposal of successions of pupils and to harness other scholars in the work. Harnack's *Texte und Untersuchungen* were aimed at research and post-doctoral scholars, Lietzmann's more to his seminarists. Each contributed massively to the expansion of early Christian scholarship in the field of textual criticism, the main tool for understanding the religious cross-currents of the Graeco-Roman period before the effective use of archaeological discoveries. By the time of his death in June 1942, no less than 170 numbers of *Kleine Texte* had been published.

The appearance of the first *Kleine Texte* had its downside. They gave the impression of Lietzmann as a 'manager' and not a 'scholar' (*Gelehrte*), undertaking too much administration at the expense of scholarship at too early a stage in his career.[10] Some of this was professional jealousy, but before he moved on he began to embark on another project which was practically to outlast him. The series of commentaries on the books of the New Testament (Handkommentar zum Neuen Testament) was languishing with the publisher, uncompleted. It was first suggested to Lietzmann to bring together a team to complete it, but Lietzmann preferred to start a new project from scratch. The result was successive volumes of the Handbuch zum Neuen Testament, begun with incredible energy and speed by Lietzmann and his friend, Erich Klostermann, in January 1905. Lietzmann himself undertook Romans, but conceived a much wider approach than a normal series of commentaries. There was an introductory volume by Paul Wendland dealing with 'Early Christian Literary Forms' and 'Hellenistic-Roman Culture', before embarking with Klostermann on volumes relating to the Gospels, Acts, the Pauline epistles, the Catholic epistles, Hebrews and Revelation. By 1941 when the series eventually closed it comprised 23 complete volumes including evidence from secular sources and papyri, a monument to the energy and vision of the original editor. And he believed that these volumes would have a practical value helping young clergy to show biblical understanding as well as piety in their sermons.

Jena

With preliminary work on Romans in hand Lietzmann moved from Bonn to Jena as extra-ordinary Professor of Church History, taking up his appointment on 1 October 1905. For the next three years he was working on his contribution to the Handbuch; *Romans* appeared in 1906 and *1 Corinthians* in 1907. The Faculty appreciated his work. His teaching-year problems lay in the past and in 1907 he was nominated as full Professor (Ordinarius) of Church History. But just as with Harnack's appointment years previously, there was strong opposition from the Lutheran Church authorities who wanted a 'strictly orthodox professor'. His candidature, however, was supported by Harnack, Loofs and Bonwetsch, also distinguished early Church historians. Eventually all obstacles were overcome, and Lietzmann entered on his career as Ordinarius on 1 June 1908.[11] Though a 'liberal' Lietzmann was always regarded as a firm Lutheran, combining an upright and caring character with great scholarly ability. His correspondence in these years touches on the whole range of German classical and patristic scholarship, including relations with Wilamovitz-Moellendorf, Reitzenstein, Hans Windisch, Wendland and Holl. With these contacts he could have settled into a scholarly routine with ever more writing, such as editing the 'Life of Symeon Stylites' (1908) published in *Texte und Untersuchungen* and his commentary on 2 Corinthians (1909) and Galatians (1910), combined with his seminars and academic meetings. But a new interest was developing, that of archaeology.

Lietzmann had not always been interested in archaeology. He was a textual scholar. In 1905, however, during a stay in Rome after visits to classical and early Christian monuments he realised their value for his work. He wrote in his diary, 'I soon saw that without an exact knowledge of archaeological sources it was impossible to obtain a clear picture of either secular or church history.'[12] On return from Rome he set about studying archaeology as a subject under Gerhard Loeschke at Bonn. In 1911 his enthusiasm for his new subject spurred him to write, 'Die Entstehung der christlichen Kunst' (The Origin of Christian Art), a contribution to an international scholarly weekly on *Kunst und Technik*.[13] A year later, a visit to Athens convinced him further of the great possibilities for the study of early Christianity that lay in archaeological research, a conviction reinforced by a study of the Theodosian land walls of Constantinople and a visit to Tunisia in 1913.

He was to use archaeology effectively, in particular, to understand the nature of the non-orthodox movements of Montanism and Donatism. It is interesting, however, that he never seems to refer to Karl Holl's significant article in *Hermes* (1908) correlating the survival of native languages in western Asia Minor, shown by inscriptions, with the incidence of non-orthodox Christian movements.[14] He never became a serious field archaeologist, or sought the practical work on Rhineland sites necessary to become one. It would seem that his work with Hermann Beyer on the Villa Torlonia catacomb, publishing the frescos and the coin finds, was his only experience in the field. Nonetheless, he showed sufficient enthusiasm for his new specialism for Karl Holl, now Professor of Church History at Berlin, to write a friendly piece of advice on 28 May 1914: 'I hear archaeology has again swallowed up all your interests. There are other things in life than science. Do please remember this.'[15]

Lietzmann was now 39. Fortunately for scholarship the war did not mean the end of his academic work in favour of the Russian front, or the trenches of Flanders. He was under considerable strain. Since 1896 he had amassed a bibliography of 132 separate scholarly contributions and in July 1914 had been elected Corresponding Member of the Göttingen Gesellschaft der Wissenschaft (Phil. Hist. Klasse).[16] In addition, his eyesight was deteriorating, made worse by the strain of concentrating on manuscript texts.

The combination of health problems ruled him out for military service. At the same time, he was becoming a public figure in Jena. In January 1914 he was elected to the City Council (*Stadtgemeinrat*) of Jena and next year became deputy chairman of the Red Cross in the City. The post brought a fundamental and fortunate change in his life. He met his future wife, a young medical student, Jutta Höfer. They worked together, became friends and married in February 1919. The marriage was a very happy one and produced three children, Sabina (1919), Joachim (1921) and Regina (1923).

In the first two years of the war, he was able to continue his work more or less untroubled. His correspondence with colleagues shows, however, that losses among promising academics were mounting,[17] and despite optimism no one could see how the war would end.[18] To his interest in archaeology he was adding an interest in the history of liturgy and an examination of the Church traditions that had brought Peter and Paul to their deaths in Rome. Could not Paul's letter to the Romans be explained best by Peter having been in Rome? Basing his research on available literary evidence, including apocryphal Acts of the Apostles, the *Liber Pontificalis*, as well as from Clement of Rome and the presbyter Gaius cited by Eusebius (*HE* ii 25, pp. 5–6) and the very recent excavations under the San Sebastiano, Lietzmann concluded that 'the tradition that existed to this day of tombs of Peter and Paul in Rome could be confirmed'. These tombs had been excavated, supporting the tradition of the transfer of the bodies of the Apostles to the site Ad Catacumbas on the Appian Way on 29 June 258, as stated by Philocalus in 354. Lietzmann now believed that 'in all probability' Peter and Paul were martyred in Roman under Nero.[19]

Not surprisingly Lietzmann's book evoked a good deal of discussion even in the middle of war. Harnack praised it warmly, though regretting that Lietzmann had not used the account preserved by Porphyry (*c*.300) cited by Macarius Magnes iii.22, that Peter 'fed his sheep for a few months in Rome before being crucified'.[20] It showed that it was believed that Peter had in fact come to Rome for a short time before being arrested and executed. Others, including Wilamovitz and Holl were equally positive,[21] but Karl Heussi, Lietzmann's colleague at Jena, was not convinced, and maintained to the end of his days (1961) that the last positive evidence for Peter's life came from Paul to the Corinthians (1 Corinthians 9.5), written *c.*54, asserting the existence of a 'party of Peter' among the Corinthian Christians.[22] Lietzmann himself updated his book in 1927, and lived just long enough to witness the beginnings of the excavations under St Peter's that uncovered the second- and third-century monumental pagan cemetery, but still left the Apostle's actual tomb a matter of debate, though, as Kurt Aland has added, the actual martyrdom of Peter in Rome is now generally accepted.[23]

He had called his work 'Liturgical and Archaeological Studies'. The history of early liturgies had already been the subject of several *Kleine Texte*, and now despite the limitations imposed by the war he planned a major contribution. His researches on Peter and Paul in Rome led a challenge to unravel confusions surrounding the Roman calendar of festivals (*Festkalender*) and thence to a study of the earliest sacramentaries, and in particular the compilation of the sacramentary of Pope Gregory I (590–604). At the time this was also being undertaken by a British scholar, H. A. Wilson, who published his results in 1915, but Lietzmann did not take this as a hindrance to his work. Careful correlation of manuscripts assisted by photographs sent from the Vatican through the good offices of Cardinals Mercati and Ratti (future Pope Pius XI and a keen antiquary) and the German occupation authorities at Cambrai enabled him to reconstruct the sacramentary which Pope Hadrian I had sent to Charlemagne sometime between 794 and 811 at Aachen.[24] The final edition was published in 1923. At the same time he was beginning to work on the manuscript traditions of the Eastern liturgies, in particular those relating to Egypt and Antioch. But the great work would have to wait until 1926 before it emerged into the light of day as *Messe und Herrenmahl*.

Even in the last fraught years of the war Lietzmann was productive and not unduly disturbed. In 1917 he was occupied in preparing the celebration commemorating the four-hundredth anniversary of Luther nailing his 95 Theses to the church door at Wittenberg. On 31 October 1917 he delivered a lecture at Jena on 'Luther's Ideals in the Past and Present' (Luthers Ideale in Vergangenheit und Gegenwart). His speech was not a great nationalist oration such as Harnack would probably have made. It was low key and concentrated on Luther and his legacy. He pointed to the breakdown of relations between the European nations, the bankruptcy of civilisation already existing but made more obvious by the war. The day was a day of repentance, meaning taking stock of oneself and a resolve to do better. That improvement would also need a radical reform of the existing provincial Church constitutions to bring about a true association with Luther's ideals, and an acceptance of the responsibilities of the universal priesthood proclaimed by Luther in 1520. For this he urged a greater lay and less state participation in Church affairs to rekindle those ideals in the hearts and minds of the German people.[25] It was a remarkable speech to be made in the fourth year of the war, when British and German armies were locked in deadly conflict on the Passchendaele front. It was an address more suited to a stressful but normal time, with its demand for a return to religion and pursuit of the ideals of the Reformation. Perhaps it shows how, even at this time, much of civilian life in Germany was as yet not severely tested.

By this time letters from friends, however, were becoming increasingly depressing. On 29 October 1916 Freiherr von Bissing, an Egyptologist, compared the damage inflicted on civilisation from the continued conflict to that resulting from the Völkerwanderung and the Thirty Years War.[26] These were merely local actions compared with what was happening now. Strife seemed to be endemic in human nature. Karl Holl's New Year greetings in 1917 hoped the year would bring peace, but a German peace.[27] Peace was what everyone wanted. At Strassburg (Strasbourg) Erich Klostermann feared for the future of the university, already very near the frontline.[28] Nathaniel Bonwetsch tells of the murder of officer cadets and the expulsion of German families from the Baltic provinces of Russia.[29] Shortages were universal.

But there was also an effort to maintain academic work and standards. Holl's letter was full of news of his patristic work. One has the impression down to October 1918 of senior scholars getting on with their studies, Karl Holl with his edition of Epiphanius' *Panarion*, Otto Seeck with his *Regesten der Kaiser und Päpste*, Richard Reitzenstein with Gnostic and Manichaean problems.[30] A significant letter from Ernst Diehl, Lietzmann's colleague at Jena, however, shows the deep sense of disillusion and despair that was prevailing by the autumn of 1918. Diehl's two journeys to the Tirol had demonstrated the extent of the economic crisis in that area even in March 1918.[31] How to get one's daily bread was on everyone's mind. Rationing allowed 1 or 2 eggs a week, and 15–20 grammes of butter. The people no longer had any energy. In October (13 October), returning from another visit, he described in bitter terms the famine that now afflicted Austria and the disasters befalling Germany with the approaching defeat of Bulgaria and Turkey. For Austria, he thought 'Jewry and the Czechs' were culprits, while 'international Jewry', the Socialists and Centre Party (Catholics) were responsible for undermining national pride and the army's will to resist.[32] The scapegoats of the future were being born. Moreover, the public had not been told the truth, fed on accounts of 'small losses'. He had no faith in a future 'President Max von Baden' if the Kaiser went, as he would. This was hardly to be contemplated. It was a letter written out of deep despair, while others described popular disorders and fears for the future. 'May God grant that our people after so many splendid deeds (throughout history) shall not finally, through itself, go down to ruin': so wrote Johannes Meinhold, the Old Testament scholar and professor at Bonn.[33]

Apart from his Luther lecture Lietzmann has left little of his thoughts at this time. He was responsible for a hospital with 1600 beds, and, as already mentioned, met there Jutta Höfer to whom he became engaged. His life was to change radically. He would continue to contribute to scholarship on a phenomenal scale, but he was no longer a bachelor totally absorbed in his published articles and reviews. The world looked different, and very quickly he adapted himself to a more mellow, family dominated life – much to the surprise of colleagues.

The years 1918–20 were among the most disastrous for humanity in a century as fraught with catastrophe as the twentieth. For the victors there was the scourge of the 'flu pandemic. For the losers, there was in addition the onset of communist-inspired revolution. Germany threatened to break up into a loose federation of communist or Left-Socialist states. 'Freistat Bayern' had its counterpart in Würtemburg, and threats of similar entities in Thuringia and Berlin itself. Only in 1921 was German unity fully restored, and meantime the organization of the Lutheran Church, previously identified with the state, had undergone huge modifications.

Lietzmann took a prominent part in averting the worst in Thuringia.[34] On Sunday, 10 November, he records how Jena was already festooned with Red posters. He met the Dean of the Faculty, Hans Heinrich Wendt, and together they resolved to confront the new situation by summoning a Church synod, which met as quickly as 15 November. This timely act prevented the Church and Theological Faculty at Jena from becoming disorganised and a victim to radical and hostile elements. Lietzmann saw that the Thuringian Evangelical Church must be reconstituted before a new secular state came into being opposed to religion in any form. To a great extent he succeeded. Relations between clergy and laity were defined. Schism between Left and Right parties was avoided, and, after several sessions, a new church constitution was agreed that allowed a good deal of freedom to clergy of different persuasions, and increased the powers of the laity in the parishes. But unfortunately, the compromise was not destined to last. In 1929 the 'German Christians' (Nazis) became the largest party in the Thuringian Church, the first German Land to fall to the Nazis.[35]

Meantime, under the shock of the communist threat throughout Germany, Lietzmann's politics moved steadily to the right. He joined the Deutsch-national Volkspartei to which he would remain loyal for the rest of his life.

Berlin

Lietzmann's chair at Jena had survived the turmoil of the years 1918–19, and he was the obvious candidate to succeed von Harnack in Berlin. But at first he refused, even when pressed by Holl and von Harnack himself. In 1921 he had become editor of the prestigious *ZNTW*. He felt at home in Jena and feared that he would not fit into the life of the capital. Gradually, not least under the economic pressures of 1923–4, his resistance was overcome. He accepted the chair. After attempting for a few months to commute between Jena and Berlin, he moved with his family to Berlin in August 1924. His promotion had given great pleasure to his mother (aunt) before she died on 31 December 1924.[36]

Lietzmann had now become a family man with three young children. He was developing family interests and hobbies. The home was the typical second-storey flat in a block in the fashionable Wilmersdorf district of Berlin. Jutta quickly settled in the Berlin professorial society while her husband was away at lectures and seminars between Monday and Thursday. In the late afternoon at 5 p.m. each day a personal assistant would arrive to act as Lietzmann's secretary, drafting speeches to the Berlin Academy of Sciences, notes for the *ZNTW* or helping to correct manuscripts for major works. For vacations, apart from continued love of astronomy, Lietzmann took up rambling and sketching, while also maintaining contact with the world of archaeology, as the writer experienced in 1938 to his great benefit.[37]

At Berlin his life was busy, in fact, as it transpired, too busy. At the same time as he was being torn between Jena and Berlin, and worried by the crisis caused by the French occupation of the Ruhr and the hyperinflation of 1923–4, he was elected a member of the Council of the *Notgemeinschaft deutscher Wissenschaft* (Organisation for Emergency Relief for German Scholarship) which involved a raft of administrative work. Only two years after his move to Berlin he was elected member of the *Kirchenväter-commission* (June 1926), which Harnack had brought into being 30 years before. An autobiography, published curiously in 1926 near

the height of his career, liturgical studies, archaeology and early
Church history were all competing for his attention. In 1926 he
published his *Messe und Herrenmahl* and next year a second edition
of *Petrus und Paulus in Rom*. That year he was elected to membership of the Prussian Academy of Sciences with the need for
another inaugural address. This also was a triumph, a voyage
through the art of Late Antiquity, concentrating on the squat and
stubby fourth-century figures on the Arch of Constantine and
contrasting them with the borrowings of the builders of the arch
from a monument of Hadrianic date.[38] The lecture had lost nothing when repeated to the seminar 10 years later. But it was all too
much. A heart attack nearly led to his early death in 1927.

His friend and colleague at Berlin, Karl Holl, had already died
after a stroke on Whitsunday 1926, at the age of just 60. Lietzmann
who gave the funeral address ought to have taken note. There is no
doubt that German scholars of the day worked with fantastic
application and intensity. Of the theologians, only Adolf Deissmann, a pioneer in the application of archaeological results to New
Testament and early Church studies, contracted out. After the
end of the war, Deissmann preferred evangelical and ecumenical
work to scholarship and in 1922 nearly became Bishop of Hesse-
Nassau though retaining his chair at Berlin. Lietzmann made a
complete recovery but was a chastened man.

Had he not recovered, his lectures, his *Kleine Texte*, *Messe und
Herrenmahl* and *Petrus und Paulus in Rom* would have ensured his
reputation as a Church historian. *Messe und Herrenmahl*, in particular, demonstrated Lietzmann's thoroughness in assembling
and analysing texts relating to early Christian liturgies, not least
the early Christian creeds, such as that preserved on the Dér
Balyzek (near Assiut) Coptic manuscript. New evidence, such as
the discovery in 1964 of a considerable part of the Nubian Monophysite eucharistic liturgy from Q'asr Ibrim, has supplemented
rather than superseded his work.[39] Detailed surveys of the leading
eastern and western eucharistic liturgies showed that the Liturgy
of Hippolytus of Rome (*c*.200), described in the *Church Order*,
formed the basis of all later liturgies in both parts of the empire.

Unlike interpretations which could be derived from the Synoptists, it was clear that Hippolytus did not associate the Eucharist with a Passover meal, a conclusion reinforced by the separation of the Eucharist from the Agape meal during the third century.[40]

From now on Lietzmann respected his health. He cut his workload drastically. He gave up the Presidency of the *Gesellschaft für Kirchen Geschichte* (Church History Society) but not the *Lutherkommission* which would involve him in commemorating the four-hundredth anniversary of the Augsburg Confession in 1930. Meantime, he went abroad, first to study in more detail than previously the construction of the Byzantine walls of Constantinople.[41] Then, returning via Rome he became H. W. Beyer's associate in excavating the Jewish catacomb in the grounds of the Villa Torlonia.[42] Here, as mentioned, he added numismatics to the list of his interests.

In 1930 he was back in full harness at the heart of the Lutheran Church celebrations. His essays on the beliefs and future of the Lutheran Church were published under the title of *Bekenntnis der Evangelischen Lutheranischen Kirche* (Confession of the Evangelical Lutheran Church).[43] A lecture at the Berlin Academy criticised the prevailing view that the Mandaean sect could trace their roots back to John the Baptist and the description the Fourth Gospel gave of Jesus. Rather, he pointed out that the Mandaeans were originally a Gnostic sect which perhaps in Islamic-Arab times had adopted a more Christian colouring. Mandaeism provided no clues as to the beliefs of the primitive Church.[44] If his views on the Mandaeans aroused controversy his lecture in the same environment on 'The Trial of Jesus' (1931) caused public debate. On the basis of the New Testament texts supplemented by references to the Mishna, Lietzmann concluded that the Jerusalem High Priesthood wanted to be rid of Jesus but had not evidence enough to condemn him on the religious charge of blasphemy. Jesus did not suffer Stephen's death by stoning. They therefore adopted a more convenient procedure of handing him over to Pilate on a political accusation that his claim to be the Messiah involved a political offence, namely, stirring up an uprising against Rome:

hence the Roman punishment of crucifixion. The blame for Jesus' death must be equally divided between the Jewish authorities and Pilate; and not laid on the Jews alone, as Matthew 27.25 and Paul (1 Thessalonians 2.15) were prepared to do.[45]

Such views would be readily acceptable today, but at the time they were controversial, not least to traditionalists represented by Martin Dibelius. He argued that the Sanhedrin had no competence to order a death penalty and that the martyrdom of Stephen was an abuse of power and hence it had handed Jesus over to Pilate simply to carry out the sentence. Lietzmann had started many years of discussion, represented not least by Paul Winter's classic study *On the Trial of Jesus*, published in 1961.[46]

Von Harnack's death on 10 June 1930 laid on Lietzmann the sad task of giving the commemorative address. He praised not only his work as a Church historian but also the universal character of his genius. His writing on the history of the Church to 312 would always be compared to that of Duchesne's master work. He was a supreme scholar and researcher particularly of the Church's institution, canon law, the Papacy, liturgy and the great Councils of the Church. And his *Das Wesen des Christentums* was the glorious sunset that 'God had let rise and set over our German people'.[47]

Lietzmann's real tribute to Harnack's *Mission und Ausbreitung* and *Marcion* was the first volume of his own *Geschichte der Alten Kirche* published in 1932 and dedicated to Harnack's memory. He had ended his autobiography in 1924 with the hope that he would be able to bring together all the disparate themes he had tackled in his articles and lectures into a single consistent whole. After his recovery from illness in 1928 he set himself this task and four years later the first volume of *Die Geschichte der Alten Kirche* (History of the Early Church) appeared. Like Harnack's first volume of *Dogmengeschichte* (History of Dogma), Lietzmann ends with the mid-second century, though he includes the Gnostics as well as Marcion. Despite writing many years before the discovery of the Nag Hammadi library, which meant that many of the Gnostic writings were not available to him, his touch was sure, though in the fashion of the day he was inclined to attribute too much in

Gnostic origins to contemporary mythology, either Zoroastrian or Egyptian, and hence to underplay that of Judaism and especially the disparate Jewish interpretations of the Genesis accounts of creation (Genesis 1–3). Another peculiarity, perhaps influenced by Duchesne's *Early History of the Church* (see pp. 134–9), was a single relatively short chapter devoted to Jesus himself, and ending:

> On a 13–14 Nisan, in the afternoon, at any rate before the end of the Passover evening Jesus had died on the Cross. Of the disciples, we hear not a word more. The words of the prophet had been fulfilled. 'The shepherd was killed and the flock scattered'. The messianic dream had ended.[48]

The narrative goes straight on to the Pauline account of the appearances (1 Corinthians 15.5–7) but apart from Mark 16.7 little more than a cursory mention of the Gospel accounts of the events in Galilee.[49]

This time controversy was muted. The work was recognised at once as a masterpiece. Translations into French and English followed rapidly. In a letter much later to Rudolf Bultmann, Lietzmann explained that he set out 'like von Ranke' to narrate 'how things really were' without prejudice or preconceptions.[50] In fact, no one, not even von Harnack, surpassed his account of the early years of the Christian mission, nor of the post-Constantinian period. It was a tragedy that sickness struck him down before he was able to take the story beyond the period of the confrontation between Theodosius I and Ambrose of Milan in 390, but his account of early monasticism in volume 4 (1944) survives as a prime authority today. With Duchesne's *Early History of the Church* (1905–10), his volumes represent the apogee of knowledge and assessment of early Church history before the great archaeological and literary discoveries of the post-war period.

At the end of 1932 Lietzmann was at the height of his influence as a historian. All research into early Christianity seemed to lead to Berlin. The *Geschichte* and his skilful editorship of the *ZNTW*

brought him world renown. The editorship had, however, involved him in controversies, some of which turned bitter. Thus, in
1926–7, a dispute with Robert Eisler's theory that the Last Supper
was a Passover meal and connected with the Coming ended
with Lietzmann not only refusing publication of the article but
also breaking off all contact with the author.[51] In 1931–2, Ernst
Lohmeyer, successively Professor of New Testament at Breslau
and Greifswald also took umbrage at the rejection of an article,[52]
while six years later an unfortunate who tried to compare
Evangelical and Catholic methods of biblical exegesis was given
short shrift when he was found to have quoted the opinions of a
Catholic critic as Lietzmann's words![53]

Meantime the second and third volumes (to the death of Julian
in 363) of the *Geschichte* had appeared (1936 and 1938) in new conditions and in a different Germany. Hitler's assumption of power
on 30 January 1933 profoundly changed Lietzmann's outlook and
ultimately the direction of his career, from one of security to one of
salvage of what could be salvaged for his subject and the German
universities.

Under Hitler's Regime 1933–42

In May 1932 Lietzmann had renewed his membership of the
Wilmersdorf branch of the Deutschnationale Volkspartei, which
he had previously left temporarily because he disagreed with
Hugenburg's parliamentary tactics which he feared were weakening the party's influence. Now he felt that everything should be
done to strengthen the hand of a national party reflecting middle-
class (*bürgerlich*) values.[54]

This was to prove in vain, and in the early years of the Nazi rule
Lietzmann, like very many others in similar positions, under-
estimated the power of the National Socialist movement and
believed wrongly that in course of time it would mellow and cool
down. On 15 May 1933 he intervened with the Ministry of Public
Worship (Kultusministerium) in favour of Professor Anton Baum-
stark of Münster who was being threatened with dismissal for his

outspoken support of the Centrum (Catholic) Party.[55] Next day he wrote to Eduard Schwartz.[56] First he thanked him for his review of *Geschichte*. Then followed interesting information relating to the first months of the Nazi government. Some colleagues had hastened to make their peace with the new regime.[57] He never hid his views. The new political slogans left him cold. He believed that though the situation was more serious than in 1918/19, it would eventually simmer down. 'Hot from the oven often means cool on the table', he maintained.[58] And, in particular, anti-Jewish agitation had not yet found support in the university. The Classicist, Eduard Norden, had been given a standing ovation by his students among whom were SA men as he entered his lecture room. And already the permanent civil servants in the Kultusministerium were succeeding in modifying the actions of the Nazi minister.[59]

Lietzmann, of course, was wrong. Matters did not improve. The 'German revolution of the National Socialists had struck much deeper roots throughout the whole of our intellectual life than anyone could have imagined the year before',[60] he wrote to Lyder Brun a fellow Church historian, on 23 February 1934. He stood firm against all attempts to force high school teachers to indoctrinate their students, and his letters show that his keenness for his subject never flagged. He speaks of 'my beloved archaeology' when the art historian Peter l'Orange sent him photographs and his study of the excavations at Dura Europos.[61] He corresponded with Franz Cumont on the latter's projected trip to the site to inspect the latest frescos from the synagogue (Esther and Ahasuerus seated on a throne with Mardocheus advancing on horseback through a crowd of onlookers), and the Mithraeum, representing a community of poor soldiers and NCOs.[62] He himself gave a lecture on Dura.

In 1935 and 1936 Lietzmann continued to work mainly on volume 2 of *Geschichte* and maintained a lively academic correspondence with colleagues. In general, Germany's relations with her neighbours and, not least, England improved. Neither the Saarland plebiscite (decisively in favour of reunification with Germany) nor the remilitarisation of the Rhineland in March 1936 resulted in the major crises that had been expected. A naval agreement was signed with Britain in 1935, and Germany took an active part during the same and following year in the negotiations which were hoped to yield to a Four Power Pact between Britain, France, Germany and Italy aimed at settling all outstanding questions between the four leading European powers. These negotiations were disrupted by Italy's invasion of Abyssinia and the impact of the Spanish Civil War in the summer of 1936, and never resumed.

Lietzmann, however, was gaining national and international recognition. In 1935, he was elected as a Member of the Academy of Science of Athens, followed in 1938 by a similar honour at Stockholm and at Vienna in 1940. He also became a member of the Deutsche archaeologische Institut, a recognition of his lasting enthusiasm for archaeology.

Nonetheless, his oppostion to the Nazi regime was growing. It was the threat to the Lutheran Church that turned misgiving into alienation. On 6 September 1933, the 'German Christians' who dominated the Old Prussian Union (of Lutheran Churches) got a resolution accepted that banned all non-Aryan clergy and church officials, including those married to a non-Aryan, from exercising their functions in the Church.[63] Lietzmann made his position clear on 19 September 1933 by associating with statements backed by other New Testament scholars, including Bultmann, Jeremias, von Soden and Deissmann, that 'according to the New Testament both Jews and Gentiles were fundamentally suitable to hold Church office',[64] and they were in their appointments solely on the basis of their beliefs, outlook and personal suitability. The statement was forwarded to the Reichsbishop Ludwig Müller, and to the Foreign Ministry. On 23 May the next year, Lietzmann followed this up by signing a sharper declaration together with Barth, Bultmann and others in the name of German university professors, protesting against the new direction being imposed on the Evangelical Church. Only Scripture and the Confessions of the Reformation demanded observance in questions which included those of Church order.[65] This declaration preceded the Barmen Declaration to which it ran parallel. The latter, however, went further in rejecting the *Führerprinzip* in Church matters, upholding the rule of Scripture and rejecting the ideas of the Reichsbishop and the 'unspiritual dictatorship of a secularised hierarchy'.[66]

The protests were unavailing. The tactics of the Nazi authorities were to let existing professors retire and then fill their places with their own creatures, while denying opponents the chance of promotion. This had its effect. H. G. Opitz whom Lietzmann had groomed to be his successor found continued exclusion from any expected academic advancement intolerable and sometime after May 1937 threw in his lot with both the 'German Christians' and the Nazi Party.[67] Little good did it do him, however. He was rejected at Marburg for a chair as 'lacking enthusiasm' and only achieved a full chair (Ordinarius) at Vienna in 1940 a year before being called up for service on the Russian front.

Lietzmann was above all 'a man of the Church' and he continued to represent its principles in his Seminar for Protestant theology. Luther was to him a heroic figure, a 'German protagonist in the service of Christ', and he drew a sharp distinction between Luther's dislike of Jewry and the measures perpetrated by the Nazis. Luther's views had nothing to do with racism or indeed any earthly considerations. They were based purely on a religious interpretation related to the practical experiences he had had with the Jews of his day. The heroes of the Old Testament were as much Luther's heroes as his own: thus, Lietzmann in the autumn of 1933, the three-hundredth-and-fiftieth anniversary of Luther's birth.[68]

Lietzmann's letters of 1935–8 show that he still felt enthusiasm for his subject. He was constantly consulted by colleagues and invited to contribute to overseas Festschrifts, such as those in honour of the Belgian scholars Cumont and Pirenne.[69] But all the time the situation for the theological faculties and for German scholarship as a whole was worsening. In July 1937, he spoke at the seventy-fifth birthday of Gustav Krüger, Professor of Church History at Giessen, of 'stormy times' and the duty of handing on to the next generation the study of Christian history.[70] The warning

went unheeded. International contacts were being restricted.
Lietzmann was unable to obtain and send abroad 60 Belgian francs
as his subscription to Franz Cumont's Festschrift.[71]

I arrived in Berlin early in December 1937, in time to be taken
by my hosts to the exhibition of 'Entarteten Kunst' – mainly holding up to ridicule and disgust the work of Marc Chagall and other
Jewish artists; and I witnessed the last, finely acted play by pupils
at the Rudolf Steiner school which the authorities were closing
down, on 1 January 1938. The situation of the Jews – my hosts,
Frau Hedwig Hackel and Dr Maass were Jews – was becoming
even more threatening. Looking out of my window on the second
floor of a block of flats, I saw scrawled in huge red letters on the
window of the chemist's shop opposite, the word *Jude*. People
round about showed the proprietor sympathy but it was a sign of
things to come.

I was readily accepted as a *Gasthörer* (visiting student) in the
seminar to which Hugh Last had recommended me. As mentioned
at the outset, the standard was very high. We were expected to be
fully acquainted with the relevant *Kleine Texte* which was to be
discussed at the weekly seminar. On occasions we would be treated
to H. G. Opitz's latest research on Athanasius. Accuracy and
simplicity were praised, obscurity and solecisms severely rebuked.
The unfortunate Volksdeutsche student from Ukraine dilated
learnedly about 'von Mommsen'. Lietzmann listened with growing impatience and finally thundered 'Mommsen war ein Demo-
krat' (Mommsen was a democrat). The class was dumbfounded
for a minute and then cheered. It was a moment not to be for-
gotten. Not all German university students were Nazis.

In the spring of 1938, Lietzmann had a further chance to make
his own views clear. For a formal lecture to the Academy he chose
the subject 'Die Anfänge des Problems Kirche und Staat' (The
Beginnings of the Problem of Church and State).[72] Even today,
more than 60 years later, I remember the scene, standing at the
back of the great Aula. There was not a seat to be had; the audience
was distinguished, uniforms in plenty, but none in brown, and
listening intently to Lietzmann's address. Like Harnack before

him, Lietzmann stressed the difference between eastern and western Christian attitudes towards the empire. This was familiar ground, but these differences led to the fateful consequence of the emperor's attempts to coerce the Copts and Syrians into accepting the state creed. This struck a chord. The applause was deafening. Without going beyond his scholarly theme, Lietzmann had struck a blow at the 'German Christians' and the government that would impose its own version of religion on the Church.

To me, a foreign student with only an imperfect knowledge of German, Lietzmann could not have been kinder. He suggested that my research for my thesis on the Donatist Church in Roman North Africa would benefit by a detailed comparison between it and the Montanists of Phrygia, both being basically biblical and prophetic movements, whose strength lay in a single province. He introduced me to Wilhelm Schepelern's work *Der Montanismus und die phrygischen Kulte* (Tübingen, 1929) that combined literary with detailed archaeological evidence concerning the Phrygian cults before arriving at the conclusion that the New Prophecy owed more to the Revelation of St John than it did to the ecstatic pagan cults.[73] When I left for Tunis on 15 March 1938 (every house as one traversed Austria displayed a Nazi flag) to continue my research, concentrating on North African Christian inscriptions, he provided me with a warm letter of introduction to Louis Poinssot the Director of Antiquities in Tunisia. Poinssot was not always an easy master, but since then my interest in Christian North Africa has never flagged.

I returned to Berlin in late June 1938 and for the next seven weeks saw more of Lietzmann and his family. Though I think his knowledge of English was quite adequate, he gave me a long review of volume 2 of *Geschichte* to translate into English. With the help of my hosts in Levetzowstrasse I succeeded in making a passable rendering; and was rewarded with two volumes of the *Geschichte* and, as a parting gift, Strack's *Hebräische Grammatik*, which, alas, I have never had cause to use.

The final meal with the Lietzmann family was an occasion tinged with sadness. The family expressed the warmest feelings towards England. Forces beyond our control, however, seemed to be propelling our countries onto different sides in a war, even if, as it happened, this was postponed for a year. Lietzmann's views when war eventually broke out on 3 September 1939 were what one would expect of a Deutsch nationale and a Lutheran champion. Even as late as the well-remembered Berlin Archaeological Congress of late August 1939 he hoped for peace,[74] but, once war had broken out, he was convinced of Germany's strength that could blockade and ultimately defeat England.[75] He attributed the war to the injustice of the Versailles Treaty and incompetence of the western politicians,[76] but, as he showed in a letter to Franz Cumont, on 3 January 1940, he feared for the lasting damage to western civilisation and the renewed unbearable sacrifices that all the combatants, French, English and German alike, would be forced to sustain. As ever, he hoped for peace.[77]

Support for Germany's cause, reflecting the outlook of his students as much as his own, did not lessen his hostility towards the Nazi Party. Since 1924 Lietzmann had been a member of the Mittwochgesellschaft (Wednesday Society). This was an old and traditional semi-political club originating in 1863 which brought together senior civil servants, academics and senior officers of the armed forces for an informal evening meeting to discuss scholarly and kindred subjects, on alternate Wednesdays throughout the year. Politics took up a good deal of time, but in October 1940 Lietzmann gave an updated version of his Academy lecture on the problems of Church and State in early Christianity. Politics, however, ruled. The prevailing outlook of the society was national/ conservative, and Lietzmann felt entirely at home. Among his colleagues were Popitz, Finance Minister in the Prussian Government and survivor from Weimar (Treasurer), General Ludwig Beck, Chairman, and Ulrich von Hassell, German Ambassador in Rome. It was through Popitz that Lietzmann was able to bring some influence to bear to secure the release from concentration camp of some Jewish colleagues, such as Paul Friedlander. Gradually, the Gesellschaft developed into a centre of anti-Nazi resistance. Popitz himself was involved in the anti-Nazi plot of 20

July 1944, arrested and executed the following February. Before illness struck him down Lietzmann himself had drafted a scheme for a reform of German universities free from Nazi influence.[78]

Despite Germany's victories over the western allies in June 1940, Lietzmann feared for the continuation of his subject and his fears were realised.[79] At 5.30 a.m. on 22 June 1941, Germany unleashed a well-planned but unprovoked attack on the Soviet Union. On some parts of the vast front extending from the Baltic to the Romanian frontier there was scant resistance. The writer has in his possession the diary of 296th Supply Company (*Trosskompanie*) which he picked up in the Grünewald in 1948 when working in Berlin as an editor of the captured German Foreign Ministry documents. The entries begin with the advance into Russia on 22 June and end on 19 July. The company moved at a leisurely pace, suffered one casualty and were either 'greeted with enthusiasm' as they approached Smolensk, or encountered no difficulty in securing supplies for their onward march. Further south, however, it was different. Around the town of Gomel the Russians put up stern and temporarily successful resistance. On 9 July, Opitz was killed – accidentally it was said – but six days later Lietzmann suffered a devastating blow with the news that his son Joachim, a junior officer in an artillery regiment, had fallen. Lietzmann never recovered from the loss. Cancer was diagnosed; he was given leave to seek recuperation in Switzerland, but died at Locarno on 25 June 1942, his great work unfinished and the tradition Harnack and he had built up in the Humboldt University left without an heir.

While in Berlin during the Airlift in 1948, I visited Frau Lietzmann in Wilmersdorf. She confirmed what her husband's writings show; he was a strong nationalist with a belief in the rightness of Germany's cause, namely, that of survival. The Allied defeat in Flanders and France had momentarily cheered him. 'Unsere deutschen Herzen klopften', as she put it. But not for long, and before he died he foresaw the ruin of the German universities as he had known them. Fortunately her daughters had survived and the elder, Sabina, was already in the USA as a correspondent for the *Frankfürter Allgemeine Zeitung* where she has remained.

Looking back, it is hard to overestimate the debt I owe to Lietzmann and his seminar. Accuracy and application were simply expected, but above all, the necessity of harnessing archaeological and literary evidence to form an adequate picture of the development of the early Church. He would have liked to have done more work in the field, but his enthusiasm for the subject never flagged. As mentioned, his recommendation on my behalf to Louis Poinssot set me on a road which has governed my life's interests. Not surprisingly, I have chosen Stéphane Gsell as a third major influence on that work.

3

Stéphane Gsell and the Recovery for Scholarship of Roman-Berber North Africa[1]

Stéphane Gsell (1864–1932) will always be associated with the recovery of evidence for the religion and life of Roman-Berber North Africa, and in particular of Donatist Numidia. At the time of writing, the area north of the Aurès mountains that Gsell and his colleague, Henri Graillot, traversed in a memorable expedition in the spring of 1893 has been, practically speaking, closed to archaeological research since 1940. The stringencies of the war and Allied occupation were followed by the growing insecurity of the countryside. Then, in 1962, the winning of Algerian independence resulted in Islamic governments less interested in recovering and preserving early Christian sites. Finally, in the 1990s the emergence of an Islamic militant movement murderously hostile to all non-Muslims has warned European scholars off Algeria. All this has prevented the resumption of archaeological research in an area once so rich in Roman, early Christian and Byzantine remains. For the recovery of so much evidence and the accurate plotting of so many sites on a map of Algeria, an enormous debt is owed to Gsell and his successors in the 1930s, especially to Louis Leschi and Andre Berthier, the curator of the Musée Gustave Mercier at Constantine, and his colleagues in the administration of the Département de Constantine.

Stéphane Gsell was born in Paris of a Swiss Protestant family of Alsatian origin, but established at St Gall for several generations.

His father was a painter, his mother a member of the Pasteur family, and in the accounts of his researches Gsell never forgot that the remains he was discovering once related to people, such as the murdered Donatist *sanctimonialis* (woman in vows) Robba whose memorial dated to AD 435, whom he discovered during his excavations at Benian in Mauretania and about whom he wrote eloquently.

Gsell's early career indicated great interest and promise in Ancient History. He entered the École Normale in 1883, gained his first *Agrégation* (the top of his year) three years later and obtained a coveted place in the École française de Rome. There he had an outstanding career. His doctoral thesis revolved round the life and reign of the emperor Domitian (81–96) (*Le règne de l'empéreur Domitien*) and even today researchers into the campaigns and organisation of the Roman provinces in that period could do worse than start with Gsell's work.[2] Careful and accurate though the study was, it is fair to say that it suffered from two defects. No clear picture of the emperor emerged as a general conclusion except that he distrusted philosophers and Roman aristocrats,[3] and little to indicate that the reign saw as a matter of policy the romanising of the provinces of the empire. The building of temples, houses and fora in Roman Britain are mentioned among Agricola's measures prior to his military campaigns in the north of the island, but not as part of a general drive towards romanisation throughout the empire.[4]

Even so, Gsell's work was attracting notice, and in 1889 he was invited to supervise and record excavations on the Etruscan cemetery of Vulci.[5] This was a rare privilege for a foreigner, but the faith of Geffroy, the Director of the École, and Prince Torlonia was not misplaced, and once again Gsell produced a comprehensive report published in 1891, characterised by accurate observation and detailed description of the finds, qualities he was to show in North Africa. Forty-five years later, in 1928, German archaeologists who resumed work at Vulci referred to Gsell's report as 'the foundation of our knowledge of the ruins of Vulci'.[6]

Another aspect of his future work was emerging while he was at the École française, namely, an interest in early Christianity. His final chapter (ch. 10) in *Domitien* deals with the emperor's actions against philosophers whom he suspected of plotting treason, and finally against converts to Judaism and Christianity. Gsell points out that Domitian had no intention of destroying the Jewish religion,[7] only of preventing its spread; and this included that of its noxious offshoot, Christianity. Gsell accepts that the execution of Flavius Clemens, Domitian's cousin, and the exiling of his wife Domitilla was on the grounds of conversion to Christianity, and that Dio Cassius' (lxvii.14) account that they were charged with atheism, 'having drifted into the customs of the Jews', means Christianity. He links these acts of repression to the story Eusebius found in Hegesippus (writing *c*.170) of an alleged hearing before Domitian himself of descendants of relatives of Jesus, on the grounds that as individuals of the distant lineage of David they could be considered a potential menace (*HE* iii.2). However, they were freed once they established that they were simple farmers and that Christ's kingdom was not earthly but at the end of the present age when Christ would return in glory. This seemingly would be a long time ahead.[8] Despite the persecution being soon over, Gsell makes the important point that whereas the persecution under Nero had had the specific aim of placating the gods who had punished Rome by causing the fire (not Nero himself!), that of Domitian was the first instance of an emperor deliberately attempting to prevent the spread of Judaism and Christianity. In his view, their religion was a threat to the imperial cult, and hence treasonable as well as an example of atheism.[9]

Gsell's remains a first-class analysis of events which, incidentally, makes sound sense of the alleged action of Septimius Severus in 202, to forbid conversion to Judaism and Christianity, and the consequent persecution of converts, such as Perpetua and her companions in Carthage.[10]

Gsell had also met Abbé Louis Duchesne while at Rome, which increased his interest in early Christianity, and his next move was to give him all the scope he needed to pursue that interest. In November 1890, a ministerial decree appointed him lecturer (*chargé de cours*) at the École des Lettres at Algiers; and four years later, in December 1894, he was promoted to be titular professor in the Chair of Antiquités d'Afrique at the École, which was soon to become a university.[11] Gsell's career opened out before him.

Arrived in Algiers, he found an opportunity to follow up a suggestion by Duchesne, namely, that he should explore the ancient port of Tipasa, west of Algiers, with a view to throwing light on the legend that the virgin Salsa, martyred at the age of 14 during the Great Persecution (303–5), had been buried there.[12] Tipasa had declined until it was totally abandoned, perhaps in the eighth century, its churches decayed and its population diminished until nothing remained. The Arab rulers of Algeria apparently did not need the port and left the whole area to become overgrown with rank vegetation, as evident in the unexcavated areas when the writer visited the site with US troops in the late summer of 1943, as when Gsell set foot on it in 1891.

Duchesne's interest in Salsa had been aroused by reading the account of her martyrdom recently published by the Bollandists.[13] The martyrologist had identified a place outside the town's ramparts as the place where the body was buried. Knowing Gsell's work at Vulci, Duchesne invited him to investigate. No prompting was needed. He had already heeded the words of Emile Masqueray and others of his generation that North Africa 'offered a vast field for the study of Christian archaeology' and he had already visited the impressive ruins of the Roman city of Madaura.[14] Helped by fellow scholars of the École française and the Curé, Abbé L. Sainte Guerand (d. 1893), he set to work in the area indicated by Duchesne, east of the town amidst a vast cemetery, whose tombs still visible in the middle of the brushwood extended from Punic times to the sixth century. He was lucky, coming upon a basilica built towards the middle of the fourth century. It had been enlarged by Bishop Potentius of Tipasa *c.*440 and again in the early Byzantine period. The whole of the centre of the church had been paved with mosaic surrounding a verse inscription honouring Salsa 'dulcior nectare semper' (always sweeter than nectar). Nearby was a tomb laid on a raised base, and in front of the inscription Gsell came upon a stone funerary memorial (*cippe*) honouring the *matrona* Fabia Salsa who had died at the age of 62 years and two months with the exact timing of her death in days and hours added.[15] It would seem, however, that the Christians who found this stone commemorating this relative of the martyr had cunningly altered the inscription so that it read 'Fabia Salsa martyr' and the age changed from 62 years and two months to 14 years.[16] Hence by the mid-fourth century, the tomb of the martyr had been associated with a memorial. All that needed to be done was the construction of a fitting basilica and inscription in mosaic in her honour.

Gsell discovered a second smaller monument to Salsa nearby,[17] but in the next three years concentrated his efforts on a site on the opposite side of the town where the landowner, M. Trémaux, encouraged him to work. There he worked on another basilica built also in the fourth century, by Bishop Alexander in honour of his predecessors, the *justi priores* first discovered by Abbé Guérand. Nine stone coffins found in a crypt below the church suggested the existence of a Christian congregation in Tipasa from the mid-third century onwards.[18] Just within the walls on the north-west promontory which formed the city boundary Gsell found (1892–3) an even larger basilica, a vast building 52m by 45m excluding the apse, with seven aisles and floors paved with mosaic.[19] It was to remain one of the largest churches ever found in North Africa and a testimony to the vibrant faith of the Christians of Tipasa from the fourth to the sixth centuries.

Meanwhile, Gsell's thoughts were turning to Numidia, or rather the swathe of country between the Aurès mountains and the brackish lakes that divide the north from the south expanses of the central Algerian high plains (see map on pp. 66–7). Since 1890 this area had begun to attract the attention of members (*scolaires*) of the École française. In that year, Auguste Audollent and Jean Letaille, alarmed at the prevalent vandalism among some of the French settlers against remains of past civilisations in North Africa, made a journey of archaeological exploration into the area east of Algiers (Mauretania Sitifensis). There they were able to recover, among other finds, the important Christian inscription from Kherbet Oum el Adham. This, a dedication by two Christians, made on 7 September 359, honoured an astonishing collection of Christian martyrs of the Valerianic and Great Persecutions, including Cyprian of Carthage (executed 14 September 258) and the martyrs of Abitina (imprisoned at Carthage 303–4), as well as fragments of 'the True Cross'. It was the earliest mention of this relic, and showed both pilgrimages from North Africa to the Holy Land and also the existence at this date of a cult of the True Cross, originating with the discoveries of the empress Helena at Jerusalem in 326.[20]

Audollent and Letaille also ranged over the country north of the Aurès which Gsell and Graillot would be surveying more thoroughly three years later. In their report the two archaeologists urged that the best way to salvage remains of the Roman period was through the establishment of local museums in prominent French settlements near extensive Roman and Byzantine ruins. Museums at Tebessa, Khenchela (Mascula), Announa and Constantine itself were the result.

Audollent and Letaille had blazed the trail. It was now time for Gsell, and his colleague Henri Graillot to follow this up. The year 1893 was an *annus mirabilis* for Gsell. He not only published the *Recherches archéologiques en Algérie*, a work of more than 400 pages, in which he describes 177 Roman remains and records 690 inscriptions, but in April and May of the same year he and Graillot undertook a journey of archaeological survey whose results have never been equalled. Three major descriptive articles in the *Mélanges* remain as a monument to their success.[21] Travelling by bicycle, mule and on foot, the two archaeologists traversed a vast area extending the whole length of the high plains between the Aurès mountains and the *chotts* (salt lakes) in central Algeria. To the west of the railway running between Constantine and north of the mountains of Batna they recorded 67 sites and recorded and mapped another 173 on the plains east of the railway. They therefore explored the whole area between Timgad in the east and Zarai in the west. Mostly their journey took them through fertile plains dotted with Roman and Byzantine remains, but broken up by the outcrops of the Aurès mountains, which sometimes reached the height of 3,000ft (1250m) above sea level. Part of this area had been explored previously in the 1850s by Colonel Carbuccia, the officer commanding the *sous-division* of Batna, and somewhat unsystematically by a succession of officers stationed at Batna or Tebessa.[22] Scholarly survey of the Roman-Berber ruins, however, challenged Gsell and Graillot (see map on pp. 66–7).

They examined carefully the surviving ruins and inscriptions, often found in the walls of modern buildings, which revealed much about the society that prevailed in the area between the second and the fourth centuries. In particular, they showed how in the period from Domitian to Trajan there was a fortified triangle of garrison posts centred in the east on Mascula (Khenchela) and then after 100 on Thamugadi (Timgad) and finally Lambaesis, which became the permanent headquarters of the Third Legion. In the second century the towns became imitations of Rome with their triumphal arches and capitols, and the ruling classes displaying their *tria nomina* on their tombstones or their membership of a civic organisation (*sodalis*) of the town.[23] In the countryside, great landholding families, such as that of Julianus Martalianus, administered their estates (*praedia*) and collected dues and taxes from their *coloni*.[24] Religion was solidly based on a Roman-Berber paganism in which sanctuaries to the native Afro-Punic god Saturn (Baal-Hammon) could be found near Liber Pater and those of 'civic', 'saving gods' and Jupiter Serapis Augustus. The long life of some of the inhabitants (one husband and wife from Henchir Ouazen near the Mascula–Thamugadi road are recorded as living to the age of 80 and 100 respectively) was a feature of the area. Such longevity could only have confirmed the healthful and saving quality of the gods.[25]

The fourth century, however, brings a dramatic change. New temples are no longer built (though some were refurbished in Julian's reign) and cemeteries no longer dominated by pagan memorials. Instead, Christianity becomes a force in southern Numidia. A great cemetery characterised by simple, uniform tile

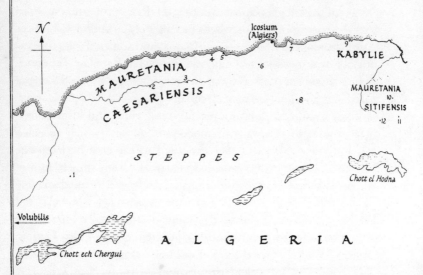

Key to numbers on the map   (Modern names are in brackets)

1. Benian (Ala Milaria)
2. Castellum Tingitanum
3. Tigava
4. Caesarea (Cherchell)
5. Tipasa
6. Tanaramusa Castra (Mouzaïaville)
7. Rusguniae (Matifou)
8. Gouea
9. Iomnium (Tigzirt)
10. Sertei
11. Thamalla (Tocqueville)
12. Equizetum
13. Satafis
14. Cuicul (Djemila)
15. Kherbet Bahrarous
16. Kherbet Bou Addoufen
17. Bir Younkene
18. Mechta Azrou
19. Azrou Zaouia
20. Bir Djedid
21. Bou Takrematem
22. Bou Kaben
23. Henchir el Bahira
24. Tiddis
25. Henchir Guessaria
26. Henchir el Ateuch
27. Henchir Akhrib
28. Zarai
29. Nif en Nisr
30. Ain Beida
31. Telergma (Ferme Laurent)
32. Bou Lhilet
33. Foum el Amba
34. Oued Rhezel
35. Seriana
36. Lambiridi
37. Foum Seffane
38. Ain Fakroun

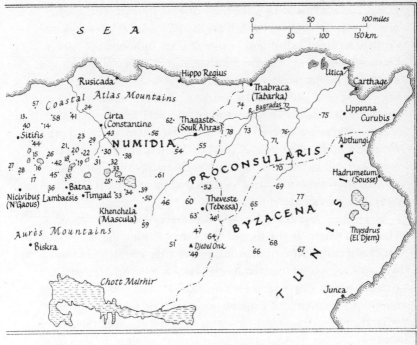

Originally appeared in Stéphane Gsell, *Atlas archéologique de l'Algérie* (Algiers, 1911)

graves laid out row on row, the body carefully preserved in plaster, grew up on the slope of the hill south of Timgad.[26] Churches and chapels replaced urban and village shrines in honour of Saturn. Outside the towns, villages increased in number and size and instead of public buildings, except for the occasional bath building,[27] were olive presses and granaries.[28] Though we know little of the detail of rural society, tribal identities were by no means dead and the colonate preserved the relatively free status accorded to its members under the terms of the Lex Mancia in the second century, and still in force during the Vandal occupation.[29] It looks as though they were egalitarian villages dominated by the Christian church, a granary and the olive press.

Gsell and Graillot observed and recorded these changes. Henchir Ouazen at the foot of the Aurès mountains, where the memorial to the octogenarian and centenarian couple were found, was now the site of 'numerous oil presses' and of an 'interesting church' where a large sarcophagus had been interred in a place of honour in the middle of a square enclosure (altar space) in front of what the two archaeologists assumed were the vanished remains of the apse.[30] Near Mascula they recorded inscriptions in honour of Saturn,[31] not dated, but probably of the second and third centuries, and also a group of elaborately carved rectangular blocks of limestone, on one of which was inscribed the Donatist watchword 'Deo laudes' (praises to God) and also an even more impressive series of panels finely decorated with a wood chip design unlike any Classical model, but inspired by native crafts in honour of the Donatist Church.[32] As the two scholars recorded, 'Everywhere churches and chapels were built, which from their architecture and the form of the Christian symbols allows one to date to the 4th, and early years of the 5th century.' 'This region', they continued, 'was the centre of Donatism, a schism whose history remains very obscure, but which appears to have been at the same time as a religious movement a sort of revival of independence among the natives.'[33] It was not surprising that it received so warm a welcome among the people living at the foot of the Aurès mountains.

In saying this about the Donatists, Gsell and Graillot were

confirming the views uttered a generation before by Adrien Berbrugger, though without the latter's condemnation of the sect.[34] Donatism was never to be popular among French scholars from one end of their occupation and settlement of Algeria to the other. Even Paul Monceaux in his series of classic volumes on the literary history of Christianity in North Africa could never bring himself to paint the Donatist leaders as other than somehow just below par, for all their positive qualities. They were 'obstinate' and 'arrogant' as well as being wrong-headed, and Donatism was always 'a sect'.[35] But from now on, the Donatists and their social background could never be left out of any account of Late Roman North Africa.

Gsell had made his name before he was 30. His discoveries dominated volume 14 of the *Mélanges*, but he was less than generous to scholars not associated with him, especially if they were Germans. Donatism and its social and economic background had been attracting research in Germany at this very time. In 1893 a Westphalian pastor, Wilhelm Thümmel, wrote a thesis devoted to an assessment of the sect. He drew attention to the origins of the schism in Numidia, to the support given by the Donatists to the native rebels Firmus and Gildo, and to the apparent coincidence of Donatism with a population speaking a native language, which Thümmel thought was Punic.[36] He had, however, never been in North Africa and was working from literary sources alone, but with a shrewd understanding of the available evidence which Gsell's and Graillot's discoveries would have reinforced.[37]

Gsell's reactions, however, illustrate the fraught relations between France and Germany at every level of society, as Harnack had experienced during his visit to Paris in 1887. Instead of an encouraging and complimentary review to a young scholar like himself with kindred interests to his own, his review in the *Mélanges* of 1895 was anything but friendly. Without giving Thümmel credit for his novel and scholarly approach to the problem of Donatism, he criticised his belief that the Donatists were 'anti-Roman'. Only the Circumcellions participated in social revolt, while many details, mainly geographical, in Thümmel's study were inaccurate.[38] In fact, Gsell was warning German scholars off North Africa. He was as keen to keep research into its antiquities in French hands as Cardinal Lavigerie had been regarding Carthage a few years before. Scholarship would be the poorer from such attitudes.

Meanwhile his career was prospering. In December 1894 he became Titular Professor of African Antiquities in the École des Lettres, soon to become a Faculty in the University of Algiers. In the same year as already mentioned he wrote up a French version of his Latin thesis on Tipasa, entitled, 'Tipasa ville de Maurétanie Césarienne'and transferred the *Chronique* of excavations and dis-coveries in North Africa from the *Revue Africaine* to the more prestigious *Mélanges*, which he continued to write until the end of 1904. In 1900 he was appointed Inspector of Antiquities in Algeria, and two years later Director of the Museum of Algerian Antiquities and Muslim Art.[39] He was already proving himself an enthusiastic visitor and advocate of the burgeoning local collec-tions of antiquities.

A relatively light load of work in the university allowed Gsell time to pursue what he was best at doing, namely, the discovery, accurate recording, and where possible, excavating Classical and early Christian sites. One excavation, at Benian (Ala Miliaria) in Oran which he published in 1899 was particularly rewarding.[40] Whereas most Christian cemeteries in North Africa give few clues as to their religious identity, at Benian Gsell came upon a small but exclusively Donatist burial ground and church. The latter had been built round the tomb of Robba, a woman in vows (*Sanctimonialis*) and *sacr*[*a*] *Dei* who had been murdered by the Catholics (*c*[*a*]*ede tradit*[*orum*]) and who deserved the 'dignity of martyr' (*meruit dignitate*[*m*] *martiri*[*i*]). She was aged 50 at the time of her death on 24 March 435, nearly a quarter of a century after the proscription of the Donatist Church by the emperor in 412. The church was built presumably in her honour, between 434 and 439. Before that, there had been burials since 422, and these continued until 446. It was a close-knit community whose leaders were buried in funerary chambers and in an adjacent crypt, containing the bodies of the Donatist Nemessanus, bishop of Ala Miliaria for 18 years. His sister, members of his clergy and probably of his successor's (Januarius[?]), resting 'in the faith of the Gospel'. As Paul Monceaux pointed out, Gsell had discovered a Christian site of first importance. It showed that in distant Mauretania, the writ of the emperor in religious matters did not always run, especially now that Mauretania was cut off by the Vandal kingdom from Carthage. There was deep sectarian ill-feeling between Donatists and Catholics in that far-off province, with the Donatists still asserting the dual primacy of martyrdom and faith in the gospel as their distinctive beliefs and worship.

In 1903, Gsell excavated a small basilica in south-western Numidia which conveyed a different message from that of Benian. Henchir Akhrib would appear to have one of many local Numidian churches, built in the fourth century, but in this case continuing through the Vandal occupation into Byzantine times. The reliquaries, however, that he uncovered told a different story from the tombs found at Benian. The main occupation was in the mid- and late sixth century. There was a dedication to the martyr Cassian, probably the same who was executed at Tingis (Tangier) in 298. The presbyter Floridus, however, commemorated the deposition of separate reliquaries in honour of Laurence the Roman deacon executed in Valerian's persecution on 6 August 258, whose cult was celebrated in Constantinople as well as Rome, and probably Julian of Antioch. Another reliquary placed under the altar commemorated the deposition of the relics of the martyrs Julian and Laurence 'by the hands of Columbus the bishop of the holy church of Nicivibus' (N'gaous) on 4 October 582 (reign of Tiberius II). The inscriptions written in barbarous script showed that the cult of relics which had been a Donatist practice in a strongly Donatist area had been transformed into part of an official Byzantine cult, in which Byzantine saints were associated with native martyrs in a single ceremony.[41] Columbus was probably the same bishop mentioned by Pope Gregory as his agent in managing the papal estates in Numidia.[42] The excavation had thrown unexpected light on the close ties between empire and Church that existed in Numidia in the latter part of the sixth century. It makes the recrudescence of Donatism on what appear to be great papal estates in the pontificate of Pope Gregory (590–604) a challenging question.

Meantime, Gsell had published another great synthesis, the two-volume *Monuments antiques de l'Algérie* (1901). In this work he showed his breadth of interests in Algeria's past, chapters being devoted to grottos and rock carvings, as well as illustrated articles on every type of Classical and Byzantine ruin, including his most recent work at Benian. The study retains its value today, because it shows the state of the remains in 1900 before the native population began to expand and French settlers, though greedy for the cut stone available from ruins, were scattered relatively thinly throughout Tunisia and Algeria. A similarly useful study of the organisation of water supplies in Roman Algeria followed the next year,[43] as a preparation for what was to prove his enduring masterpiece, the *Atlas archéologique de l'Algérie* (1902–11).

The decade 1901–11 marked the high point in Gsell's career in Algeria. His work in the university flourished. He was beginning to train competent assistants and successors. One was Felix de Pachtère (d. 1916) whose study of an inscription from Lamasba detailing how, in the reign of Elagabalus (218–22), a group of farmers was arranging the distribution of water supplies for their holdings, remains the best work on the subject today.[44] He himself cooperated with C. A. Joly on excavations at Annoucoper (Thibilis),[45] and was also interesting himself increasingly in the art and archaeology of the Arab population. In 1905 he organised an Exposition d'Art Musulman at the Medersa in Algiers, and planned, but never completed, a history of Arab Muslim art in Algeria. Now, he began to be recognised for his worth. In 1902 he was elected Correspondant de l'Institut, and next year appointed Chevalier of the Légion d'honneur. But unlike von Harnack, whose ability in his own field he equalled, further honours came slowly. He was never promoted to Officier in the Legion d'honneur and had to wait until 1923 before he was elected member of the Académie des Inscriptions et Belles Lettres, scant recompense for the brilliant work to which he had devoted his life in Algeria. He was outspoken, being strongly critical of what he considered to be a waste of money. He protested against the expenditure of 500,000 francs on the recovery of the town plan of Timgad. Rural archaeology could have used the money better.[46] This criticism was not calculated to make him popular with the powers-that-be in Paris. Some wrote him off as a *bouru*, obsessed with his studies, with no time for outside life. Perhaps he was too stern a critic of his colleagues.

After nine years the *Atlas* was finally completed in 1911.[47] It was a prodigious work, founded on a special edition of the current military 1/200,000 map. It was divided up into 50 compact areas; in each there was a numbered entry corresponding to a surviving ruin or other remain. There were a very great many: Batna, for instance, Bou Taleb (the area between the salt lakes and foothills of the Aurès), Constantine, Theveste all contributed hundreds of ancient remains. The whole work included 10,000 sites amounting to 510 pages in double columns. Each entry was carefully catalogued, with a description of the ruin and a reference where possible to any literature describing it, or the number of a published inscription in the *Corpus Inscriptionum Latinorum*. It was a prodigious work, of lasting value, a tribute to Gsell's patience, observation on the spot, and attention to detail. As with the *Monuments* the timing could not have been better, for the same reasons. Many areas, particularly north of the Aurès, were sparsely inhabited and often the ruins and their buildings could be observed above the surface. The same could be said of this countryside in the 1930s when a combination of field work by scholars of the École française and additional surveys by a combination of staff from the Musée Gustave Mercier at Constantine, administrators of the *communes mixtes* and settlers enabled further sites to be explored, before the Second World War and its aftermath closed down much of central Algeria to scholarly research.[48]

The years 1910–11, however, also brought tragedy to Gsell from which he never completely recovered. He had married late, in 1909, but his wife died the next year in giving birth to a son. Gsell was heartbroken, and could no longer abide to stay in the country he now associated with this tragedy. Fortunately, he was elected to a chair of the History of North Africa at the Collège de France in 1911 and left Algiers early in the next year. This did not mean a complete parting, for he retained the position of Inspector of Antiquities in Algeria, to which was added in 1919 that of Inspector-General of archaeological and scientific museums in Algeria. This kept him in touch, and in 1914 he published jointly with his pupil Charles A. Joly an account of the survey and specimen excavation of the large urban sites of Khamissa, Mdaourouch and Announa in the north-central part of Algeria.[49]

From now on, however, his life was centred on the Collège de France and Paris. Too old (he was 50 when war broke out) to be involved in the fighting in the First World War, he continued to teach, and to consolidate the results of his researches of the previous 25 years. In 1915 he contributed a study of Herodotus, inaugurating a series undertaken by the university of Algiers of Textes relatifs à l'histoire de l'Afrique du Nord.[50] At the same time he began to collect material for a corpus of *Insciptions latines de l'Algérie*, the first volume consisting of inscriptions from the north and east part of Algeria, the Consular Province of Numidia in Roman times. It was to be continued after Gsell's death by P. F. Pflaum who published a second volume of Algerian inscriptions in 1957.

Gsell's real aim, however, and all-consuming object of his researches for the rest of his life, was a history of North Africa from the earliest times to the end of the Byzantine period.[51] His inaugural lecture at the Collège de France was entitled 'Histoire ancienne d'Afrique' and it prepared the way. From 1913 to 1928 he produced eight comprehensive volumes, but the end of the eighth volume had only brought the story down to the death of King Juba II of Mauretania in AD 39.[52] The Roman period had scarcely begun. The work had been planned and carried into practice on too massive a scale. Much of Volume 1 was taken up with a detailed geographical description of North Africa, region by region. From his study of the level of the Algerian *chotts*, Gsell concluded that the climate had not changed since Roman times. There was still the abundant rainfall on the coast contrasted with the uncertain but dry climate inland. Texts indicated that harvests could be missed owing to lack of rain. Camels were being used to transport goods from semi-desert areas inland to the Tripolitanian ports in the third century. Romanised town and steppe existed within striking distance of each other, and hence the nomadic pillager was never far away. Exceptions were the fertile valley of the Medjerda, sustaining scores of Romanised settlements, and the olive growing areas south of Theveste and north of the Aurès.[53] These chapters displayed an enormous detailed knowledge of the historical geography of those people whose story he set out to tell. They also paved the way for another professor at Algiers University, E. F. Gautier, to write his classic, *Le Passé de l'Afrique du Nord* (1937).

Subsequent volumes told the story in detail of the Carthaginian state, its conquests in North Africa and Spain, its wars with Rome and its downfall through the combination of Roman superiority on land and sea, and the enmity of Massinissa and the Numidians. In the fifth and sixth volumes (publ. in 1927) he returned to his beloved Numidians, describing Berber society in the time of Massinissa (d. 148 BC) and Juba I, tribe by tribe, detailing their way of life, relations between rulers and subjects, their dwellings and their crops, and famous Numidian horses. The eighth volume, published in 1928, recounted the rise and fall of Juba's Mauretanian kingdom in the far west of North Africa, and its cession to Rome on the death of Juba II in AD 39. It was a magnificent work but, as one critic pointed out, Gsell seldom allowed himself to go beyond his texts. A little more analysis and boldness in their interpretation would have been welcome.[54] One finds, in fact, the same strength and weakness in Gsell's *magnum opus* as in his early work on the emperor Domitian.

Gsell intended to continue his work at least as far as the Vandal invasion of 429. Notes on texts of Tertullian and on Père Lavigerie's excavation of the Basilica Majorum outside the walls of Carthage, handed to the writer by M. Esquer, librarian of the city library at Tunis, in 1938, demonstrate his interest in Christian North Africa beyond the frontiers of Numidia. It is a pity that he never continued his history into the Roman period where he would have made a lasting contribution. He never lost, however, his zeal for North Africa. His long article 'La Tripolitaine et la Sahara au IIIe siècle de notre ère', published in 1926, showed how the Berber nomads, learning to domesticate the camel, came to dominate the steppes bordering the Sahara, and was another fundamental study. A reader would have been able to appreciate how the Vandal and Byzantine occupations eventually collapsed in face of the continuous pressure of raiders, whether Berber or Arab, dominating the Saharan oases.[55] Another article, written in 1928, 'Le christianisme en Oranie avant la conquête arabe', summed up his discoveries west of Algiers over the previous 30 years.[56]

In 1930, Gsell presided over the fifth international archaeological Congress at Algiers and, in October 1931, the celebration of the fiftieth anniversary of the founding of the École française de Rome. On both occasions he received congratulations and tributes from its members. He was only 67, but he was ageing fast, faster than he realised. In the late autumn of that year he was struck down by a severe illness. He seemed to have recovered well, but early on New Year's Day 1932 he suffered a massive heart attack and died the same morning. Two posthumous articles, on the Martyrs of Ammaedara[57] and the churches recently discovered at Thelepte,[58] bear witness to an abiding interest in all things connected with the life and archaeology of North Africa.

Stéphane Gsell is not an easy man to sum up. His best work was done, with great enterprise by any form of transport to hand before he was 30, discovering, surveying and recording the innumerable Roman–Berber ruins north of the Aurès. This work culminated in his masterpiece, the *Atlas archéologique de l'Algérie* (1911), dedicated to his late wife. He never really recovered from her death the previous year. The impression he leaves after that is of a very private man who devoted his energies to his work in the Collège de France and his publication of his monumental eight-volume *Histoire de l'Afrique du Nord*.[59] He does not seem to have been involved in any great controversies such as enlivened the career of von Harnack, nor in opposition to the Nazi regime that consumed so much of Lietzmann's final period. Gsell was an impressive public speaker. He deserved fully his friend J. P. Luciani's verdict that he was 'l'homme juste qui vécut et mourut sans faiblesse'.[60] His greatest pleasure would have been, as he said, to have had a settlement in Algeria named after him.[61] It may have been a shy and brusque manner that prevented him from forming the friendships necessary for gaining senior appointments and awards. The few photographs of him that survive, such as that taken in April 1930, show a man in a dark suit, of medium height and sturdy build, with a firm gaze;[62] but the appearance concealed also a generosity of spirit towards his former pupils in Algiers, as well as a love for the Algerian *bled* (countryside).

He will be remembered as the scholar who above all others explored and put on record the social and religious history of Roman-Berber Algeria, placing both aspects on the irrefutable foundation of archaeological evidence, thus freeing future research from dependence on texts, overwhelmingly compiled by orthodox writers. Like his contemporary, Sir William Ramsay, he had the heart of an explorer, with Ramsay's single-mindedness but without Ramsay's thrusting arrogance. In the decade after his death a new generation of scholars, brilliant *scolaires* of the École française as well as established archaeologists, such as Louis Leschi and André Berthier, continued his work. The world of Classical, early Christian and Byzantine studies has been made infinitely poorer by the succession of events since 1940, which have effectively closed off central Algeria to scholarly research in the writer's lifetime.

The years, however, immediately following Gsell's death were the most important to date in the archaeological exploration of Algeria, specially from its Christian remains. Year after year, between 1932 and 1939 youthful *scolaires* from the École française de Rome would set out to Algeria and work on a Christian site that promised fruitful results. One of the earliest forays was that of Willian Seston at Ain Tamda (Mauretania) in 1927, which he believed was a monastery, but was more likely a granary attached to a basilica.[63] He was followed in 1932 by Marcel Simon working on a basilica at Henchir el Ateuch 50km south-east of Setif dating to *c.*380–450,[64] richly decorated with plaster plaques on the walls, where he found a quantity of fragments of liturgical glass vessels,[65] but no inscriptions. More fortunate with regard to the latter were P. Cayrel and Pierre Courcelle who carried out successive seasons of work at Ksar el Kelb (Vegesela) in south-central Algeria between 1933 and 1936 on what proved to be an important Donatist basilica dedicated to the martyred Bishop Marculus.[66] The latter met his end at the hands of the Imperial commissioners Paul and Macarius in either 347 or 348. The identification of Marculus as the honoured martyr was shown by an inscription, 'Hic memoria Domini Marchuli' and the Donatist allegiance by another on the top of the vault across the entrance 'Deo laudes H(ic) omnes dicamus'. Eight tombs dedicated to confessors (probably victims of the Macarian persecution) had been placed beneath the apse of the semicircular presbyterium at the east end of the church.[67] This work was followed by that of M. Labrousse in 1937 at Henchir Tarlist, also in central Algeria, which proved to be of a basilica of Byzantine date,[68] and finally in 1938 by Jean Guey working on a Christian site at Drah Souid, also in south-central Algeria.[69]

Over all these excavations presided the figure of André Berthier (1907–2000) and his two friends, Maurice Martin, *propriétaire* of a farm at M'Chira south of Château du Rummel, and Fernand Logeart, Administrateur du Commune Mixte of Ain Mlila, who provided the necessary official backing for Berthier's work.[70]

The contribution to the archaeology of central Algeria made by these three researchers cannot be overestimated. At this time Roman-Berber remains, especially the remains of circular 'barrows' and vestiges of Christianity, were so numerous in the *Département* of Constantine as to defy an accurate count. The area eventually selected by Berthier for research measured 110km broad and 40km wide and comprised the area of the Chotts where Gsell himself had worked in his journeys with Henri Graillot in 1893–4.[71] Over 70 Christian sites were surveyed with excavations in many of them between 1934 and 1940, and the results published under the stress of war and German occupation of a large part of France, at Algiers in 1942.[72] In addition, Berthier carried out with Martin notable excavations on churches at Bou Takrematen (perhaps the onetime Roman town of Nova Sparsa)[73] and at Sila and Sigus on the northern fringe of the area explored.[74]

André Berthier was not a professional archaeologist. His early studies at Senlis, near his birthplace at Beaumont sur Oise, and then at Paris, were designed to prepare for study at the École des Chartes from which he graduated in 1931. Afer a year's military service he was appointed at the age of 25 as Head of the Archives Department of the *Département* of Constantine. Soon he became Curator of the Musée Gustave Mercier in Constantine and editor of the longstanding archaeological and cultural periodical, the *Receuil de Constantine*. After the Algerian war of 1954–62 his tact and abilities were recognised by the new Algerian rulers, and after carrying out notable campaigns of excavation in the Roman city of Tiddis, he returned to France only in 1975. He was employed by the Archives Nationales until he retired at the age of 70 in 1978, but remained in contact with scholarship until his death in 2000.[75]

Berthier had seen at once the chance which his appointment gave him of following up Gsell's within central Algeria and, inspired by the example of his predecessors at the Musée, Jeanne and Pierre Alquier, set to work. Thanks to a letter of introduction from Louis Poinssot, Director of Antiquities in Tunisia, I came into contact with him in the late spring of 1938 and at the same time the next year, Noel Duval in his *Memoir* in *Antiquitée Tardive* devoted to Berthier's life describes my arrival on the Algerian scene as a 'coup de foudre',[76] which helped to give a new direction and impetus to the Christian archaeology of Algeria. In fact, I was able to accompany Berthier and his colleagues on a series of surveys and inspections of *chantiers* (working groups) directed by Algerian foremen, and in June 1939 was entrusted with the site of Kherbet Baharous, some 12 miles south of St Arnaud, to complete an excavation of the surrounds of an olive press discovered by

Berthier[77] and assess the site as a typical olive-producing area. The excavations at one time seemed on the point of total failure, until I decided to investigate some bumpy ground just 4m north of the olive press. This time my luck held. Digging soon revealed a well-built three-naved 17m long and 9m wide basilica associated with a granary which was appearing just to the west. A coin of Constantius II (337–61) low in the deposit covering the basilica and another of Gallienus resting on the original ground level helped to fix the building and complex as fourth century.[78] Honour was saved, and Berthier's immediate reaction, 'Vous avez gaspillé 5,000 francs' (You have wasted 5,000 francs) was turned into lavish praise.

In fact the real service I was able to render to Berthier's team was to link their discoveries on the ground with texts relating to Donatism found in Optatus of Milevis' *De Schismate Donatistarum* written *c*.365 and Augustine's attacks on the movement some 40 years later. The conclusion to be drawn from both writers was that 'Consular Numidia' (i.e. eastern and central Algeria) was the heartland of the Donatist Church,[79] and here on the ground was the evidence. There were the 'basilicas non necessarias', complained of by Optatus[80] – six at Oued Rzel alone[81] – the universal cult of martyrs, the occasional Deo Laudes inscription and the absence of any site which would be distinguished as 'Catholic'. The criticisms levelled at Berthier and his judgements by Noel Duval towards the end of his *Memoir* were not well founded.[82] Despite all, Donatist Numidia remains intact. There were few, if any, 'false martyrs'.[83]

One criticism, however, could be made, a failure too often to date the evidence accurately, and worse, to distinguish between the fourth- and sixth-century buildings. The North African villages appear to have survived the Vandal occupation (429–534) practically unscathed, but one finds in Byzantine times the cult of martyrs, reinforced by overseas saints, becoming a symbol of loyalty not to Rome but to the Byzantine state.[84] More observation on the ground for evidence for two or more periods of building would have been of great assistance to later generations of scholars.

There was also too great a desire to find caskets or pots containing relics (*les reliquaires*) which needed to be unearthed strictly in the context of the excavation as a whole.

But no praise can be too high for Berthier, his colleagues and their superior, Louis Leschi, Inspecteur Général d'Antiquités, for their work in the decade before the Second World War. Without it, Gsell's work would have been left incomplete, begging more questions than it answered, leaving a plethora of individual sites on his map without unifying features or dating, to be lost beneath the plough of the growing Berber-Arab population in Algeria.

I was able to visit Kherbet Baharous once more during my service with the Political Intelligence Department of the Foreign Office (Psychological Warfare Branch) in 1943. I met my old foreman who had conscientiously kept a small silver object – perhaps a brooch – decorated with circular Berber designs. There was nothing to be done, so I handed it back to him suggesting he gave it to the nearest museum. It was an unquiet time, in which I already felt French authority, so firm in 1939, slipping away. At that period I had hoped that archaeology would help mould the peoples of the south and north shores of the Mediterranean together, and that we, uninvolved with the quarrels arising from the Muslim conquest of the south, would be able to assist in bringing this about. It proved to be an idle vision of youth, as I found in March 1944 when, as Head of the Political Intelligence for North Africa (PWB 'D' Section) based in Tunis, I suggested to my French colleagues that France should seek to turn her possessions in North Africa into a Dominion, as we were planning for India. The answer was strongly negative. There was no Lord Lugard among the French colonial administrators. I went on to join the German Section of the PID/PWB in Italy. Today, nothing could be further from the possible. The study, however, of the history of the Donatist movement through the remains recorded by Stéphane Gsell and his successors has been among the guiding influences in my approach to the story of the Christian Church.

4

Sir William Mitchell Ramsay (1851–1939): Native and Early Christian in Asia Minor

'In the contact of East and West originates the movement of history.'[1] The historical position of Christianity could not be rightly understood without its relation to that immemorial meeting and conflict.[2] Thus, wrote Sir William Ramsay in 1906 in the Preface to his *Letters to the Seven Churches of Asia*. This passion to understand what he believed to be 'the collision between East and West throughout history', had been a leading but underlying interest he had fostered 'since early youth'.[3] He saw Christianity as the religion which associated East and West 'in the higher range of thought than either can reach alone'.[4] It formed a bridge and link between them. These ideas provided the key, first, to his undying interest in the history and geography of the Roman provinces of Phrygia and Galatia, and then his intense pre-occupation with Luke and Paul, the accuracy of the story told in Acts 13–21 and Paul's letter to the Galatians. In pursuit of these aims he laid the foundations for the archaeological exploration of the central and southern part of Asia Minor as surely as his contemporary Stéphane Gsell was recovering the evidence for a distinctive Roman-Berber culture and religion in central Algeria (ancient Numidia).

William Mitchell Ramsay was a Glaswegian, born in that city on 18 March 1851. His family came from Alloa and were reasonably well off. Though his father, Thomas Ramsay, died in 1857 when

William was six, the family was able to send him away to school to the Gymnasium at Old Aberdeen, and thence to Aberdeen University. From there he gained a scholarship to St John's College, Oxford, and, after obtaining a First Class in Honour Moderations in 1873, spent the next year at the university at Göttingen. This proved to be one of the critical points in his life.

In front of the Preface to his *St Paul the Traveller and the Roman Citizen*, published in 1896, Ramsay reproduced a letter to his uncle Andrew Mitchell written from King's College, Aberdeen, on 17 September of the previous year. In this he describes how his stay in Göttingen in the Long Vacation of 1874 had been 'a critical point in my life'. His studies with Professor Theodor Benfrey not only introduced him to 'modern methods of literary investigation' but turned his thoughts 'towards the borderlands between European and Asiatic civilisation'. This chance he felt after 20 years he owed to his uncle, Mitchell, and wrote to acknowledge his debt publicly.

His time at Oxford was fully occupied. He studied Greek under Jowett of Balliol and Sayce, and epigraphy under Sir Charles Newton, Keeper of Greek and Roman Antiquity in the British Museum. All this, as well as his degree, for which he had to study Paul's letter to the Galatians, he recalled more than 50 years later, were essential preparations for his life's work in Asia Minor.[5]

Meanwhile, he had married Agnes Dick in 1878. She came from a strongly Wee Free background, her father being prominent in the schism that disrupted the Church of Scotland in 1843. She bore him two sons, the younger being killed in action in 1915, and four daughters:[6] Margaret and Mary were good scholars, especially Margaret, who held the Crown Robertson Fellowship at Aberdeen University in 1904 and wrote a distinguished article in the development of provincial art in Phrygia and Isauria for *Studies in the Eastern Roman Provinces* (1906). Agnes accompanied her husband on his first visit to Asia Minor in 1880, and subsequently in 1884 and 1886. Later, when the family was growing up, she was with him on a memorable visit to Constantinople during the revolution there in 1909.

Ramsay's chance came in 1879, when a studentship was advertised for travel and research in Greek lands. His rival for the appointment was none other than Oscar Wilde, who was ostensibly more qualified than Ramsay, but fluffed his chances by overpraising Roman statues in the British Museum when the object of the travel would be Greece. On his appointment, Charles Newton advised Ramsay not to centre his research in Athens, where the French and Germans already predominated, but to go to Asia Minor, and work on the remains of ancient Greek civilisation there.[7]

Ramsay accepted the advice and in May 1880 set out with his wife for Smyrna (lzmir). There, he was lucky enough to meet (Sir) Colonel Charles Wilson who had the title of Consul-General in Anatolia, who advised him not to confine himself to the Graeco-Roman sites on the coast but to travel inland. He should try to follow and if possible improve on the work carried out by the two French scholars Lebas and Waddington, who had travelled, noting and recording inscriptions in the inland provinces of Asia Minor over 30 years before, in 1843–4.[8]

As Ramsay generously acknowledges, he was not the first of his generation in the field. He had been anticipated by two young French scholars, Louis Duchesne and Maxime Collignon, who had set out boldly but inadequately equipped into Anatolia in 1876, sponsored by the newly founded École française d'Athènes.[9] He was to be luckier.

When Ramsay embarked on his first expedition in October 1881, in company with Colonel Wilson and members of his staff, the political situation was more favourable to exploration by non-Muslims. The British benefited in particular, owing to the improvement of relations between Great Britain and Turkey following the Congress of Berlin in 1878. Nonetheless, travelling in Anatolia in the 1880s was a harsh experience. In 1885, Ramsay describes how two years before, accompanied by the Virginian scholar from Amhurst University, J. R. S. Sterret, he was aiming at the site of Hierapolis. 'Before ascending the steep range of mountains extending north-east south-west we encamped for the

night at a village called Mandanaa or Ak Tekesme close under
their foot.'[10] Another laborious climb next day brought them
to a cave, and there they found inscriptions on the walls dedicated
to the goddess Meter Leto which they copied before moving
on to another exacting day's work. Enterprise had brought its
reward.

Ramsay's first expedition in 1881 had been even more fruitful.
His party arrived at a series of ruins of Greco-Roman towns in the
valley of the River Glaukos, a tributary of the Maeander. These
included Otrous and Hieropolis known to Church historians from
their bishops' opposition to Montanism (Eusebius, *HE* v.16.3 and
5). Eumeneia lay to the east and Pepuza, the Montanist centre to
the west (see Map). At Kelendres, the probable site of Otrous,
Ramsay discovered a funerary inscription commemorating a certain Alexander, son of Antonius, dated precisely to AD 216. These
funerary inscriptions were often lengthy, with the object of defin-
ing ownership and right of inheritance, and hence the threat of
dire punishment in case of unauthorised disturbance. They were
legal documents, the title deeds of a family.

Alexander's epitaph was peculiar. As mentioned, the first lines
read, 'I, a citizen of a distinguished (*eklektes*) city made this [tomb]
while I was still alive that my body may have a resting place in the
eyes of men (*phaneroi*)'. Further on, it claimed that Alexander had
been 'a disciple (*mathétés*) of the holy shepherd'. The phrasing at
once suggested to Ramsay that Alexander had been a Christian,
and he determined to research further on his return to Britain.[11]
Before he did so, he met Waddington, now a diplomat and soon to
be French Ambassador in London. Waddington inspired the
young scholar further, and in particular showed how his work in
fixing the location of sites could be helped by the study of the
coinage of the Greek cities in Asia Minor.[12] In 1882 he put his fine
collection at Ramsay's disposal. As there were no excavations,
without its help and that of the British Museum collection his
studies, particularly of the cities visited by St Paul and those in the
book of Revelation, would have been less convincing.

Ramsay returned to Britain and in 1882 published an article in the *Journal of Hellenic Studies*, established in 1880. In this he was able to demonstrate the link between the Alexander inscription and the language of the late fourth century *Vita Abercii*. This celebrated the life of Avircius Marcellus, the anti-Montanist bishop of Hieropolis, who flourished *c*.190.[13] Sentences used in the *Vita* were evidently well enough known in the early third century to be used on a tombstone of a prominent Christian of a neighbouring town.

This was an outstanding discovery in itself, but it was followed by one with which Ramsay would always be associated. He returned to the Otrous area in 1883, with Sterret. The latter had been trained through the Asia Minor Exploration Fund and proved an invaluable colleague. Exploring the ruins of a bath house at the hot springs three miles south of the site of Hieropolis they came on three fragments of what appeared to be a large and richly decorated pagan altar. They looked more closely. To their surprise they could read words such as *ichthun* (fish), 'golden', 'Euphratcn' (the river Euphrates) and 'golden-sandalled queen'. Soon, Ramsay was able to make out that the owner of what proved to be an epitaph and not an altar was, like Alexander, 'a citizen of a distinguished (or elect) city' and a 'servant of the shepherd'. Further, it revealed his name, Avircius Marcellus, who at the age of 72 had set up the memorial in his lifetime recording his journeys from the furthest east of the Roman empire, Nisibis, to Rome. On these, he had been accompanied 'by a pure virgin with bread and wine' for him and his friends to partake. He had also been 'accompanied by Paul with Faith leading the way', and he had found 'all gathered together', that is, no dissenters.[14] Ramsay's find was the earliest dated Christian inscription (and remains so), as well as evidence supporting Eusebius, citing the late second-century writer Hegesippus,[15] that at this period the Greek-speaking Church in Asia Minor was united (except for the Montanist dissenters). Ramsay duly reported the discovery in the *Journal of Hellenic Studies* but for the time being it made little stir among Continental scholars. In 1888 he returned to the site and organised the transfer of the inscription to the Lateran Museum. Though a strong

Presbyterian himself he had no doubt either of the Christian significance of the discovery, nor where the inscription would be best housed and studied.

The controversy that broke out in 1894–5 following Adolf von Harnack's intervention has already been narrated.[16] Suffice it to say that as Ramsay's description of his discovery in *Cities and Bishoprics in Phrygia* (1895–7) makes clear, he never wavered for a moment from his first assessment of the inscription. It remains one of the great archaeological discoveries adding to our knowledge of the early Church. If Ramsay had done nothing more, his place in the history of archaeology and early Christianity would have been secure. The years 1882–91 were full for Ramsay in Asia Minor. Every year saw him on a new expedition; every year was a new harvest of inscriptions. In 1882, again travelling with Colonel Wilson and aided by the General Manager of the Ottoman Railway, Mr Barfield, he fixed the site of Akroenos, where for the first time Byzantines defeated the Arabs in a major engagement in Asia Minor, in 739. Next year he published 450 inscriptions in the *Journal of Hellenic Studies*, that he and Sterrett had found in Phrygia, describing his article as 'Cities and Bishoprics in Phrygia', a title used 15 years later for his *magnum opus*.[17] He was also starting to collect material for *The Historical Geography of Asia Minor*, published in 1890 (after the loss of nearly the entire manuscript while travelling by train to Aberdeen). In 1884, he was back in Phrygia, this time accompanied by his wife and Sterrett. The party spent a considerable time among the ruins of Eumeneia (Ishekli) which he had examined there years before. Among the tombstones found on this occasion were 26, which as well as a reference to a sum to be paid to the treasury if the owner's tomb was disturbed included the additional threat that the offender would have 'to account to God' or 'to the living God' or 'to God the Judge'. These could be Jewish, 'the living God' (*ton zónta théon*) being a normal description of God by the Jews of the Dispersion; but in the third century, the date of most of these inscriptions, the Christians would be careful not to draw too much attention to themselves, and the formulae would suit that purpose.[18] In addition an inscription from Philomelium where there was a Christian community in the 160s (Eusebius, *HE* iv.15.3) and another from Iconium add the words 'At the Pasché [God] will judge in the future the living and the dead'.[19] Another 'living God' inscription had been set up for a bishop in the fourth century.[20] The Christian attribution seemed incontrovertible. The formulae, however, could hardly have caused offence, and, as Ramsay claimed, 'no violent break between pagan and Christian culture had taken place', in Eumeneia, a comparatively wealthy town.[21] What the Christians sought was legality rather than absolute concealment.

Ramsay was content to look at the evidence for early Christianity in Asia Minor through the eyes of a Classical historian. He saw archaeology as a means of interpreting the wealth of meaning that underlay the literary references.[22] He was then writing about the Church in the early Roman empire and Acts, but his attitude to evidence from other periods was the same. His interest at this time was Phrygia, its ancient peoples and civilisation, as much as Christianity, and he devoted a substantial article in the *Journal of Hellenic Studies* of 1888 mainly to 'sepulchral customs in ancient Phrygia', where he discussed in detail the significance of the false door, altar and lion symbols on Roman-Phrygian monuments. The lion he believed had been ultimately the inspiration for the Mycenaean Lion gateways in mainland Greece.[23] The previous year he had been leading another expedition in Phrygia accompanied by his wife, Dr Brown and D. G. H. Hogarth of Magdalen College, Oxford. Examples of Phrygian art had again been their main objective, but on the site of the town of Dionysopolis his party had come on the remains of a temple dedicated to Artemis Leto and Apollo Lairbenos.[24] Phrases used by suppliants to the deities asking pardon for misdemeanours carved as inscriptions included acclamations, 'Great Apollo' and 'Great Artemis'.[25] Ramsay saw at once that the religion practised at Dionysopolis and Ephesus was the same. The shouts of the crowd against Paul, 'Great is Artemis' actually happened and indicated an eyewitness account of the episode recorded in Acts 19.22–41.[26]

One group of inscriptions discovered in the Tembris Valley in

1886 found Ramsay less sure-footed. Waddington had already come upon some memorials on which the dedicant had openly confessed his Christianity.[27] Ramsay found three more and in 1888 published these with Waddington's discovery in the *Expositor*.[28] Today, thanks to further work by Ramsay's pupil, J. G. C. Anderson, and his successor in the next generation of exploration, William Calder, it would seem almost certain that these inscriptions proclaiming their dedicators 'Christians for Christians' are Montanists.[29] Ramsay, however, while registering their peculiarity, attributed this to the arrival in northern Phrygia of rigidly inclined missionaries from Bithynia. A lax administration, he thought, in this out of the way corner of the province would have enabled 'a community of little social organisation and great individuality' to proclaim its religion without fear.[30] His views about the social organisation of the Tembris Valley farmers were speculative, though until more work in the field is undertaken they remain one possibility. More likely is that these Tembris Valley farmers were converted in large measure to Montanism during the third century. Until then, Mēn was the great god of the territory, known as *patrios theos*, the Saturn of Phrygia.

Meantime, Ramsay's successes were inspiring others to follow. The Frenchmen Foutrier, Radet and Leschat based on Smyrna, struck eastwards into Lydia. Hogarth continued to work in Phrygia; Theodore Bent and E. C. Hicks went further south and explored parts of eastern Cilicia. Bent sailed along the south coast of Turkey, stopping at likely find-spots. On one occasion he records literally stumbling across 'extensive city ruins' at Lydae and evidence of 'a Roman palace or residence of the Proconsul at Patara'.[31] It was a period in which every type of archaeological discovery was possible; remains of towns could be found standing; and substantial academic articles written by the fortunate explorers.

Ramsay, of course, was one of the main beneficiaries. His career prospered. In 1885 he was elected to a newly created chair of Classical Archaeology sponsored by Lincoln and Merton colleges. Next year he was recalled to Aberdeen as Professor of Humanity, which he retained until he retired in 1911.[32] Unlike Harnack for much of his life and Gsell, he was from the outset an international scholar, contributing to foreign journals, particularly the *Bulletin de Correspondance hellénique* published by the École française d'Athènes. He corresponded with Mommsen, and in 1893 received a gold medal from Pope Leo XIII. He spanned national and ecclesiastical rivalries of the time. As one notable French scholar, M. G. Perrot commented, Ramsay set future bibliographers a task 'to track down all his scattered contributions, in Heaven knows how many different periodicals which contain his precious studies. What a lot of trouble a book would have saved!'[33]

Ramsay obliged. In 1890 he published a detailed monograph on *The Historical Geography of Asia Minor*, a vast reference work and a gazeteer of every known major site in Graeco-Roman Asia Minor, republished 72 years later in its original form. Four years before, Ramsay had hoped to 'make a study of the local history of the whole central plateau of Asia Minor, from the beginning of recorded history to the Mohammedan conquest', and this was the result.[34] The book opens with Ramsay's credo. Asia Minor was 'like a bridge between Asia and Europe', and, a little further on, 'the very character of the country has marked it out as a battle-ground between the Oriental and the European spirit',[35] much to the disadvantage of the former. As mentioned, these restraints he was to repeat 15 years later. During his travels in Phrygia he had mused whether the Phrygians and Carians were an 'Aryan people', European conquerors better equipped in war 'than opponents armed in slighter Oriental style'.[36] For a scholar and man of action of the time as was Ramsay in the 1880s the superiority of the 'Aryan Europeans' over 'Asiatics' was simply a fact of life.

In his book Ramsay aimed to lay the foundations on which the history of Asia Minor could be built.[37] Topography and its influence on the life of the inhabitants were essential. 'False topography meant false history', he declared. So, every scrap of evidence, literary and archaeological, was drawn into service. To his own researches on the ground were added information gleaned from Classical and Patristic texts, not least the letters of Basil of

Caesarea, the *Acta* of Church Councils, the list of bishoprics drawn up by the Byzantine ecclesiastical geographer in the *Synekdemos* of Hierocles (*fl.* 530), and the *Acta Sanctorum*. He was able thereby to correct mistakes made even by contemporary geographers such as Kiepert and establish the framework of an accurate survey of Greco-Roman and Byzantine Asia Minor and also the gradual penetration of Islam, first, under the Arabs and then under the Turks into this once-Christian territory. He concentrated first on the roads, tracing their main lines in ancient times from the coastal cities of Smyrna and Ephesus, testing the accuracy of the Antonine Itinerary, Peutinger Table, Strabo and Ptolemy against other textual evidence reinforced by his own discoveries. He pointed out how in the reigns of Diocletian and Constantine the road system was modified so as to give more importance to roads directed towards first Nicomedia and then Constantinople rather than the seaports serving Italy and Rome. 'The centre of attraction was no longer Rome . . . and the roads which served only for Roman traffic sank rapidly into mere cross-country paths.'[38] This enabled him, in turn, to explain the increase in the prosperity of the northern half of the Asia Minor plateau, between the reigns of Constantine and Justinian. The configuration of the Byzantine road system also provided the key to the strategy of the Comneni emperors in their desperate and unsuccessful efforts to oust the Turks from Asia Minor in the twelfth century.

The second part of the work was a vast gazetteer in which the major roads, cities, bishoprics and, where possible, the imperial estates were located and described, province by province. On the way, the author considered how far native language and nomenclature was replacing the Greco-Roman during the later Byzantine period. The return of long-submerged native culture in much of Asia Minor could be documented as it had been in Roman North Africa and even in sub-Roman Britain.[39] The whole work is a tribute to the enormous learning and enterprise of its author in this early stage in his career.[40] Others would build on his discoveries, but meantime he had compiled an accurate map for areas that previously had been either blank or, worse, inaccurately described.

By 1889 Ramsay was already feeling the strain of having to fulfil the duties of a professor and continuing explorations in Asia Minor. The publication of the *Historical Geography* marks a caesura in his career. He became ill with cholera, and, after a final journey to Apamea and the surrounding country in 1891, remained in Britain for the next eight years.

Ramsay's researches had included detailed study of the topography and available history of the bishoprics of Asia Minor. Though Christianity had figured, there had been no particularly Christian slant to his research. Now, this was to change. Spurred on by a respect for the work of Bishop Lightfoot (d. 1889) and perhaps by a reminiscence of having to read Galatians in detail as a requirement for the Oxford Final Schools he began to turn to the career and ideas of Paul as an essential part of the history of Christianity in Asia Minor. His first article featuring Paul appeared in the *Expositor* of October 1888, and thereafter the apostle and his work were never far from his research.[41]

Back in Britain the books whose absence Professor Perrot had so much regretted began to come thick and fast. Ramsay found himself in demand as a lecturer and some of his most notable books from 1891 onwards were the revised texts of his lectures – delivered, as appears to have been true both of Britain and Germany in the 1890s, in a prolix and rotund style. The first of these studies, *The Church in the Roman Empire to A.D. 170* was based on lectures given at Mansfield College, Oxford in May–June 1892. Only part of the second section was devoted to the history of the Church from 64 (the Neronian persecution) to 170, midway through the reign of Marcus Aurelius (161–80). The rest was occupied by Pauline and kindred studies, including a chapter (ch. 16) devoted to the legend of Paul and Thecla, the outline narrative of which, Ramsay believed, went back to the first century. Ramsay's explanation for the Pauline character of the earlier chapters was that Paul's career provided the best available account of the social and political conditions in Asia Minor in the mid-first century. The history of the Church threw light on many problems of Roman history.[42] He considered that the narrative contained in Acts 13 onwards was an accurate record of events.

To prove his point, Ramsay chooses the Acts account of St Paul's stay at Ephesus.[43] The three years that Paul spent there and his active mission from that base suggests that he may have planned Ephesus to be the centre for the communities he founded in Asia Minor. Acts 19.23–41 tells the story of the upsurge of violence against Paul by the silversmiths led by Demetrius and other traders whose living depended on sales to pilgrims to the temple of Artemis of models in clay or silver of the temple. Ramsay argued the opinion of Canon Hick, a well-read opponent, that had someone wanted to invent the story he would have made the priests of the temple the prime movers in the disturbances.[44] But that was not the case. Trouble came from traders who sold models of the temple to be carried in procession, and those made of silver would bring in a handsome profit. The priests did not feel threatened and were not overly concerned. The traders were; and the city council was terrified lest a riot got out of hand and resulted in the provincial governor using troops to quell it. The cry 'Great is Artemis', Ramsay showed convincingly, was the same as that already mentioned as having been found on the inscription in 1887 at the temple of Artemis–Leto at Dionysopolis.[45]

Elsewhere, Ramsay argued forcefully against Lightfoot and others who supported the 'North Galatian' theory of the route of Paul's missions.[46] Most New Testament scholars at the time set the missionary journeys of St Paul and his letter to the Galatians in North Galatia, that is, the country of the Asiatic Galatians of Celtic origin which would have included territory as far north as the provincial capital Ancyra (Ankara), which was partly Celtic-speaking. Ramsay, however, putting together text and topography concluded that Galatia must mean the inhabitants of the Roman province of Galatia which included parts of Phrygia, Lycaonia and Pisidia where the normal language was Greek and the people knew themselves as Greeks.[47] The 'South Galatian' theory, however, was more important than merely an alternative description of the area covered by Paul's mission. Ramsay believed that the right identification of the churches addressed by Paul in Galatians was essential for understanding the growth of the Church down to AD 150. As he saw it, the new religion progressed from Syrian Antioch to the Cicilian Gates and thence into Asia Minor, through Lycaonia along the main roads to Ephesus, and from Ephesus across the Aegean to Corinth and, finally, Rome. A subsidiary line of mission followed the land route to Philadelphia, Troas and thence to Philippi and via the Egnatian Way to Thessalonica. This latter line of communications enabled churches to be founded in Cappadocia and Pontus in the 80s and 90s. Ramsay had sometimes harsh things to say about those who flew in the face of what he believed clear evidence to maintain traditional opinion.[48] Ramsay could argue, however, that there were no churches mentioned in Paul's time as being founded in the area covered by North Galatia.

Ramsay's theory, worked out in detail by its author, makes sense, so did his avowed method of reinforcing evidence from the well-known texts of Tacitus, Suetonius and Pliny on the relations of Church and empire, with archaeological, topographical and numismatic material. This is how a historian of the early Church would approach the subject a century later. And one would agree with Ramsay that Acts, even though revised and finally compiled 20 years or so after Paul's death, was founded on events recorded by a contemporary, and provided an accurate picture of life and government in western Asia Minor in the 50s and 60s AD. It could not be a work by some unknown writer in the second century.[49]

Much of this was elaborated in Ramsay's second course of lectures in Mansfield College under the title 'St Paul the Traveller and the Roman Citizen' (1896). Once again, one finds his contempt for the lower orders of Graeco-Roman society in Asia Minor. He speaks of the 'moral degradation of the lower classes', 'grossly superstitious rustics' and priestly colleges that were on the side of 'stagnation, social anarchy, and enslavement of the people to the priests'.[50] In fact, he saw the story of Asia Minor since Graeco-Roman times as a process of degeneration. Christianity as preached by Paul opposed these influences and on this issue he was on the same side as the empire. Both would further universal citizenship and equality of rights founded on a universal religion and unified Church, but in Rome's case on the cult of Dea Roma and the emperor.[51] Ramsay saw the universal Christian religion as the natural successor to the claims of the immortal gods of Rome.

In these lectures also, Ramsay continued to define his aim, to interpret his subject as a department of history. He places the author of Acts 'among the historians of first rank', various details of whose narrative 'showed marvellous truth'. Luke in his view was 'a great historian'[52] and he rejected ideas common at the time that the author had clipped up older documents and patched together the fragments in a more or less intelligent way enabling the critic to pick out what documents or incidents were genuine and what were not.[53] He was to defend Luke's reputation a few years later in *Was Christ Born at Bethlehem?* (1898), pointing to his literary skill, unity of style, and command of historical detail shown in the first chapters of the Gospel.[54]

Ramsay's great advantage over his (and Luke's) critics was that he knew at first hand the location of the Pauline cities and their environment. It was a great pity that the Gallio inscription, fixing Paul's stay in Corinth as AD 51–2, had not yet been found.[55] This resulted in his chronology which placed Paul's controversy with the Judaic emissaries in Galatia in these years as mistaken. His verse-by-verse commentary on Acts, however, emphasising Paul's versatility, shown by his ability to combine Jewish and Hellenistic religious ideas and his genius for organisation, are surely correct and should stand the test of time. In his *Cities of St Paul* (1906), he would have more to say about the synthesis of Greek and Jewish philosophy that Paul imbibed in his early years at Tarsus.[56]

In this period, however, Ramsay will be remembered most for his two-volume study of *Cities and Bishoprics in Phrygia* (Oxford, 1895, 1897). The concept had been with him since he had written two articles with the same title in the 1880s. Here, he was able to consolidate the material he had accumulated during his journeys and studies and set it down as a *magnum opus*. This result was an immensely valuable survey of evidence relating to the life, religion, Christianisation and ultimately Islamisation of the people of Phrygia. Some material, such as his account of the discovery of the Abercius inscription, he had described before. Elsewhere, a pagan inscription from Oturak dated to the end of the reign of the emperor Maximin (312–13) records a succession of four pagan priests, one of whom, the priestess Spitale, claimed to have 'ransomed many from evil torments' (Christianity?).[57]

As was evident, however, from *St Paul the Traveller and the Roman Citizen* (1896), Ramsay had become acutely interested in Jewish-Christian religions in the first centuries AD. He considered rightly that the Jews in Asia Minor formed 'an active, intelligent and prosperous minority', which 'must have exercised a strong influence on their neighbours'.[58] Phrygian towns, such as Eumeneia, Dokimion, Iconium and Akmonia, provided evidence for a thriving Jewish community. At Akmonia he found a funerary inscription dating AD 60–80 of Julia Severa, a lady of royal Phrygian or Galatian descent, who was also a Jewess and leader of a synagogue.[59] Another inscription found near Hierapolis mentions an orphanage, either Jewish or Christian (*ergazia thremmatiké*).[60] Such evidence confirmed the account given by Luke in Acts 13.30 that at the time of Paul's first mission there were 'devout and honourable women' devoted to Judaism, but in this case not at all favourable to the dissident version offered by the Apostles.

Paul himself Ramsay was to describe as the son of a prominent family in Tarsus, a city that had had a large Jewish population since its foundation by the Seleuceids *c*.170 BC.[61] Despite his education as a Pharisee in Jerusalem, Paul was always influenced by the mixed Hellenic-Jewish background of his native city. Ramsay believed that in Palestine he had seen how the Hasmonaean dynasty had been unable to preserve the Jewish nation from Roman domination, and Pharisaism itself was too exclusive to exert an influence on the pagan world. God's promises to Israel could only be fulfilled if Gentiles also were included. His aim (which Herod the Great had shared in the sphere of politics) was to achieve unity between Jew and Greek by raising the Greeks to the Jewish level of morality and approach to God. As his fellow citizen Athenodorus had preached freedom from passions so Paul preached freedom from the Law. This message was to be carried throughout the civilised world. Jesus was Messiah for the Jews and Saviour for the Greeks. He was the Heavenly Man, sent by God to free humanity from superstition, idolatry and servitude to the powers of fate.[62]

In 1899 Ramsay resolved to undertake further exploration in Asia Minor. So far as he was concerned, things had not been going well. He complained that while up to 1892 exploration of the hinterland had been largely a British enterprise, this had now been taken over by other nationals.[63] Symbolic of this had been Franz Cumont's publication in 1895 of his first catalogue of Christian inscriptions in Asia Minor. Meantime, between 1894 and 1896, British exploration had 'nearly ceased',[64] the reason as usual being finance, coupled with the fact that in Scotland such activity was not universally approved. Scholars should be teaching elementary pupils.[65] Ramsay sought to remedy this by aiding the foundation in 1897 of a Wilson Fellowship for archaeological exploration of Asia Minor. J. G. C. Anderson was the first holder and made good use of it in his exploration of the Tembris Valley area. He was followed by T. Callander, another of Ramsay's students, who worked in Lycaonia and Isauria in 1904. Even so, funding remained on a hand-to-mouth basis.

Ramsay took up the challenge. His spell of work between 1899 and 1914 was almost as productive as the first. He was now 'a great man'. To his LLD, proudly displayed on the spine of *St Paul the Traveller and the Roman Citizen*, were now added DCL, and founder membership of the British Academy (1901). In 1904 he received the Victoria Gold Medal for Research from the Royal Geographical Society and two years later was knighted, a richly deserved honour. As noted above, two of his daughters shared their father's interests. Margaret becoming Croom Robertson Fellow in the Humanities in Aberdeen University in 1904 and Mary contributing artistic drawings in *Studies in the East Roman Provinces* (1906).

The Wilson Fellowship was not altogether successful, for in

1904 and 1905 Ramsay found himself accepting it, as there were no other suitable candidates. He was now working with Callander along the borderlands of Lycaonia and Isauria identifying among other discoveries the site of Savatra.[66]

In 1905, however, a new chapter opened. He had made Konia (Iconium) his base, and in that year was visited by Gertrude Bell who, after exploring early Christian sites in northern Syria, had moved up into southern Turkey (there was no frontier, as both were part of the Ottoman empire) and had started work among the churches that occupied the plateau centred on the settlement of Maden Shehir (Byzantine Barata) near Karamanlis.[67] From 1900 onwards this had proved a magnet for explorers. In turn, Anderson, Smirnov, Crowfoot and Holtzmann had visited the site, inspected the 22 standing remains of churches and the other churches and church buildings in the Kara Dagh mountain complex to the north. Holtzmann in particular, from Hamburg, had made detailed plans of some of the ruins. The Byzantine site in fact included almost every type of church built between the fifth and eleventh centuries and the almost intact ruin of a large monastery. It had survived the seventh-century Arab raids and flourished in the time of the Byzantine resurgence under John Tzimisces and Basil I (960–1025). The Kara Dagh had served as a refuge.[68]

Gertrude Bell asked Ramsay for help in deciphering an inscription she had found there. Next year Ramsay had urged the need for a proper exploration of the site, and in 1907 joined Bell in an expedition on the site. The spectacular results were published jointly within two years, and because of the continuous pillage of the area for stone by the increasing local population *The Thousand and One Churches* remains the standard work describing it.[69]

Ramsay made one other notable find in the years 1904–5, namely, the series of inscriptions from a site west of Godane on the Roman imperial estate (*regio*) centred on Pisidian Antioch. The Tekmoreian Brethren were an exclusive, religious group who conducted a mystical form of worship of the deities of the country, especially Artemis, and the emperors. It represented the alliance between ancient Phrygian worship and the imperial cult during the third century, and in the latter part of the century developed as an opponent of Christianity.[70] Ramsay was inclined to connect the numbers of inscriptions of that period to the deepening hostility between the two religions that resulted in the Great Persecution and destruction of Christian communities in Phrygia.

Ramsay's expeditions between 1899 and 1914 were less spartan than those of the 1880s. As well as his designated successors as field archaeologists and Classical historians, Anderson and the young William Calder, he was now often accompanied by his wife and daughter, Margaret. In 1909 he describes in a full-length book and in graphic detail how in April he and his companions bound for Asia Minor were delayed for 17 days by the events of a revolution that raged in and around Constantinople. The Revolution of April 1909 was the second of the two outbreaks – the first was in July 1908 – that brought the Young Turks to power in the Ottoman empire.[71] Two factions, the Liberals (the party in power) and the Freedom Party were rivals, and in the background were pro-British and pro-German parties, with the latter the stronger.[72] Constantinople was not safe for foreigners; yet Margaret Ramsay's exclamation when the family had reached Berlin on the first stage of their journey from England 'Could we not go straight on and be there when the fighting begins?'[73] sums up the sense of imperial superiority which the British felt towards 'the Orientals'. Nothing could happen to them!

Ramsay's detailed diary of the events of April and May 1909 shows that he could easily have been a foreign correspondent as well as an archaeologist. He interviewed Young Turks whom he met on the train to Constantinople, while Mrs Ramsay took pictures of the Soldiers of Liberty en route to the capital, and commented on the unfortunate consequences for Britain of ill-informed articles in *The Times*, in contrast to those of the Italian and German press.[74] He recorded the growth of anti-Christian feeling, the alternating hope and despair in the city as the prospect of civil war threatened, fulfilled by the entry of the 'Army of Liberty . . . into the city on 24 April and the surrender of the government forces'. He noted all this before being able to move on into Anatolia and his excavations 11 days later. For May he records his journey through Asia Minor to his work near Konia, much to the displeasure of British officials who tried in vain to dissuade him from his journey.[75] He also records the not unjustified fears of the Christians in Konia.[76]

Ramsay was never short of a word, and his books produced at this time would not disappoint. *The Letters to the Seven Churches* (1906) was written in the high noon of Edwardian assurance and prosperity. It reflects the sense of superiority tinged with anxiety of the European and, in particular, the Briton in regard to the East. The sentence with which this chapter opens, of conflict between East and West, captures the mood. In a book written in the aftermath of the Turkish victories in Thessaly over the Greeks in 1897 entitled *Impressions of Turkey*, Ramsay had warned that 'Mohammedanism and Orientalism have gathered strength to defy the feeling of Europe'.[77] As already mentioned he believed that the Christianity of St Paul and his successors provided the basis for a synthesis, a 'higher plane on which Asia and Europe may mix and meet'.[78] The direction of Christianity was towards an intermingling of European and Asiatic nature and ideas. The *Seven Churches* was written to further the understanding of that synthesis; just as the original Apocalypse, for all its Jewish models, was written to be read and understood by the Graeco-Asiatic public.[79]

The result was a book in which he stated his belief that the seven churches stood for the whole Church in the province of Asia, and in turn stood for the Church of Christ as it existed in the last decade of the first century.[80] The seven churches themselves headed groups of local churches. In contrast to Paul, the writer of the Apocalypse regarded the imperial government as Antichrist, 'the inevitable enemy of Christianity'.[81] The comparisons and contrasts which characterise the letters to the churches were between the power of God and that of his enemies, the empire, the pagan cities, the Jews and heretical Nicolaitans. The 'crown of life' promised to Smyrna contrasted with the splendid buildings of the city, called 'the crown of Smyrna'.[82]

The second major work of this period (*Luke the Physician* was a collection of articles) was his *Cities of St Paul* (1907). The series of lectures given, again at Mansfield College, marks the high point of Ramsay's intellectual achievement. His audience could have been gripped as intensely as Harnack's seven years before when he delivered *What Is Christianity?* (English translation). Apart from Ramsay's characterisation of Paul as the man who sought the coalescence of a universalised Hellenism with a universalised Hebraism,[83] there was a refreshing if controversial understanding of currents of thought in the reign of Augustus and his successors and their relevance to the birth of the new religion.

Ramsay had been no friend of Latin/Roman studies before he became Professor, but as Professor of Humanity these had to take up a large part of the syllabus. He came to appreciate both the immediacy of the writers of the age of Augustus and the importance of Rome and its writers in influencing the government of the Asiatic provinces where his own interests lay. *Cities of St Paul* contained detailed descriptions of Tarsus and other cities in southern Asia Minor where Paul had preached, but he also took the opportunity to discuss the relations between Horace and Virgil and their attitude towards the transition from republic to empire in the years following Julius Caesar's murder (44 BC).[84] While Horace could see no salvation outside supernatural aid, a new God was needed.[85] Virgil in contrast became the prophet of the new age of Italy. The *Fourth Eclogue* (written in 40 BC) was a glorification of Italy and Rome. The young child destined to govern the realm was not a reference to an expected son of Octavian,[86] but an idealised concept of a Saviour fulfilling the needs of the time.[87] The incipient empire was the world's hope. Ramsay believed that while the imperial cult became one expression of that hope, Pauline Christianity was the alternative.[88] It is not surprising that in the fourth century, when the Old Testament and its prophecies exercised less influence on would-be converts to Christianity, many of these including the emperor Constantine sought a path to the faith via Virgil's *Fourth Eclogue*.

Ramsay retired from his chair in 1911. He could not have fore-

seen that he still had 28 years before him. At 60, however, he had
accomplished an enormous amount, not least for his university.
The *Studies in the History and Art of the East Roman Provinces*
(1906) which he edited to celebrate the fourth centenary of the
university was a summary of his discoveries in the previous 25
years. His daughter, Margaret, contributed the first essay, a
detailed discussion of Phrygian and Isaurian funerary art, to show
how in the third century Hellenistic and Roman artistic traditions
were giving way to revived native forms, which would find full
expression in Christianity.[89] Anderson continued this theme in his
article on Paganism and Christianity in Northern Phrygia. He
took up the story of the Tembris Valley *Christianoi Christianois*
inscriptions describing how 9 out of 15 epitaphs from this region
belonged to this group and, where there was evidence, it was dated
between 249 and 279.[90] After the end of World War I, Calder was
to continue these researches in detail, concluding that the inscriptions were the work of Montanist *coloni*.[91]

In the years before his retirement Ramsay had been insistent
that funds were needed if British pre-eminence in archaeological
work in Asia Minor was to be maintained. A base from which
students could work was needed at the cost of £300 a year.[92] The
appeal made in the course of a lecture to the British Academy in
1901 fell on deaf ears. Funding for archaeological discoveries has
seldom come high on the agenda of public bodies. In August 1914
war broke out with England and Germany on different sides. On 5
November, Turkey declared war on the Allies, and British interest
in Turkish archaeology ceased for a decade.

Had it been 1939 and the Second World War, Ramsay's talents
would have been immensely useful. His knowledge of Turkish
topography apart, his keen observation of the people and understanding of their outlook would have made him invaluable in
political intelligence and in PWB (Psychological Warfare Branch).
But neither wireless nor even leaflet warfare existed in this
conflict, and his biographers say little about Ramsay's wartime
career. He was Romanes Lecturer at Oxford in 1914 and soon after
left for the University of Virginia, to return in 1915 to write 'The

Making of a University: What We Have to Learn from America'.[93] The same year he gave the Gifford Lectures in Edinburgh University on 'Asianic Elements in Greek Civilisation' (not published until 1927, enabling him to add studies made between 1919 and 1924). The basic question he tried to answer was 'Who were the sons of Yavan, the Old Ionians who represent the Greek race in ancient Hebrew tradition (Genesis 10.4)?'[94] It was as far removed from the practicalities of war as can be imagined, and contrasts with Harnack's passionate commitment to the German cause. Ramsay, however, delved back into a possible Hittite past and made excursion into Anatolian prehistoric cults – 'Wolf-priests and others'[95] – demonstrating the depth of his knowledge of the area, knowledge which never seems to have been used by either the Government or the Allies.

In the years either side of the Armistice Ramsay continued to write extensively, notably three series of studies in the Roman Province of Galatia, published in the *Journal of Roman Studies* in 1917, 1918 and 1921, and he returned to the Tekmoreians in an article in the *Journal of Hellenic Studies* of 1918. His continued lively interest in current affairs was marked by articles on conditions in Asia Minor in 1919 and a strong line against the proposed partition of Anatolia in favour of the Greeks. This ended in the summer of 1922 when the Turks completely defeated the Greek army that had rashly advanced from Smyrna as far as Afyon. The defeated rabble was given no respite. Smyrna fell, and on 8–10 September a gigantic fire destroyed much of the Greek quarter of the city. Ramsay's hope of an Asia Minor shared by the Turks as soldiers and the Greeks as traders evaporated overnight.[96]

The Festschrift entitled *Anatolian Studies* and edited by William H. Buckler and William Calder was published and presented to Ramsay in 1923. It summed up his lifelong interests with a panorama of the history and civilisation of Asia Minor from Hellenistic times to Byzantium. A balance was maintained between Classical and Christian themes, and between literary, epigraphic and numismatic evidence that furthered his understanding of the subject. French, German, Austrian and Belgian scholars

were among the 32 contributors. There were notable articles.
Hogarth, Ramsay's companion in the 1880s, wrote on Hittite
monuments of Southern Asia Minor,[97] Franz Cumont on the
Roman annexation of Polemoniac Pontus and Armenia Minor
in the reign of Nero,[98] Calder on the epigraphy of the Christian
heresies in Anatolia[99] and, perhaps most important of all, W. H.
Buckler's study of little-chronicled labour disputes in the province
of Asia, the violent upsurge of trouble among the bakers at
Ephesus, builders at Pergamum, and again among builders in
the reign of Zeno (474–91).[100] The Festschrift was a magnificent
tribute to Ramsay from his fellow scholars.

A similar Festschrift marking his eightieth birthday was organised by Henri Grégoire in 1931. Grégoire describes the scene at
Christchurch, Oxford, where a symposium was held in Ramsay's
honour.[101] The man himself was described as jovial and 'youthful',
immensely pleased at the honour he was receiving. This time the
emphasis was on Ramsay's echo in Continental scholarship, the 35
contributors to a 970-page issue of *Byzantion* being mainly overseas scholars. It was a fitting mark of the worldwide respect in
which Ramsay was now held.

Yet in other ways the twenties had not been an easy decade.
Many of his ideas and aims had ceased to be relevant. True, there
was still a latent threat (and still is)[102] of Islam against Christianity.
Turkey itself might be a secular state and the Caliphate abolished
but Islam was capable of stirring itself throughout the Arab world
and as far as Indonesia. But his hopes from a Graeco-Turkish
rapprochement were buried in the Turkish victory over the
Greeks and the Treaty of Lausanne in 1923. Then there were personal tensions. What caused him to resign from the British
Academy in 1924 is not at all clear. Anderson in his biography in
the *Dictionary of National Biography* throws no light on the affair.
Family problems, too, were becoming more pressing. Agnes died
in 1928, their Golden Wedding year. Ramsay moved south, to
Bournemouth, where he met and married Phyllis Eileen (née
Thoroughgood) from Old Bosham in Hants. They had nearly ten
years together.

The match proved a success, for during the thirties, despite advancing years, Ramsay remained an active scholar. The Roman empire in Asia Minor and its Byzantine successor in Asia Minor continued to hold his interest. He planned a final extensive work on the 'Social Basis of Roman Power in Asia Minor', to be published in a number of parts. As it was, he only completed Part 1, which was in page proof when he died. Thanks to his lifelong associate J. C. G. Anderson and his daughter Margaret it was published in 1941, as *Social Basis of Roman Power in Asia Minor* (reprinted 1967). The result showed that the author had lost none of his skills as a historian, epigraphist and geographer. The key to the romanisation of the provinces of Asia Minor lay, he believed, with the great families. In many cases these were descended from the priest-rulers of the temples through which the ordinary inhabitants were controlled throughout their lives. Members of these families, already great landowners, were made Roman citizens and became local dignitaries in the cities of Asia Minor. Their influence was reinforced by the numerous class of veterans from the Roman army who, as tribesmen by origin, were able to bring elements of Roman civilisation to their people and substitute Roman imperial patriotism for its antithesis, tribal patriotism. Society was formed into an ordered system obedient to the emperor and his representatives. As in his other major works, Ramsay followed this outline with the detailed history of romanised families from their epitaphs, and the careers of officials who served in Asia Minor. It was a tragedy that he had not time to consolidate this raw material into a major synthesis and, perhaps as Gsell had attempted for North Africa, write a continuous history of Asia Minor from the Hellenistic kingdoms to the fall of Byzantine power.

Ramsay died at his retirement home in Bournemouth on 24 April 1939 at the age of 88. Great Britain was still at peace, and the British empire still enjoyed its long and not unprosperous Indian summer. But, after Hitler's march into Prague on 15 March, few doubted that another conflict with Germany was in the offing. Ramsay had witnessed immense changes during his lifetime, not least in attitudes towards different races and geographical areas. It was no longer possible to discuss Mediterranean civilisation as 'degenerate' and the history at least of east Mediterranean countries as one of decline.[103]

Sir George Reid's portrait of Ramsay in Aberdeen University shows firm, enquiring features dominated by an aquiline nose, and a steady gaze that promised little comfort for fools. Harnack thought his enthusiasm for inscriptions let his imagination run away with him. 'Sometimes he hears the grass grow',[104] he commented. Harnack's contemporary, Adolf Deissmann, who had a far better grasp of the nature and value of archaeological material, was warm in his praise:[105] he made us study on the ground problems previously confined to the study. The most searching criticism comes from Arthur Wright, a pupil who became Fellow of King's College, Cambridge. Ramsay, he wrote on the fly-leaf of his copy of *St Paul the Traveller and the Roman Citizen*, was 'arbitrary and headstrong' and 'one who makes everyone yield to his views'. Wright found some errors in the book in front of him, and one should balance his views against praise from Henri Grégoire as a jovial man who combined humour with faith.

Today one would regard his lifelong concern with what he believed to be unbridgeable differences between East and West as wrongheaded – too reminiscent of Kipling:

And east is east and west is west
And never the twain shall meet.

Even in the first decade of the twentieth century, the successive inventions of the motor car, aeroplane and wireless telegraphy were beginning to unite the world. 'Globalisation' was being prepared. Great Britain could not afford the narrow nationalism and the imperialistic views of the 1880s and 1890s. In the 1930s, the last decade of Ramsay's life, all this was becoming self-evident. Even without World War II, the political and economic superiority of the western Europeans could not have survived. Yet with all his faults, Ramsay remains the outstanding scholar with a great determination to pursue aims that he set himself. He was a keen observer of events, interested in public affairs, though unlike Harnack he lacked the opportunity to participate effectively. But his love was Phrygia. He opened up Phrygia and south and western Anatolia to archaeological and especially early Christian scholarship. He was concerned with facts on the ground, with topography, and with 'South Galatia' as the area of St Paul's missionary journeys. He stood outside the theological and nationalistic quarrels that followed his discovery of the Abercius inscription. He provided the evidence, and gave his own views. Let the continentals wrangle about its precise significance. British scholars such as J. G. C. Anderson, W. M. Calder, Seton Lloyd and now Stephen Mitchell have followed in his footsteps, but without his pioneering enthusiasm and majestic scholarship their efforts would have been seriously handicapped and less successful today.

The author owes his months in Asia Minor with the British School at Ankara during his tenure of the S. A. Cook Bye Fellowship at Gonville and Caius in 1953 to the inspiration of Sir William Ramsay. He visited the Bin Bir Kilisse (Thousand and One Churches) and found a rock carving dedication to the goddess Gaia on the way up the path that led to the site, but much of what Ramsay had seen and illustrated in *Luke, the Physician* had disappeared. In the museum of Afyon he identified an inscription from Suhmenli (Soa) as a third-century lawsuit between two villages contesting their respective responsibilities for *angareia* in their district; and, at Apamea, he identified an inscribed stone which was serving as a breakfast table with the headman as a dedication in honour of Augustus' birthday. The British School and its work, not least in encouraging its visitors to travel in the interior of Asia Minor, owes a great deal to Ramsay's example.

5

Mgr Louis Duchesne (1843–1922):
Critical Churchman and Historian[1]

During my undergraduate and postgraduate years at Oxford (1934–40) Louis Duchesne's three-volume *Early History of the Church* shared with Benjamin Kidd's equally massive *History of the Church to AD 461* the undivided attention of candidates in the Honour School of Theology and also of those historians who took the early period of European history (285–604). The third edition of volume 3 (1924), which covered in detail the great Christological controversies of the first half of the fifth century, centred on the rival theologies of Alexandria, Antioch, Constantinople and Rome, had been translated and extensively indexed by Claude Jenkins, Professor of Ecclesiastical History at King's College, London, but also a canon of Christ Church, Oxford, it was said, as a labour of love. Duchesne himself had been honoured at both Oxford and Cambridge.

But these were the views of non-Catholic universities. Despite all he achieved, much of Duchesne's life was beset with controversy with his own church. In the era of Vatican I his fairness of mind combined with profound and critical scholarship rendered him unpopular and, by some, suspected of heresy. Yet with Harnack, whose work on occasion he criticised strongly, he shares the claim to be one of the founders of the movement which has helped to remove the history of early Christianity from the realm of apologetics and hagiography to a historical study, integrated into the study of the general history of the Roman empire in the first six centuries AD.

Early Life and Early Problems 1843–77

Louis Duchesne's early years gave little hint of what lay ahead. He was born at Saint-Servan not far from St Malo in northern Brittany on 13 September 1843, the sixth child of a seafaring family. He retained a strong affection for his native province belonging to its historical and cultural societies and returning there year after year each summer for rest, relaxation and religious retreat. His parents had a more than conventional piety. While his father died tragically at sea in 1847, his mother who lived on until October 1889 exercised a strong influence on him. Every year he would return to Saint-Servan on a retreat organised by her. A letter to J. B. de Rossi after her death expresses his affection for her sincere and tolerant outlook 'unburdened by excess, hypocrisy and terror'.[2] Her influence may be counted among those that moved the young Duchesne towards a calling of the priesthood and, within that, to be primarily a teacher.

He showed early promise as a student at the grande séminaire of St Charles at Saint Brieuc, Saint-Servan's episcopal town, and by 1863 the two strands in his future career were beginning to emerge. Apart from his fascination for the visible remains of early cultures in Brittany he became interested in the Bollandists' *Acta Sanctorum*, reprinted in 1863. At the same time he was already contemplating a vocation in the priesthood. Rome beckoned, and there he would come into contact with another determining factor in his life, namely, de Rossi's publication in 1861 of *Inscriptiones christianae* and, two years later, the first volume of *Roma Sotterranea*. Scholarly research and Catholicism were to remain the hallmarks of his career – head and heart that he was never quite able to reconcile.

The liberal-minded bishop of St Brieuc, Mgr David, was sympathetic, and on 6 November 1863 Duchesne was admitted to the Collège romain, founded by Ignatius Loyola in 1553, as a 'candidat libre', to participate in courses of dogmatic and moral theology.[3] He remained there two years but, as he says himself, he was 'less interested in the lectures than in visiting the catacombs, Classical ruins, and the museums', and 'more than once I left the learned professors to their lectures' with that aim in mind.[4] Not surprisingly, he returned to St Brieuc with not quite unstinted praise. His abilities were recognised but also a certain lack of tact which raised a question whether he was really fitted for the priesthood. 'Il n'est pas assez discrète', it was said of him.[5] But Duchesne persevered. Back at St Charles in 1866 he was appointed professor of literature and sciences where he remained for the next four years. He was ordained priest in December 1867 and at this stage was an ardent Infallibilist. He showed he had little use for the Gallican hesitation of Mgr David and on 4 March 1870 was among the clerical signatories of a pro forma petition urging Pius IX to proclaim the doctrine of the Infallibility trusting that 'God and His Immaculate Mother' would enable the Pope to 'pursue and terminate the Holy Council of the Vatican'.[6] He was never to express himself in such terms again.

The rift with David was healed at least visibly. Duchesne stayed at St Charles until 1871, when he took the chance of moving to Paris to accept an appointment at the École des larmes. This was then a sort of ecclesiastical Institut des hautes Études founded in 1845 by Mgr Affre to serve as a centre for the higher and more scientific education of the clergy and prepare them for university standard exams. From the outset the École had cultivated contacts with the Sorbonne, and students were able to follow courses there. Duchesne took advantage of this. At this moment, an École pratique des hautes Études was coming into being within the Sorbonne, in which emphasis was laid on tutorials as well as the traditional oratorical set lectures. Duchesne chose philosophy and Greek antiquities as his themes for 1871–2, and the latter choice enabled him to take the first step towards carving out a career at the École française de Rome.[7] Duchesne had benefited from distinguished masters at the École pratique, not least Tournier, for introducing him to Greek philosophy, and he took his *licensié ès lettres* on 27 July 1872. His all round knowledge of the Classics and his archaeological interest now fitted him to become one of the first students at the newly founded École française de Rome. These years were a milestone in forming his outlook on the relations between history and theology.

The École at this stage had been established by a decree of the Thiers government on 25 March 1873, at first as an outstation of the older École française d'Athènes. In July Duchesne acquired a dual role of a researcher into manuscripts in the Vatican still on the books of the École pratique, while becoming associated with the beginnings of teaching Greek palaeography to students at the new École at Rome at the end of 1873 with a salary of 2,000 francs.[8]

The decade 1870–80 was a great period for the founding of overseas schools of research by the Great Powers in central and western Europe. The Powers were rivals in scholarship as in so much else, and the French, defeated by Prussia in 1870–1, were determined not to suffer any further humiliations through yielding to a superiority of German scholarship. There was an underlying anti-German motive in founding the École française de Rome.[9] The British also followed the French by founding schools of Roman Studies and Hellenic studies at Rome and Athens, and also pressed on with archaeological exploration in Palestine. And, in addition, the discovery of the manuscript of the *Didache* in 1875 by Bryennios in the library of the Jerusalem monastery of the Holy Sepulchre at Constantinople gave a new impetus to European Patristic scholarship.[10]

Unfortunately, the great majority of French clergy had no enthusiasm for those movements. Edmond Le Blant found that his research into the material remains of the early Christian Church in Gaul was not always well received. Some clerics believed criticism of traditional theories was 'odieux'.[11] Overall, hung the view that it was *scientia inflat*, that is, science inflated pride. Much of the Catholic Church in the West still clung to the idea that there were divinely fixed bounds to human knowledge, and that 'curiosity' beyond these was sinful. Duchesne would be increasingly unable to reconcile his critical scholarship with the intellectual positions taken by his Church. Now a member of the École française he was despatched in the summer of 1874 (with the necessary authorising letter from the minister) by Albert

Dumont, its Director on a confidential mission with Charles Bayet to Epirus, Salonica and the monastery library on Mount Athos in the search for new manuscripts of Homer. Dumont was among those determined that the Germans should not claim superiority in higher learning. Duchesne succeeded, recovering 24 scholia almost all hitherto unedited for the use of the future editors of the poet. As a bonus, he was able to copy 140 Greek inscriptions laid bare by the demolition of the ramparts of Salonica. He also visited Patmos and recovered scholia of Demosthenes and Thucydides and a manuscript of a third-century treatise by Julius Africanus (*fl.* AD 220–30) on the science of measurement – altogether a very successful piece of work, which was fully recognised in Geffroy's report in the *Revue des Deux Mondes* of 15 August 1876.[12]

Duchesne had put the École française de Rome on the map. Not surprisingly after a year working for his thesis on manuscripts relating to the *Liber Pontificalis* and Macarius Magnes in the Vatican library he was invited to participate in an expedition to Asia Minor. His companion this time was Maxime Collignon, and the object was to find and copy inscriptions and identify ruins in the country along the southern seaboard of Asia Minor. They set off on 9 May 1876. Here, too, one may detect the latent rivalry between the European powers. Only five years had elapsed since Schliemann's sensational discoveries on the site of Troy, while in 1880 William Ramsay was to begin his discoveries in Phrygia which would alter for ever the course of research in the heartland of early Christianity. This time, however, Duchesne and Collignon were less fortunate. News of the assassination of the French and German consuls in Salonica and the abdication of the Sultan Abd-el-Aziz had made the Turks suspicious of westerners, and Duchesne found the villagers he met for the most part unhelpful. His expedition lasted until 16 July, and by that time he had found evidences of Byzantine Christianity in Lycia (Kaunos) and Cilicia (Ermenele and Mut) and Christian buildings in Sifilke, Korikos and Sebaste. This was not a big harvest, but despite its relative shortcomings his report filled much of the second part of the first volume of the *Bulletin de Correspondance hellénique* (1877).[13]

Duchesne, however, was not destined to be a French Ramsay. The demands of his thesis and its aftermath pulled him ever more through library work, lectures and writings into a normal (in his case not so normal) academic career. At first, he had considered (like the present writer) embarking on a thesis on the subject of the persecutions against the Christians but by early 1874 he had decided finally on a study of the *Liber Pontificalis* within the framework of his priestly status. The *Liber* is a collection of biographical notices of the popes, arranged chronologically, including their name, their family and place of birth, the length of their pontificate, their place of burial and the length of any interregnum after their death. Some entries contain precious information about liturgical changes, the building of churches, reception of gifts and the number of priests and deacons in Rome. In Constantine's reign the *Liber* records the emperor's numerous benefactions to the Church, beginning in *c*.314 with the Lateran palace, valuable evidence for his progress towards conversion to Christianity; and under Xystus III the efforts of the pope and emperor Valentinian III to repair the losses in goods and chattels suffered by the Church in Rome through Alaric's occupation of the city in 410.[14] Properly handled the *Liber* is a mine of information regarding the history of the early and mediaeval papacy.

Duchesne went to work to ensure that it was properly handled. His first task was to establish a reliable text, which resulted in a comparison and collation of 98 separate versions, 36 preserved mostly in the Vatican Library; for the remainder he visited French, Swiss and Italian centres and carried out a lively and successful correspondence with scholars who had assisted his research. At this stage his industry and energy stand comparison with Harnack's visiting an obscure monastery in south Italy to search for a fresh manuscript of the Apostolic Fathers.[15] He was able to establish first, two major families of manuscript tradition, the Lucca (Class A) and the Naples, considerably later (Class B). He concluded that A originated not long after the death of Pope

Felix IV in 530, while there was a second edition associated with the short-lived reign of Pope Conon (686–7). The accounts of the popes after Pelagius II (579–90) were written by contemporaries, and the work was continued in various forms until the pontificate of Martin V (d. 1431). Duchesne, however, showed that the Felician catalogue itself was only a résumé of an earlier edition compiled in the reign of Pope Hormisdas (514–23) and that, far from being a strictly historical account of the lives and actions of the popes, the *Liber* reflected the acrid quarrels at the beginning of the sixth century that surrounded the succession to the papacy following the death of Anastasius II in 498. The antipope Laurence represented a Byzantine element in the Church and Senate whereas his successful rival Symmachus (498–514) reflected the growing Italianate consciousness of the Roman clergy. Both produced their own accounts of past popes to justify their claims to the succession, of which the survivor provided the basis for the compilation of the *Liber* under Hormisdas. While the *Chronography of 354* was the most important source for the early popes to Liberius (352–66), the *Liber* biographies also contained unreliable and legendary material. Thus, that of Pope Urban (222–30) drew on material from the *Passion* of St Cecilia.[16] Apart from factual information that could be checked from other sources, the main value of the *Liber* was to demonstrate the state of the Church of Rome in the early sixth century, its buildings and landed wealth, as well as its liturgy. It was also a crucial witness to the topography of Rome itself at that period.

Duchesne finished his work early in 1877. The reactions to his thesis, published as *Études sur le Liber Pontificalis*, were mixed. On the one hand, he was warmly though discreetly praised by J. B. de Rossi whom he had met in July 1873 through the good offices of Léon Renier (1809–87) the outstanding North African archaeologist and epigraphist.[17] De Rossi and Duchesne became firm friends, demonstrated by the 593 letters exchanged between them between 1873 and 1894 – fantastic until one remembers one is dealing with a period practically without telephones. On the other hand, there was the far more serious opposition of conservative clerics in the Vatican. Cardinal Pitra, the Librarian of the Vatican Library (d. 1889) who had encouraged his work on Macarius Magnes, while praising the thesis as 'méritoire' criticised it as being 'more German than French',[18] insufficiently Catholic and missing the opportunity to submit a truly orthodox dogmatic thesis worthy of presentation to believers and unbelievers alike.[19] In particular, Duchesne was charged with throwing doubt on the reality of Constantine's baptism by Pope Silvester. There was too, the shadow of Ernest Renan and his *Vie de Jésus* (1863) that hardened attitudes towards critical judgements of the early history of the Church. Was Duchesne to be another Renan, asked Mgr Freppel, Bishop of Angers?[20] Duchesne, in fact, had little use for Renan. In an article in *Revue du Monde catholique* in 1877 he pointed to his own beliefs in the supernatural, the divinity of Christ demonstrated by miracles,which Renan rejected.[21] Nonetheless the thesis was submitted to the Congregation of the Index and only in January 1878 was found acceptable, provided a second edition was published taking into account a list of 19 'remarks' made by three theologians and canonists who had examined the work plus 4 'general comments' by Pitra.[22] Historical criticism had gained the day, but only just. Duchesne was encouraged to work further.

The Maturing Scholar 1877–85

Duchesne had introduced critical scholarship into Roman Catholic historical studies. How was his career to develop? One may regret that he did not continue with the pursuit of early Christian archaeology of Asia Minor. His successful Latin thesis on Macarius of Magnesia published in 1877 and his expedition with Collignon would have provided a basis for other journeys. Charles Bayet characterised him as an 'archéologue militant' always out for adventure (13 April 1875).[23] His publication in 1878 of an important inscription recording the dedication of a *martyrion* in honour of St Christopher on 22 September 452 on the site of Chalcedon, the scene of the great Council of the previous year, pointed in that direction.[24] The zeal also with which he entered the fray following Harnack's comments on the religious allegiance of its dedicant, Avircius Marcellus (see above, p. 22) in 1894–5 shows that the archaeology of Asia Minor still held a place in his affections. However, Paris and Rome, whether secular or religious, were from now on to benefit from his scholarship, and unfortunately his addiction to controversies.

He was now docteur ès lettres. Was his senior teaching career to be in the Sorbonne or the Institut catholique de Paris? His choice was to mark profoundly the rest of his career. Duchesne had already been considered for the chair at the latter in 1876, and despite the controversy which his *Etudes sur le Liber Pontificalis* was arousing, he made a deliberate choice for a chair at the Institut. His aim was, as he wrote on 21 November 1885, 'to contribute to initiate clergy into sound methods of work'.[25] His nomination, however, was delayed. Not only had his studies offended, but questions were raised about his suitability to teach in a Catholic institute. He was accused by an abbé in Saint-Servan itself of liberalism, of walking out of church during a litany in honour of the Virgin Mary in the Marian Month which he characterised as a 'devotionette', and that he had frequently referred to Pope Pius IX as 'Jean Mastaï'.[26] Duchesne denied all this in a letter to his old friend from Rome days, Mgr d'Hulst, now Secretary to the Institute. After hesitation the electors on 24 January 1877 nominated him unanimously first to a chair of Christian archaeology and then, when there were insufficient funds to sustain it, to a chair of history. Duchesne would be free to include archaeology, not least epigraphy. Strongly encouraged by de Rossi,[27] to whom he had turned for advice as 'his master', he accepted the nomination.

Between 1877 and 1885 Duchesne taught at the Institut. His courses followed what today would be considered conventional lines. Roman administration from Augustus to Diocletian, the early Christian martyrologies, the Roman empire during the era of the persecutions, a comparison between Donatism and Arianism, and Christian epigraphy, filled the years to 1882.[28] Duchesne was able to draw on his thesis to describe the evolution of the *tituli*, or ecclesiastical districts in Rome, and the progressive foundation of churches in the city. Regarding the former, he could show how after the Gothic wars in the mid-sixth century the 14 *regiones* established by Augustus ceased to exist and had been replaced by 7 ecclesiastical divisions represented by the 7 diaconates first recorded in the pontificate of Pope Fabian (236–49).

These were among the best years of Duchesne's life. He had a secure position, teaching clergy subjects he loved, and preparing material for his great work on the early history of the Church. While he was Secretary of the School of Theology he suffered little interference from the bishops, then arguing among themselves how to promote the teaching of theology outside Paris. In 1881 he was also able to found in succession to the failing *Echo* an important journal, the *Bulletin Critique de littérature, d'histoire et de théologie* which gave him an outlet for his own views and sometimes those of his opponents. It was dedicated as the editor wrote in the first number to 'absolute impartiality'. The readership would be mainly clergy, and the aim, as always with Duchesne, to raise their critical standards.

It was with the same aim in mind that he opened his course in 1879–80 with an inaugural lecture during which he told his hearers that 'studies should be rigorous in terms of science based on original texts' and that 'true science does not disturb the faith'.[29] This was always his credo. He himself (like Harnack), as he wrote to a pupil and later fellow Church historian, Pierre Batiffol, 'accepted the transcendent superiority of Christianity over all religions and its intimate alliance with conscience'.[30] To Alfred Loisy, one of his most gifted pupils, he admitted that one had to accept disagreements in the Synoptic Gospels over events in the New Testament, and 'to leave to scholastics attempts to harmonise the Birth genealogies', but 'though one could launch one's boat into the midst of a storm, the moment Christ was there, there was no danger'. Neither the doctrine of the Trinity nor the Incarnation troubled him.[31] It was over their attitudes towards Ernest Renan that their friendship eventually broke down. Loisy took Renan seriously, Duchesne with a liberal pinch of salt.[32] With

Batiffol the disagreement which occurred in 1898 was in the opposite direction, Duchesne accusing his former pupil (25 February 1898) of 'astonishing orthodoxy' even 'aggression'.[33] The fact was that Batiffol, as shown in his later scholarly works, though a critic, was fundamentally a loyalist in his attitude towards the beliefs of his Church.[34]

There were many clergy whose orthodoxy was 'aggressive' and were also in a position to damage Duchesne's career. The trouble started in the summer of 1882 when a Parisian priest, Abbé Rambouillet, objected to the contents of lithographed synopses of Duchesne's lectures on Christian origins, which he had handed out to his students at the end of the course, thus making them public.[35] Rambouillet made his views known in two articles attacking Duchesne in the *Revue des sciences ecclésiastiques* (published at Lille, July and August 1882). Duchesne had been lecturing on the development of Trinitarian doctrine from the second century to the Council of Nicaea (325). He had pointed out that the efforts of Hermas and Justin Martyr to relate the divinity of Jesus Christ to the role of the Holy Spirit had resulted in 'bizarreries théologiques' and that similar efforts by Hippolytus and Tertullian to oppose Modalism had led these theologians to 'near heresy'. Also he did not call the Apologists 'Church Fathers'. Rambouillet objected to this apparent downgrading of the second-century theologians and asserted that faith in the Trinity and consubstantiality of the Son with the Father had always from the earliest time been consistent. Duchesne dismissed his opponent's views as 'ce fatras informe et furibonde', and replied in detail to Rambouillet in the December number of the *Revue* in an article entitled 'Les témoins antenicéens du dogme de la Trinité', preceded by a 'Prologue' by Mgr d'Hulst, Rector of the Institut.

He had meantime requested a year's sabbatical from the Institut catholique in order to prepare his fuller publication of the *Liber Pontificalis*. The request gave rise to rumours that he was being sacked by the Institut, which was not true. In October 1882, however, the students at the Institut de Saint Sulpice were forbidden by their rector, Mgr Icard, to attend Duchesne's lectures, and it was clear that Rambouillet had powerful supporters among the Parisian clergy.[36] Duchesne had hoped to find support from Cardinal Newman on the basis of the latter's latest work, translated as *Mémoires sur les causes d'Arianisme* (published in 1874 in *Tracts theological and ecclesiastical*) but all Newman did was to send him in March 1882 a pedantic and rather patronising letter regretting that he had used the first and not the final 1881 edition of his work on the Arians.

Duchesne's article in the *Revue* had not stilled controversy. Rebuff by Newman was a setback; more serious was the intervention of Cardinal Franzelin, Professor at the Collège romain. He thought Duchesne was treading a dangerous path with his views. He was concerned in particular to protect the orthodoxy of Pope Callistus and to deny, against Duchesne, that Callistus' concept of the Trinity was that refuted by Tertullian in *Adversus Praxean*, though it appeared to coincide with Hippolytus' criticism of Callistus' views in the *Philosophiumena* (9.12.15–19). In a long letter in reply, Duchesne suggested that the problems were not those of truth versus heresy, but of an increasing clarification of doctrine 'from the less clear to the more clear towards the truth'.[37]

The matter might have ended there, but Duchesne's exaggerated language inflamed controversy, not for the first or last time. 'Bizarreries théologiques' could not be accepted as a description of orthodox Patristic thought even in the second century, while it could be argued today that Duchesne's use of such terms demonstrated that he had failed to immerse himself in the thought and outlook of Christians of that period. All this was to be remembered against him.

The immediate upshot was that the Institut had to accept a second professor of ecclesiastical history (Abbé Largent) to teach the early period, while Duchesne, after a period of leave, returned to concentrate on the early Middle Ages and the religious history of the Greek East. His lectures, and the tutorials he had now introduced, were less controversial. The affairs, however, had left their mark. As he wrote to Georg Waitz, with whom he had scholarly disagreement on the dates of the editions of the *Liber Pontificalis*, in April 1884, 'the freedom of spirit with which he was obliged to treat these questions was not always judged favourably by those around him', and he had suffered much.[38]

But worse was to follow. Next year, he was embroiled in a con-troversy that went beyond the bounds of the Institut catholique. How did Christianity originate in France? This had been Edmond Le Blant's field of research since 1848, when he had obtained from the Republican Ministère d'instruction publique leave to travel throughout France to collate inscriptions referring to early Christianity that had found their way into private collections as well as museums. Le Blant published two volumes of *Inscriptions chrétiennes de la Gaule antérieure au viiie siecle, remises et annotées* in 1856 and 1865. They showed that, so far as material remains were concerned, Christianity did not take a significant hold in Gaul until the middle of the fourth century.[39]

There were, however, many in senior positions in the Roman Catholic Church in France who preferred to believe in the found-ation of the major sees in Gaul by the Apostles or other individuals mentioned in the New Testament. Thus Paris would owe its foundation to Denis the Areopagite, and Mary Magdalene accom-panied by Martha and Lazarus landed in southern Gaul to found the see of Aix-en-Provence.[40] These beliefs were not accepted as simply monkish theories of the early Middle Ages, like that associating Joseph of Arimathea with Glastonbury, but held passionately as literally true and providing the title deeds of the bishoprics concerned. Duchesne was not welcome for exposing their falsity.

He had already got himself into difficulties through his insist-ence that a hypogaeum found in a Christian cemetery near Poitiers in 1878 was of seventh or eighth-century date. This was clear from the approximate dating of the tomb of a certain Mellebaudis the principal tomb in the cemetery. This contained the relics of the Seventy-two Martyrs along with other relics. Duchesne main-tained that these were not connected with Poitiers or even with Gaul, but were originally Roman and belonged to a collection made by Mellebaudis and buried with him. He published his view in the *Bulletin critique* of 1 April 1884. His opponents, however, included prominent local clergy in Poitou and they reacted vigorously, but Duchesne was vindicated by scholars writing in the prestigious *Bulletin de l'Académie des inscriptions et des belles lettres* and in that of the Société nationale des Antiquaires de France (December 1884). Unfortunately, the affair earned him the ill will of influential clergy in western France.[41]

More serious was the controversy that now embroiled him with Mgr Bernadou, Archbishop of Sens. Duchesne had been invited by Abbé Henault, a priest in the diocese of Chartres, to review a book by him (*Les Origines chrétiennes de la Gaule*) on the foundation of churches in the dioceses of Chartres, Sens, Troyes and Orléans. Duchesne accepted for the *Bulletin critique*, but took the opportunity to point out that there was no proof for apostolic nor even for very early foundation for these sees, the earliest recorded bishop of Sens, Agroceius, for example, being recorded as bishop only in 472.[42] Not surprisingly, Mgr Bernadou was furious not only with Duchesne but with the Institut catholique for tolerating him. He denounced the Institut as a 'sorbonne moderne' affected by 'le virus libéral'. Duchesne himself was weakening the Church by his rejection of the apostolic tradition of his see. He was a 'Jansenist', 'throwing the saints out of their niches'. Duchesne himself was threatened with denunciation to Rome, and this time earned a rebuke, though a mild one, from his friend, the Rector, Mgr d'Hulst.[43]

If this were not enough, the first months of 1885 brought an attack on his scholarship relating to the *Liber Pontificalis*. The first fascicule of his *magnum opus* had appeared in 1884 and had been preceded by articles in the *Mélanges de l'École française de Rome* (1883) and the *Revue des questions historiques* (1884). The first was devoted to the succession of Pope Felix IV in 530.[44] In what today seems like just a good scholarly article Duchesne pointed out, as he had in his thesis, that for the previous 32 years the Papacy had been riven by factional strife fuelled by rivalries between a pro-Byzantine and an Italianate party favourable to the Ostrogothic king, Theodoric, and his successors. Felix represented the ideas of the latter party and on his deathbed (he died on 22 September 530) he attempted to bequeath the pontificate to his ally, Boniface. For the moment he failed, because the Alexandrian supporter of Justinian, Dioscorus was elected, but he survived only 28 days, when the succession passed without serious dispute to Boniface II. Felix's attempt to assure Boniface's succession was proved from newly found contemporary documents. The authenticity of these Duchesne demonstrated and in addition pointed out that it was not unusual for bishops to nominate their successors, as Augustine of Hippo had Heraclius in 426.[45] But these procedures were uncanonical and the revelation that they had been employed by a pope caused scandal.

In his second article on Pelagius and Vigilius, Duchesne had criticised the latter sharply, as an intriguer of doubtful orthodoxy and a plaything of the rival influences of the deacon Pelagius and Justinian.[46] This time, he was challenged by a historian, Dom Chamard, a Benedictine monk of Ligugé. Chamard believed that writing Church history must have a 'mission of edification' which allowed faults by clergy to be extenuated while lay interventions in ecclesiastical affairs were to be attacked. He accused Duchesne of 'excessive freedom of thought in regard to matters touching the sovereign Popes and decisions of the Church'.[47] His method was clean contrary to Duchesne's which was to ascertain the facts and let them speak for themselves. Chamard was a formidable enemy, not least because he was on good terms with de Rossi. In October 1884 he wrote to the latter expressing his surprise at de Rossi's friendship with Duchesne. Duchesne he described as 'un rationaliste en soutane', from henceforth 'on the Index' so far as 'true French clergy were concerned'.[48]

In the summer of 1885 the combination of attacks had become too much for Duchesne. He accepted a year's leave from the Institut and in August 1885 considered resignation altogether. Even de Rossi was critical of his Vigilius article as leaving him with 'a bad impression' when he first read it – too critical of Vigilius.[49] For a moment, Duchesne thought of life in a rural parish. He feared 'the storm would not pass', but wiser counsels prevailed.

De Rossi wrote to the Institut on his behalf (17 September),[50] pointing out that Duchesne had preferred its membership to that of the Sorbonne and commending his critical scholarship. But the Rubicon had been crossed. The year's leave beginning on 22 August 1885 extended into ten, by which time Duchesne had been nominated Director of the École française de Rome. He would never again teach full time in a Catholic institute. His path now lay with the exploration of Church history as history rather than as a means of 'instructing the clergy'.

Paris and Rome

Despite this disaster Duchesne still wanted to 'serve the Church by history conscientiously revealed and studied without prejudice' (*franchement*).[51] Without cutting himself off entirely from the Institut catholique, he found a teaching post as 'maître de conférences' in the secular École pratique des hautes études (24 November 1885) which he held for ten years. But in this he became a salaried official at a time when tensions between the state and the Catholic Church were increasing until the final separation was imposed by the Combes government in 1905. To de Rossi he described his new role as a 'bigamous marriage' and to von Hügel as a 'hybrid'.[52] He spent much of his year of *congé* prepreparing Volume 1 of the *Liber Pontificalis* for publication by the École française de Rome. At the École he found freedom, freedom to diversify his studies to teach early Christian epigraphy on the basis of Cumont's (and Ramsay's) work on Christian inscriptions in Asia Minor, as well as the organisation of the Church in Gaul and in mediaeval Rome, and to prepare a general study of the Church in the Greek-speaking East to the eleventh century.[53] Much of this work would find expression eventually in the three volumes of the *Early History of the Church* and *The Church in the Sixth Century*. He was already known even as a Chargé de cours internationally as a scholarly priest who studied his original sources.

His position in the École pratique, however, opened the way to further secular advance. After two failures in 1887 he was elected to the Académie des inscriptions et des belles lettres in December 1888, warmly supported by de Rossi, the Africanist Gaston Boissier and Le Blant. His early work in Greece and Asia Minor, as well as his interest in the origins of the Church in Gaul, had borne fruit. He was able to pay his personal tribute to de Rossi in presenting the *Mélanges de Rossi* on the latter's seventieth birthday (1892). Speaking of his own experience he pointed out how no one other than de Rossi was able to inspire young French scholars with a taste and respect for Roman history. He had made the potentially dull subject of early ecclesiastical history live.

All this time Duchesne was able to write. His bibliography for 1892 contains the second volume of the *Liber Pontificalis* and ten articles. Meanwhile, he had been turning to a close study of the development of Christian liturgy.[54] In 1889 he published *Les Origines du culte chrétien*, a formidable book of 500 pages based on his lecture notes at the Institut catholique and 'written for beginners'. In fact, it was a considerable work of scholarship which went into five editions to 1925. Its simple style belied the author's examination of 90 separate manuscripts dealing with early western liturgies. His first edition concentrated on the Latin Church to Charlemagne (but included a long chapter on the Eastern Mass), discussing continued Jewish influence on early Christian rites,[55] especially their apocalyptic tendency, now vindicated by the analysis of the Dead Sea Scrolls. Only in the fourth century, however, did liturgical books appear. The authorities seized 35 books from the library of the church at Cirta (Numidia) during the Great Persecution, though what percentage of those were liturgical as against scriptural is not known.[56] The development of Christian ceremonies, baptism, ordination, clerical dress, rites of marriage and the reconciliation of penitents followed. So far, so good, but Duchesne entered controversy by suggesting that the Gallican rite, used by Caesarius of Arles, Germanus of Paris and Gregory of Tours was associated with Milan rather than Rome. He pointed out how the early Anglo-Saxon liturgical books were 'far from containing the Roman liturgy in an absolutely pure form. Gallican details abounded'.[57] Today, reviewers would have discussed the theory; and the author would, on the whole, seem to be vindicated. The oriental influences in Milan may be associated with the activity of the Cappadocian bishop Auxentius (355–74).[58] Milan's general influence on the church in Gaul would explain these influences on the Gallican and, apparently to judge from the hexameter inscribed on a silver bowl from Water Newton, the Romano-British liturgy.[59] But the idea that Milan had made a greater contribution to Gallic worship than Rome shocked some contemporaries. Duchesne, however, pressed on. Further editions concentrated more on the Eastern rites, including the Monophysite, while Wilson's discovery in 1915 of the Gregorian Sacramentery in use in the Church under Charlemagne enabled Duchesne's work on its successive editions to keep abreast with discoveries.[60]

Again, despite his claim that his work, though a historical study, should not diminish merited respect for the 'venerable rites of our ancient mother the Catholic Church',[61] he was sharply criticised. His study did not allow sufficiently for 'the supernatural element'; while others including Auguste Sabatier, professor in the faculty of Protestant theology in Paris, blamed him for being 'too ultramontane'.[62] In face of such divergent criticisms it seems that Duchesne had struck the right note for the great majority of his readers.

His research continued. A notable article in the *Mélanges* of 1890 vindicated the Appendix to Optatus of Milevis, *De Schismate Donatistarum*, a key series of documents used by the Catholics against the Donatists.[63] In 1883 a German scholar, Daniel Voelter had published, under the title of *Der Ursprung des Donatismus* (Freiburg, 1883) a detailed study of the documents which formed the Appendix to Optatus. The dossier contained *inter alia* a record of the hearing at Cirta before the Curator, Munatius Felix, on 19 May 303 at which the clergy of the church in the town handed over copies of the Scriptures and church valuables to the state's representative. One of those implicated in this act of betrayal was the sub-deacon, Silvanus who subsequently became bishop and a leader of the Donatist movement. Another document concerned

the trial of Silvanus before the Consularis of Numidia, Zeno-
philus, at Timgad on 20 December 320.[64] There, his misdeeds
were brutally exposed and the Donatist movement thereby dis-
credited. There were other documents, such as the letter of the
emperor Constantine to officials in North Africa following the outbreak of the Donatist dispute in 312 and his letter to the bishops
assembled at the council at Arles on 1 August 314 in an effort to
heal the consequent rupture in Carthage, as well as verbatim
reports of proceedings in the North African courts at the time of
the Great Persecution. These documents had formed the basis of
Optatus' defence of the Catholic position during the 360s, and
were used by Augustine in his attack on the Donatists at the
Conference of Carthage in June 411. Voelter, however, satisfied
himself that many of these documents had been interpolated or
falsified. His ideas received backing from the distinguished
German historian Otto Seeck, in 1889, who while upholding
the authenticity of most of the documents cast doubt on those
relating to the Council of Cirta in May 305, and the instructions
sent by Constantine to the Council of Arles, which he placed in
316.[65]

Unfortunately for these objections, Duchesne was able to show
from a ninth-century manuscript from the Abbey of Cormé near
Tours (Parisinus, 1711) that the dossier formed a single whole and
must have been compiled between February 330, the date of the
last document, and 347 when the Catholics gained a period of
ascendancy. He was also able to reconstruct many of the pieces
missing from Optatus' dossier.[66] The demonstration was complete
and compelling. Apart from doubt whether Constantine's message
to the bishops at Arles on the result of their deliberations reflected
the emperor's own beliefs about a 'judgement of Christ' or those of
his Christian advisers,[67] Duchesne's results stand today. They
were not the result of any anti-German bias. He was a friend
though a critic of Georg Waitz a fellow researcher on the *Liber
Pontificalis* and an admirer of Mommsen, whose edition of that
work published in *Monumenta Germaniae historia* (*MGH*) in 1898
he praised,[68] but as always he aimed at establishing historical truth,

as he was to show five years later when he challenged Harnack's interpretation of the Abercius inscription.

He showed the same qualities in two other topics which he explored between 1890 and 1893. The first was directly associated with the *Liber Pontificalis* and took the form of a series of studies on the topography of Christian Rome.[69] In contrast to de Rossi, Duchesne worked from documents, concentrating on those relating to the Vatican area and papal burials. In 1891 with the same method, not least using the *Passio Sebastiani* and seventh-century *Itinerary of Salzburg*, he anticipated the discovery in 1915 of the chapel below the San Sebastiano on the Via Appia where the relics of St Peter and Paul were brought in 258 during the Valerianic persecution (257–9), and restored to their former resting place in the Vatican in Constantine's reign.[70] On the basis of this and other research he was urged, not least by Mgr d'Hulst, to set down to write a major work on the history of the Church of Rome, or even, the Church in North Africa, inspired by his interest in Gsell's discoveries relating to the martyr Salsa at Tipasa in 1890.[71]

Gsell's work in North Africa was not the only discovery relating to saints and martyrs at this time. In 1892 Austrian archaeologists working at Ephesus had discovered 'the house of the Virgin Mary'. Duchesne had already interested himself, as we have seen, in the alleged apostolic foundation of major bishoprics in Gaul. He now wrote studies on St Martial of Limoges, St Denis and St Barnabas, this last in honour of de Rossi.[72] At the same time, he was collaborating with de Rossi in a new major work preparing an edition of the Jerome Martyrology. He was able to show that not only did the Martyrology originate in Nicomedia 50 years before Jerome's principal years of activity (400–20) but also many of the entries were derived from a sixth-century Italian text. This masterpiece of joint critical scholarship was completed just before Duchesne's friend and mentor died on 24 September 1894.[73]

There was the usual criticism, this time, however, largely from the German Protestant side. Duchesne had pointed out rightly that the Martyrology preserved important traces of genuine *Acta Martyrum* from a number of Roman provinces, not least the

Gallic. Bruno Krusch, one of the collaborators in the *MGH*, considered that Duchesne had been too indulgent to the *Passiones* of
some of those recorded in the Martyrology.[74] The controversy
lasted until 1898 and provoked Duchesne to the statement that in
judging ecclesiastical tradition he was better placed than lay
Protestants and freethinkers.[75]

Preparation of the Martyrology led on to Duchesne tackling
seriously the question of the origins of the churches in Gaul, in
which he had been involved a decade before. In this study he was
now aided by the Bollandists seeking to classify saints by region,
provinces and dioceses, beginning with the earliest and moving
forward in chronological order. Once again, *Les Fastes épiscopaux
de l'ancienne Gaule* which appeared at the same time as *Jerome* in
1894 aroused fierce controversy, with monks and clergy uniting to
uphold the legendary foundation of their institutions.[76] It was with
general relief that the 'Dénicheur des saintes' accepted his
appointment from Raymond Poincaré as Director of the École
française de Rome on 27 March 1895, as successor to Auguste
Geffroy. He ended his association with the Institut catholique
from which he had been 'on leave' for ten years. In that period,
however, he had established himself as a premier historian of the
early Church devoted to the truthful interpretation of facts, loyal
to his Church but regardless of ecclesiastical interests. In the university he had been promoted to Directeur d'études in 1892; he
was ripe for further secular advancement.

Directeur de l'École française de Rome

Duchesne was to remain Director for the next 27 years, until his
death in April 1922. Before taking up his appointment he had been
involved in another issue, this time in the service of the Church,
which was to have lasting effects on the relations between the
Roman and Anglican Communions. This is not the place to
attempt to outline the complicated discussions between representatives of the two churches from 1889 until the intransigent papal
pronouncement, *Apostolicae Curae*, declaring Anglican Orders

'utterly null and completely void', in 1896. Given the unbending hostility of Cardinal Vaughan and Dom Gasquet and the intellectualist critic Edmond Bishop, there was never much chance of their succeeding. Duchesne was drawn in through friendship with Abbé Portal, a Lazarist, and his reaction to a pamphlet written by Portal and the Revd F. W. Puller somewhat inconsequentially rejecting the validity of Anglican Orders.[77] Duchesne wrote to Portal on 13 April 1894, objecting. He maintained that the Orders were valid, accepting the Augustinian view against the Donatists (*De Baptismo contra Donatistas*) that the sacramental reality was independent of the personal faith of the administrator.[78] The object, as he wrote in the *Bulletin critique* in July of the same year, should be to lessen so far as possible the 'distance that divided us from certain Christian groupings'. He believed that Pope Leo XIII also considered that it was best to 'bind together the fasces of the forces of religion in face of the very numerous enemies of the faith'.[79] With this Lord Halifax and other promoters of Anglican–Roman reunion would have agreed.

Duchesne, however, always insisted that in any scheme of reunion Rome must be in the driving-seat.[80] Conditional reordinations were essential. At this time research had not shown that Christianity was in every probability introduced into Britain, Gaul and the Rhineland provinces of the empire either by merchants from the eastern provinces (as at Lyons) or by Christian soldiers in the second half of the second century.[81] Rome was not a missionary centre for this part of the empire. In addition, in Britain the Church in the fourth century followed the general line of the other western churches, particularly the Gallic, of supporting Athanasius of Alexandria against the emperor Constantius II, but without any special reference to Rome. Duchesne, however, regarded the mission of Augustine of Canterbury sent by Pope Gregory to England in 597 as the origin of the Church in England. He insisted that through the early Anglo-Saxon period 'the Church of England was a colony of the Church of Rome'.[82] 'Ubi Petrus, ibi Ecclesia', he wrote to Lord Halifax in July 1894.[83] In his view, despite its faults, the Catholic Church was Roman.

Such views were unacceptable on the English side of the
Channel by Christians whether Anglo-Catholics or Evangelicals.
The fact was that a chasm separated their outlook regarding critical scholarship and the understanding of the Bible from their
Roman Catholic counterparts. The Church of Westcott and Hort
had little in common with that of Chamard and Bernadou.
Moreover, this was the time when the Church of England was
beginning to become the worldwide Anglican Communion and
Great Britain itself was moving towards the height of its imperial
power. To have accepted Duchesne's thesis and the Roman interpretation of Archbishop Parker's consecration in 1559 in dubious
surroundings and with it practical submission to Rome would
have been intolerable.

Duchesne, however, gained prestige with Leo XIII though
losing it with more liberal-minded French clergy, including
Portal. His installation as Director was attended by Cardinal
Parocchi who saluted him as a worthy successor of de Rossi. He
remained the Pope's adviser on Anglican Orders and in 1896 wrote
Autonomies ecclésiastiques: églises séparées, concentrating on the
Eastern schismatic churches but vindicating the Roman position.
The book was translated into English in 1907. Duchesne meanwhile had been promoted to the rank of Apostolic Protonotary
with the title of Monseigneur, in 1900, and became counsellor to
the Congregation of Indulgences and Relics. From the Republic
came his nomination as Commandeur of the Legion d'honneur,
as part of the celebrations to mark the twenty-fifth anniversary of
the École française de Rome. Meantime, in 1896, he had received
an Honorary Degree from Cambridge. At the age of 58 the
clouds seemed to be behind him and he appeared destined for both
an influential ecclesiastical and secular career, and perhaps a
Cardinal's hat.

In addition, his long period of office in the École française de
Rome was being extraordinarily successful. His appointment was
immensely popular among young clergy in Rome. The work of the
promising French scholars who became its members reflected
Duchesne's own interests. Critical study of Antiquity and the

Middle Ages included both investigation of material remains on the ground and to a lesser extent research on manuscripts, though the Middle Ages were included in the range of the École's interests. Originally, Duchesne wanted to encourage archaeological work in Italy, but stringent laws aimed at discouraging excavations by foreign scholars (Stéphane Gsell's work on the Etruscan cemetery at Velletri was an exception) turned his attention to North Africa. Here, in both Algeria and Tunisia, he was successful. He was able to build on the programme of his predecessor and the publication of Audollent's and Gsell and Graillot's expeditions in Algeria published in the *Mélanges* between 1890 and 1894 (see above, pp. 65–9). He saw Roman North Africa as the 'terrain privilégié'[84] for French archaeology and he was richly rewarded. Between 1902 and 1914, the *Mélanges* contained a notable succession of important articles recording the discoveries of French scholars. Gsell's report on the Byzantine church at Henchir Akhrib including a collection of dated reliquaries (see above, p. 71) was followed by Jerome Carcopino's report in 1906 on the inscription of Ain el Djemala with its information about the proprietory rites of the *coloni* on the Imperial estates in second-century Proconsular Africa[85] and Félix-Georges de Pachtère's discovery of an inscription which showed how the latter distributed their limited water supplies (1908).[86] He was openly welcoming to his students; their work was encouraged and where necessary redirected towards more profitable enterprises than they had themselves proposed. His attention was repaid with their lasting affection. He was proving himself in every way a worthy heir of de Rossi. Amid all this successful literary and administrative work Duchesne remained a man of prayer, so concentrated on his daily conduct of the Mass that on one occasion even a drunken, raucous disturbance in his church near the Farnese Palace (Santa Maria della Monte) could not deflect his meditation. He never realised anything had been amiss, he told a friend.[87]

Yet clouds continued to build. What went wrong to the extent that the Italian translation of volume 2 of *The Early History of the Church* should be placed on the Index (22 January 1912) along with

the other volumes and the author's historical scholarship dis-
credited among Roman Catholics? The answer may be found in
the Modernist Movement,[88] and perhaps to an extent in his association with Mme Augustine Bulteau.[89]

Duchesne was not a philosopher and never pretended to be one.
He established his criticism of the Old Testament in particular,
the Pentateuch and early Church history on the basis of fact and
his understanding of situations described by the texts. He avoided
theology where possible; he had little sympathy with the philo-
sophic arguments of his Modernist contemporaries. As he wrote to
von Hügel on 28 November 1902, he was unable to accept the
negative exegesis of Scripture undertaken by Hébert, Loisy and
Tyrrell 'and other neo-Gnostics'.[90] Anyone, he wrote to his same
correspondent on 8 June 1906, who reduced Jesus to 'the son of
Joseph' and denied the Resurrection 'had no right to call themselves Christians'.[91] There must be limits to criticism, but where
did they lie? The Church was a permanence whatever the failings
of individuals, including a 'narrow-minded and limited Pope'.
Christianity in this world must be reckoned as religion itself.[92]

He was, however, walking a tightrope. There was no gainsaying
that he had left the Institut catholique under a cloud. He had been
too subjective, it was said. Even Maurice d'Hulst, the Rector, had
reproached him for 'having too little taste and too little esteem for
theology'.[93] Later, when *Études sur le Liber Pontificalis* appeared,
powerful voices, such as those of the Benedictine Cardinal Pitra
and Cardinal Richard, the co-adjutor Archbishop of Paris, had
criticised the work for its use of non-Catholic sources, especially
'those from the other side of the Rhine'.[94] Duchesne himself
had written to von Hügel in 1885 that while Renan could be
accused of creating 'agitation intellectuelle' Catholic exegesis of
the Scriptures was on the eve of being transformed. Revolution
must be avoided.[95] False exegesis dishonoured Scripture and
'turned the masses from the Church' (Palm Sunday 1885).[96] As
always he feared for the future of the Church. A few years later, in
1888, he criticised orthodox theologians for failing to take into
account modern criticism concerning the authorship and content

of the Pentateuch. Since 1882 he had come to the conclusion that this did contain legendary material.[97] Ten years later, in April 1891, he had reproached those who opposed the critical study of Scripture as 'asses' and 'poltroons'. There were 'Areopagites' in Rome, half-learned and not to be taken seriously.[98] This strong language was not easy to reconcile with devotion to the Roman See. Not surprisingly Duchesne was regarded by many as 'a liberal' and even the 'founder of Modernism'. He would have repudiated this title.[99]

Modernism as a movement within the Roman Catholic Church was on its scholarly side devoted to upholding the results of critical scholarship of the Scriptures and the early history of the Church. There had been no 'vaccination' of unhindered quest after the truth in these fields as undergone by Protestant scholars, as Duchesne ruefully confided to René Massigli, a young Protestant scholar whom he befriended at the École française after his arrival there in 1910.[100] There was in fact nothing of the *Essays and Reviews* and *Lux Mundi* tradition of fair-minded and critical study of evidence interpreting Scripture, taking account of the latest archaeological discoveries, that characterised Anglican theological scholarship of the time. Tied to Tridentine orthodoxy, often buttressed by early mediaeval legend, the Roman Catholic Church was unprepared for the threat that was arising in the 1890s among clergy, particularly in Italy and France, to its established beliefs.

Alfred Loisy, a Hebraist and biblical critic, one of the clergy most associated with the movement, had been a pupil of Duchesne in the Institut catholique in 1881. Duchesne had inspired him by his lectures on biblical criticism, pointing out *inter alia* contradictions in the narratives of the Resurrection.[101] There had been a period of estrangement, but this had ended in 1895, though in March 1899 Duchesne warned him 'that you are going so far ahead of us that we shall only be capable of not understanding you'.[102] Three years later, Loisy's *L'Évangile et l'Église* though intended, as we have seen (p. 25), as an answer to Harnack's *Das Wesen des Christentums* (What Is Christianity?), caused a storm and was immediately condemned by the Archbishop of Paris. Loisy's argument that Jesus did not found a church nor institute the sacraments, but that this did not detract from their central place in Christianity, did not convince. This and its sequel *Le Quatrième évangile*, were placed on the Index in 1903. Loisy resigned his post in the École des hautes études (1904) and abandoned his office of priest two years later. He was excommunicated in 1908. At the time, however, of complete separation between the Roman Catholic Church and the French Republic (1905) Loisy was not long unemployed, becoming professor of the history of religions in the Collège de France in 1909, a post which he held until 1930.[103]

By this time Modernism had been condemned by Pope Pius X (1903–14) in the decree *Lamentabili* (July 1907) and the encyclical *Pascendi Gregis* (8 September 1907), where it was described as 'the synthesis of all heresies'; and in 1910 the Pope introduced the 'anti-Modernist oath'. What effect were these measures to have on Duchesne?

Duchesne had, as we have seen, enjoyed reasonably good relations with Pope Leo XIII. Under the more limited Pius X this was to change, until the crisis which engulfed him in 1911–13 when as mentioned his *Histoire ancienne de l'Église* as put on the Index. He had been drawn into Modernist circles in Rome not long after his arrival as Director of the École française,[104] but while he remained on good terms with Modernists, including Loisy, Marcel Hébert and Albert Houtin, he kept just the right side of current controversy, though not without criticism. 'He did not easily appreciate the work of others in a consistent manner',[105] it was said of him. He preferred to write history and he shared Batiffol's innate loyalty to the Church. When the blow fell, it was harder for him to bear.

The Shadow of the Index

The *L'Histoire ancienne de l'Église* had been in Duchesne's mind since the 1880s when he was lithographing résumés of his lectures for his students at the Institut catholique. He had been urged to write such a history by de Rossi (May 1885), von Hügel (1892–3) and by Cardinal Parrochi; but each time he had hesitated to write a broad-brush work covering the whole of early Church history.[106] It was Mme Bulteau who persuaded him finally to write. 'Go on, go on', his 'Mother Abbess' had ordered; and, as was often to happen in Duchesne's last 20 years, she was obeyed.[107] By July 1905, volume 1 was ready for the printer. By April 1906, the first edition had been exhausted. A second volume was begun in March 1907 and published in December 1909. Next year, the most difficult volume, that concerned with the great Christological controversies, appeared and Duchesne began on what he intended as a fourth volume taking the story to the death of Pope Gregory the Great in 604.

It was a magnificent effort, something that Harnack himself had failed to achieve. Translations were made into English and Spanish in 1909 and 1910 respectively. It was praised by Norman Baynes as a 'masterpiece'. And then came the project for a translation into Italian.

Reading Duchesne, first as a research student in the late 1930s and then as a junior lecturer in the Divinity Faculty in Cambridge in the 1950s, I relied on *L'Histoire* and Lietzmann for study and lectures. Both histories were in many ways practically interchangeable, telling the same tale almost in the same way, following out the development of the Church from Judaistic sect to world religion. On the way there were third-century persecutions and the conversion of Constantine, and in Duchesne (Lietzmann's work did not go beyond Ambrose's confrontation with Theodosius in 391) the irreversible progress of Church doctrine from Nicaea to Constantinople despite the efforts of Arians and Apollinarians. Then beyond, the story was taken into the fifth century with its climax at the Council of Chalcedon in 451. It was a well-told tale based on information provided by Eusebius of Caesarea to whom Duchesne paid tribute as a genuine historian, 'the father of ecclesiastical history',[108] and his successors. There were just enough footnotes to glimpse the immense learning and authority of the author. It was a tour de force and volume 1 obtained an imprimatur.

But an attentive and less friendly reader could have found much to worry him. In his brief introduction to volume 1 Duchesne also paid tribute to 'Harnack and his school' collecting documents for a 'great synthesis' of early Christian history. *Texte und Untersuchungen* had kept the scientific world abreast of their progress,[109] and though praise was lavished on Tillemont and his seventeenth-century contemporaries and 'the wild theories' of the Tübingen school dismissed, the debt to 'beyond the Rhine' was obvious. Duchesne's forceful rejection of the 'folly of some of the legends'[110] and, in the introduction to volume 3, his 'dismissal of the quarrels of theologians' would not endear him to those who had suffered from his exposure of the legendary and his caustic comments about Roman Catholic historical studies while he was in Paris. Equally, critics could comment on the lack of a chapter devoted to Jesus. Did Duchesne think he founded the Church, or not? The origins of the church in Rome were also left in doubt; the presence of Peter there under Claudius in *c*.42, dismissed as resting on 'too insecure foundations'[111] while placing his first arrival in Rome *c*.62 'about the time Paul regained his liberty'[112] would have raised eyebrows. Paul and even some Jewish predecessors such as Prisca and Aquila, and not Peter, were perhaps the true founders of the church in Rome.

The real problem, however, lay with volume 2. Loyal as always to the Roman See, Duchesne presented the first two volumes of the *Histoire* to Pius X on 22 March 1910. They received a cordial but guarded welcome and the French edition received an imprimatur.[113] Perhaps if the author had forborne from an Italian translation nothing further would have happened. Volume 2 deals with the period from the Great Persecution (303–12) to the death of Theodosius in 395. From a distance of nearly a century, it is difficult to see what the storm was about. The right people, such as the Arians, were rejected. The colourful career of 'the godless deacon' Aetius was fairly but critically described.[114] Few tears were shed for Constantius II, Julian or the Donatists. There is a hint of irony in the 'roseate accounts' of pilgrimage centres in Palestine visited by Gregory of Nyssa in 381,[115] and perhaps more than a hint that the famous shrine of St James the Apostle at Compostella in Galicia may have been of Priscillianist origin.[116] The *cause célèbre* of the fall of Pope Liberius was treated factually according to the evidence provided by Athanasius and Hilary of Poitiers, and he allowed that the pope in all probability signed the creed of the first Council of Sirmium of 351 that condemned the heretic Photinus and not 'the Blasphemy of Sirmium' of six years later.[117]

Why the fuss? The trouble lay with the Italian clergy and the publicity it controlled. Elements of the Italian Catholic press led by *L'Unità cattòlica* from Florence mounted a furious attack on the work: Duchesne had argued that the action of the Church had been solely the work of men, not of God, an accusation repeated during the course of the next year. Moreover, Duchesne had failed to describe the organisation of the Roman Church and the *History* had little use for Christian mysticism. An article in the summer of 1910 not only attacked *L'Histoire* but called Duchesne's orthodoxy into question. This was taken up more seriously by the *Osservatore Romano* on 6 August. The aim was to prevent an Italian translation of *L'Histoire*. Rivalry between publishing houses for the publication rights had become mixed up with the anti-Modernist tide of opinion prevailing among powerful groups of clergy in France and Italy. Duchesne was caught in the middle.[118] A compromise appeared to be reached whereby in exchange for an Italian imprimatur the work would be subjected to a thoroughgoing revision. But whatever the possibilities of this, they were overtaken by the election of Duchesne to the Académie française on 21 January 1911.

There had been some desperate intrigues before Duchesne was elected – he was scurrilously accused of personal failings;[119] but on his election he was congratulated by Cardinal Aghardi, Bishop of Albano, and the even more influential Cardinal Rampolla, Secretary of the Congregation of the Sacred Office. His enemies, however, did not give up. Duchesne had, in fact, played into their hands by his inaugural speech in the Academy, where it appears that not having much to say about the contributions of his predecessor in his chair, Cardinal Mathieu, Archbishop of Toulouse (d. 1908), he allowed himself to call into question the value of cardinals in general, and even the alleged debts of his former adversary Mgr Freppel, Bishop of Angers.[120] In view of the separation between Church and State begun in February 1905 this was dangerous territory, for Duchesne appeared to be putting himself unreservedly on the side of the state.

The French Catholic press and in particular the Jesuits now took up the cause of *Unità*. There was anger especially that Duchesne had defeated Mgr Baudrillart, the Catholic candidate for Mgr Mathieu's chair in the Académie. *L'Histoire* was attacked in a brochure called the *Appunti sereni*, composed largely of articles in the *Unità* for representing an evolutionary theory of the Church, as a development from Judaism. This resulted in the Christian cult being partly Jewish and partly pagan. Renewed attacks were made on Duchesne's views concerning the birth of the Church at Jerusalem, and of the foundation of the church of Rome independently of the presence of Peter.[121] The *Dépêche de Nice* saw Duchesne as 'le chef de l'école moderniste, c'est à dire scientifique' (29 January 1911). *L'Univers* of 8 February described his speech to the Académie as 'vide de foi'.[122]

Duchesne hesitated to reply to his detractors, but by the summer of 1911 the 'case' of the three volumes of *L'Histoire* had reached the Roman Curia. His opponent was no less a person than Cardinal Gaetano De Lai, Secretary of the Consistorial Congregation. He came to the conclusion that Duchesne had written his *History* in 'a spirit of demolition'.[123] The books were therefore to be completely avoided for use by the youth and particularly in the seminaries. Duchesne took up the challenge. On 7 July 1911 he wrote to Pope Pius that in accordance with the latter's request he intended to refute publicly the attacks made on *L'Histoire* by *Unità*. He had already defended himself in an open letter entitled 'Lettre à un Ami', written at the end of June.[124] He accepted that the Holy Spirit had been at work in the history of the Church; but there had been errors – God moved in a mysterious way – and it was the duty of the historian to see clearly what had happened in the past and explain this to his contemporaries with clarity.[125] The historian in his case was a man of faith working for the Church and religious truth, but also observing the discipline of a historian.[126] The attacks by *Unità* had been malicious and unfair. Pius, however, had denounced the Modernists in *Pascendi* for having differentiated between the 'realm of faith and the realm of history' and 'the Christ of faith and Christ of history', and was not wholly convinced. He awaited Duchesne's 'Protestation'.

In the event, the 'Protestation' was overtaken by events. The accusations levelled by *Unità* carried the day. On 1 September the Sacred Congregation of the Consistory addressed a circular to the bishops of Italy forbidding the reading of *L'Histoire ancienne de l'Église* in seminaries, a decision made public three days later.[127] Though Duchesne enjoyed some support among the cardinals (for instance, Cardinal Capecelatro), the die was cast. De Lai insisted that the volumes virtually deprived the Church of the supernatural charismas on which it was founded and without which it could not progress. *L'Histoire* was placed on the Index on 22 January 1912. The decision was announced in the *Osservatore Romano* on 30 January. A few days later Duchesne made an abject submission to Cardinal della Volpe, Prefect of the Index.[128]

So far as Duchesne's creative work went, this was the end. The Index prevented further major studies. He had failed to achieve his long cherished ideal of a history of the Church 'absolument orthodoxe et inexorablement scientifique'[129] already taught to his pupils at the Institut catholique in the 1880s. He had sailed too close to the wind. It was bad luck that the controversy over *L'Histoire* should have become caught up with the wider controversy over Modernism. Not only the Church in France, however, but the Roman Catholic Church generally was unready for an early Church history as Duchesne had written it. 'Rival schools of theology dashing themselves into collision, parties waxing hot and engaging in strife', gave no favours to the ultimately victorious orthodoxy in the events preceding Ephesus and Chalcedon. Christian unity was sacrificed to 'the unprofitable defence of personal feeling'.[130] So much for St Cyril of Alexandria. So much for theology. He had written in a way calculated to scandalise the faithful.[131]

It would take another decade dominated by the horrors of the First World War and the revolutionary changes in religious beliefs and attitudes that resulted from these before even the most moderate historical account of the Passions of the martyrs, by Hippolyte Delehaye, a Bollandist, published in 1921, would receive an imprimatur.[132] Moreover, Duchesne's friendship with Loisy and Buonaiuti, brilliant historian of the Church in North Africa though he was, [133] counted against him. Another point, even if not decisive in itself, forfeited sympathy. Pius X told him at his audience that his volume 2 though satisfactory was 'talvolta un puo crudo' (at times a bit rough),[134] and that was true of the man himself. He was too combative; alongside his faith there was a streak of cynicism and irreverence. 'I am not a theologian', he wrote to von Hügel, 'that is why I can praise God with joy. The dead cannot praise Thee, but we who are living.'[135] No resurrection then, to eternal life. And in the same vein to describe to Mme Bulteau the dead Leo XIII as a 'papal mummy',[136] for whom few had said prayers at his funeral, showed a lack of good taste.

It all added up. Duchesne was, however, saved from despair, from a quarter unlooked for in a Monseigneur, Mme Augustine Bulteau (1869–1922).[137] She had married Jules Ricard in 1880; they had two daughters, but had divorced in 1896. Duchesne came across her salon in the Avenue Wagram, Paris, in 1902, a salon frequented by authors, such as Leon Daudet, historians and painters. Augustine Bulteau presided over intellectual Paris. She was highly intelligent herself, a feminist at a time when few existed in France, physically not outstandingly attractive, but with a presence, and she captivated Duchesne.[138] Between 12 December 1902 and 30 March 1922, a correspondence between them stretched to 530 letters – almost as many as with de Rossi. For Duchesne she was a mother figure, 'the abbess', 'his magician, Circe', 'princess', and their love was mutual. It had, however, to be suppressed. Most of Duchesne's letters are on scholarly matters, though they contain some biting criticisms of the Curia and the Vatican. In the

years following the placing of *L'Histoire* on the Index her friendship sustained him. In other circumstances they would have been
ideally man and wife.

Duchesne now went into semi-retirement though he published
more articles on the topography of Rome in the Middle Ages
(*Mélanges* 34 and 35). But for the most part, he buried himself in
the library and the administration of the École française, and he
bought a property in his native Saint-Servan for vacations. The
war enabled him to perform final services for France. He worked
hard to ensure that the French cause was represented effectively
against the powerful German influence on the new Pope, Benedict
XV (1914–22).[139] Trusted by the French government, he kept
influential members informed of papal views, and also of the
gradual change of attitude by the Italian government towards the
Allies. He was on occasion consulted by senior Vatican officials, in
particular in 1917 by Cardinal Gasparri on the foundation of a
Pontifical Oriental Institute, aimed at buttressing the position of
the Catholics in the Middle East, to which he attached great
importance.[140] So far as the Orthodox Communions in the East
were concerned he counselled that the Vatican should aim at
negotiated union rather than renewed subjection to the Latin
Church.[141] Finally, through his old pupil, Louis Canet, he paved
the way for a rapprochement between the Catholic Church and the
French Republic which took place during 1921.[142]

Despite all these services and frequent contact with cardinals
his major contribution, *L'Histoire*, remained on the Index,[143] and
he lived his days under its shadow. He continued to work to the
end. His final article published in the *Mélanges* of 1921–2 traced
the long history of the church and its relics dedicated to the
martyr, Laurence, on the Via Tiburtina from Constantine's original building of a *memoria* in his honour to its restoration by Pius
IX.[144] It was as well documented and concise as ever, but this
achievement belied his mood. In these years he feared, as he had
far back in the 1880s, for the future of the Christian religion itself.
On 25 July 1917, one of the worst moments of the war for France,
he wrote, that events were moving 'towards an obliteration of

religion' rather than the arrival of a new religious system (*d'un nouveau système religieux*).[145] It was always his worry as far back as 1882 and was one of the factors that influenced him as a historian of the early Church. It was not mere pessimism.

Regarding volume 4, the first four chapters, dealing with the religious policy of the Emperor Anastasius (491–518) and leading on to the disputes between the Empress Theodora (d. 548) and Pope Vigilius (537–55), appeared in the *Mélanges* of 1913, 1915 and 1916,[146] but it was becoming a struggle. He felt he could not go on. On 25 June 1920 he wrote to Loisy: 'La cruelle vieillesse s'appesant il sur moi, j'ai peine à écrire avec des doigts affaiblis et les yeux tout à larmes, elle n'empêche pas le souvenir.'[147] The final chapter was never completed, ending with the future Pope Gregory being sent by Pelagius II to represent the Holy See at Constantinople. It had begun on a note of depression, a description of the wretched state of the city of Rome in the last decades of the sixth century, a reflection perhaps also of the mind of the author. Henri Quentin in his introduction to *L'Église au VIe siècle* (English translation 1925) refers to Duchesne's expressions of sympathy and support for Pope Gregory, and also for Pope Martin I (d. 655), in the latter's handling of the Monothelite controversy. It may be that he wished, as Quentin claims, that his final work should have 'the blessing of his superiors'.[148] In any event, he did not wish to die, like Loisy, outside the Church of his baptism. On 11 April 1922 he received the blessing of Pope Pius XI, who as Cardinal Ratti had been his friend, and who knew the value of archaeology in the study of the early Church. But the purple that he perhaps had hoped for did not come. He died ten days later, on the evening of 21 April. A final picture of him shows a sad, frail old man in cassock and biretta holding a not too willing black and white cat.[149] On 1 July 1924 the incomplete volume 4 of *L'Histoire* received a 'Nihil Obstat'.

At heart, Duchesne wanted to remain 'fidelis' to his 'old mother' the Church and not least to the church of his birthplace, Saint-Servan; but he could never reconcile his critical sense as a historian with this aim. His head had driven him far from the

Roman Catholicism of his age. In England he would have been ideally suited to a chair at Oxbridge or London. His colleagues would have been scholars such as William Bright, H. B. Swete and Claude Jenkins himself, kindred spirits, combining a devout Christianity with a keen critical sense. He would have (and did) found a ready acceptance for his views without the permanently distracting hassle of hostile inquisition by ecclesiastical superiors. He would also have been able to enjoy a happy married life which his correspondence with Mme Bulteau shows he yearned, and which perhaps would have softened the acerbity of some of his judgements. It is with a note of personal tragedy that Louis Duchesne, the greatest of the French early Church historians, left the scene with much still to fulfil.

Long after his death no less than two large volumes in the *Collections de l'École française de Rome* have been dedicated to his memory, another to his correspondence with de Rossi, and his Scripta Minora reprinting his contributions towards understanding the topography of the City of Rome in the Middle Ages. One includes an opening Allocution by Paul VI, a fine graceful tribute,[150] but also the criticism that Duchesne 'neglected the transcendent coefficient of the history of the Church'. For the early Church historian today, however, he remains the Master.

6

Norman Hepburn Baynes (1877–1961): Byzantine Scholarship[1]

Norman Baynes shared with his friend Hugh Last, Camden Professor of Ancient History and later Master of Brasenose College, Oxford, the supervision of my thesis which was eventually published in 1952 as *The Donatist Church: A Movement of Protest in Roman North Africa*. This was republished after three editions, by the Oxford University Press among its Oxford Scholarly Classics in 2000, and it will probably be assessed as an early attempt to integrate the social and economic with the religious history of Roman North Africa from the third to the fifth centuries AD. Its aim was to move that study from the discussion of one or other aspect of Augustinian theology to the history of a popular religious movement which Augustine opposed, and preceded the permanent conversion of the North African to Islam in the eighth century.

Baynes was both friend and supervisor and in the former quality saw me through a gloomy period of my life in the autumn of 1939 and a minor crisis in my early scholarly career, as I explained in the Introduction. I owe an immense debt of gratitude to him. His collection of essays inscribed to me in a wavering hand 'in friendship' sums up our relationship. When I first met him on my election to the Craven Fellowship at Oxford in the summer of 1937 he had been for many years an eminent senior scholar, Professor of Byzantine History at University College, London, and the writer, *inter alia*, of a classic account of the conversion of Constantine to Christianity. He was an ideal choice to guide the studies of a keen and energetic but not too disciplined young scholar.

Norman Baynes was born on 29 May 1877, the son of two generations of Baptist ministers. His father, Alfred Henry Baynes, was for 30 years General Secretary of the Baptist Missionary Society and his mother was the daughter of a Baptist minister. His grandfather had been for more than 40 years the Baptist minister at Wellington in Somerset. Baynes therefore had the strong Christian family background that other scholars studied here have had and, like them, a background that moulded his character and ideas. He had a firm social conscience derived from his family and shown throughout his career.[2]

Serious-minded and studious, he had no great love of organised games in an age when these were the breath of life at schools such as Eastbourne College where he was educated. But his scholarship and hard work were respected and one permanent influence derived from these early years was a prolonged stay at Tübingen University whence he gained a fluent knowledge of German. This was to stand him in good stead for an immensely valuable contribution during the Second World War, namely, his translation of Hitler's speeches and his Romanes Lecture of June 1942.

Baynes went on to New College, Oxford, in 1896 and took a First Class in Honour Mods and a Second in *Literae Humaniores* ('Greats'). Like Duchesne, he never felt drawn to philosophy (which influenced his final results) but had the natural gifts of a historian of what is known now as Late Antiquity. He won the Marquis of Lothian Prize in 1901 and the Arnold Essay Prize in 1903. In both these essays he took subjects to which he was to devote himself later on, namely, the emperor Heraclius (610–41), of which an early essay published in 1904 showed promise,[3] and the military reforms of Diocletian and Constantine. He was further inspired to work in this field by a meeting with J. B. Bury in Cambridge in the same year.

Nonetheless, he did not look for a tutorship in Ancient History. Instead he chose Law for his profession. It was not a surprising choice and with his application to detail coupled with innate skills as an actor he might have developed into a barrister on the model of Marshall Hall. In the decade before the First World War he studied in the Chambers of R. J. Parker, later a Lord of Appeal, and until 1916 was for some time a tutor under the Law Society. The war, however, was to influence a decisive change of direction. Previously he had also considered a career in politics. He was invited by the Liberal Party Whip to stand for one of two seats in the London area, but after much thought he declined.

All the time, the lure of study of East Rome and its problems had been tugging at him. In 1910 he published a considerable and authoritative article in the *English Historical Review* on the relations between 'Rome and Armenia in the Fourth Century'.[4] Baynes emphasised the contribution of the Armenian writer Faustus of Byzantium towards understanding these. Comparing the accounts of Faustus with that of Ammianus Marcellinus, he showed how, sandwiched between the two empires, Armenia, in general, favoured Rome against Persia in the reigns of Constantine and Constantius II. This was not least thanks to the influence exercised by the see of Caesarea on the Armenian Church. Armenia, however, could never shake off threats from its Persian neighbour, and the permission given by Jovian (363–4) in July 363 to the Persian king Sapor 'to conquer half of Armenia' as well as to take over the fortress and trading centre of Nisibis gave the Persians the edge temporarily. Fire temples of Zoroastrianism began to replace churches and for a few years Armenia became part of Sapor's dominions under the client King Pap. Once again, however, the situation changed. Faustus emphasised the purely Armenian victory (the Romans only shared in the booty!) over the Persians in 372, and tells for the first time of active Roman participation in the war in the following year. King Pap was eventually murdered. The Armenians decided, however, that they could not for ever be at war with either Rome or Persia. Diplomacy took over and in 387 the country was effectively partitioned between the two empires, to Faustus' deep-felt disgust.

Baynes's aim was to vindicate Faustus as a historian, but the grasp of detail shown by the article, not least in the footnotes, shows that he had mastered not only Lauer's translation of Faustus but also the work of the German philologists and historians who had studied the same question. It is difficult to think that after this well-documented contribution he would have been able to give his exclusive attention to the Bar.

In fact, he followed 'Faustus' with three other Late Antique and Byzantine studies. In 1911 he contributed two chapters in volume 1 of the *Cambridge Mediaeval History* (ed. Gwatkin and Whitney) on Constantine's successors to Jovian; and the struggle with Persia and 'The Dynasty of Valentinian and Theodosius the Great'. Both were in the best tradition of British narrative history writing. The accounts are set round the principal political and military figures of the day and the events in which they participated. In both, the story moves along serenely; all the main events of both periods have been thoroughly researched and verdicts pronounced. On Constantius II, the 'task of maintaining the greatness of Rome was subtly confused with the duty of self-preservation',[5] a description worthy of Ammianus Marcellinus. Julian's campaign against the Persians is concisely chronicled, as are the events which preceded the humiliation of the emperor Theodosius by Ambrose of Milan in 390. But even here one might complain that there were some questions that Baynes did not seem aware of, let alone answer. Thus why in supressing the revolt and invasion of 367 in Britain did Count Theodosius (the emperor's father) set up his head-quarters in London if the main threat to the provinces came from the Caledonian peoples of the north? Surely he would have marched straight to York? The answer may be that the Saxons were the main peril, indicated by the death of Nectaridus, Count (commander) of the Saxon shore fortresses, and the capture of the general Fullofaudes.[6] The peril lay in the east of Britain and not least on the imperial estate that covered much of the east Midlands.[7] It was from here that grain had contributed much towards the supply of Julian's armies on the lower Rhine.[8] The Saxons may have noted the fact. And of Julian himself, there are the outlines of, but not the evidence for, a depth of understanding demanded by this complex character who substituted King Helios for Christ the King in his own thoughts and hoped, in vain as it proved, that the empire would do likewise.

Baynes had described himself as 'M. A. Barrister at Law' on the title pages, and the same for his contribution to volume 2 of the *Cambridge Mediaeval History* in 1913. His chapter entitled 'The Successors of Justinian' covered the period 565–630. It begins with a continuance of the long saga of the Roman or rather Byzantine relations with Persia, recounts the new threats posed by the Avars and Slavs in the 580s, and continues with the reign of the emperor Maurice and disasters under his supplanter, Phocas. It ends on the premature note of triumph with the recapture of Jerusalem and restoration of the True Cross in 630, only to portray the aged emperor Heraclius about to contemplate disasters at the hands of the Arabs and, in the west, the Spanish Visigoths. But, we also are reminded of Heraclius' efforts as a general and an administrator who sought to keep the Latin and Greek halves of the empire together. And, we are left with the unexpressed question, could anyone else have done better?[9]

These studies, together with his shorter article in the *English Historical Review* of 1912 on the 'Restoration of the True Cross' were marking him out as a historian of the later Roman empire and a future successor to J. B. Bury.[10] In 1913 he accepted an appointment as an assistant in the Department of History at University College, London, at the salary of £40 p.a. His scope as well as his future home were being decided even before the outbreak of war.

War service involved intelligence work in Watergate House which enabled him to begin seriously his long connection with University College, London, at first through continuing his evening classes. He now made up his mind that history and not law was his *métier*: 'I determined to abandon the teaching and practice of the law and to devote myself to the teaching of history.' This resolve coupled with his connection with London University led him to turn down an offer from New College to return to Oxford after the end of the war.[11] While he retained a strong allegiance to his old university he was, as he said, 'essentially a cockney and belonged to a cockney university'. He was to remain at University College for the remainder of his career.

He had started late even by wartime standards. Though he had given his first history lecture on Ancient History to the university Evening School of History on 8 October 1913, more than four years of war had intervened. But he was accepted readily at University College. In 1919 he became Reader in the History of the Roman Empire in London University and became a member of the Professorial Board of his college He continued to further the work of the Evening School of History. Between 1919 and 1933 he was associated with this diploma-giving body, and became its director on the resignation of the Tudor-period historian, A. F. Pollard in 1927. He continued until he in turn resigned in 1933.[12] So much for Baynes's career as his standing in the field of Ancient History became increasingly authoritative.

By 1922 the first of a steady stream of articles and learned reviews began to appear. In that year he wrote at length for the *Journal of Roman Studies* on Bury's *History of the Late Roman Empire*.[13] He concentrated on two incidents in the early years of the fifth century on which he disagreed with Bury.[14] On the one hand, Bury believed that Alaric, after his defeat at Pollentia in 402, withdrew from Italy and then reinvaded from the north-east the next year. On the other hand, Baynes considered the engagement at Verona was simply a major incident during Alaric's retreat after Pollentia. The invasion, however, determined Honorius to vacate Milan in the autumn of 402 for the security of the marshlands around Ravenna and take the latter as his capital. Defeat by Stilicho made Alaric more amenable to serve the Alan general's purposes in 405 and with his troops to ensure the restoration of western authority in Illyricum, important as a prime recruiting ground for the Roman armies.[15] Against both Bury and Mommsen, Baynes maintained that Stilicho's consistent aim had been to guide the policies of both Arcadius and Honorius in accordance with the will of their father, Theodosius I, but not at the cost of civil war between the two halves of the empire.[16] It was only after Gainas the Goth's revolt against Arcadius in 401, its failure and the Roman-nationalist reaction in Constantinople, that Stilicho chose a second course, namely, to use Alaric to secure Illyricum for the west. A second part of the review puts forward the view that the revolt of the Roman garrison in Britain in 406, and its choice of Constantine as usurping emperor the next year, 'sprang from the fact that its members had grown tired of life in our much-harassed island' and 'hankered for the fleshpots of Provence'.[17] Unflattering to our national pride, adds Baynes, but a reminder that Britain was dispensable – not least since the Lower Rhine frontier whose troops British grain had supplied was no longer defensible.

This, and other shorter articles covering both the period from Diocletian to Constantine,[18] and the negotiations between Justinian and the Ostrogothic queen Amalasuntha in 533–4,[19] established Baynes as among the premier British historians of the Later Roman Empire in succession to Bury. The review article on Stilicho and the Barbarian Invasions was compulsory reading for those of us in the 1930s who had embarked upon 'St Augustine' as our Special Subject in the Oxford Modern History School. Our scant knowledge of Greek was always tested in the exam by key passages of Zosimus Books 5 and 6 relating to the fall of Stilicho and the events leading to the evacuation of Roman Britain by the Roman legions and administration in 410.[20] Was there a popular uprising in what remained of the Romano-British towns and some form of declaration of independence, as hinted by Zosimus's writing more than half a century after the event? Or, even, was the process of withdrawal more gradual, to the extent of the maintenance of a garrison at Richborough (Rutupiae) for another ten years? The question still provides scope for scholarly articles today (2002).[21]

Baynes's next major research had a less lasting impact. The *Historia Augusta* is a collection of biographies of Roman emperors, including claimants to the throne and usurpers from Hadrian (117–38) to Numerian (283–4). The work is modelled on Suetonius' imperial biographies and purports to have been composed by six different authors writing between the latter part of the reign of Diocletian and the earlier years of Constantine (295–325) with considerable attention to Constantine's father, Constantius (d. 306). The authors quote public records and other supposed official documents extensively and provide accounts, often scandalous, of the private and sometimes the public lives of their subjects. It's a scurrilous history, but is it more?[22]

Since accounts by pagan authors break off with Dio Cassius in 229 and Herodian in 238 a consistent account of mid-third century history from a pagan viewpoint would be extremely welcome. Unfortunately, the *Historia* does not fulfil that purpose. Down to 1889 it was accepted that, though badly flawed, the accounts could be accepted as reasonably accurate and were the work of the six authors named. In that year, however, a young German scholar, Hermann Dessau, exploded this theory, maintaining that the *Historia* was the fabrication of one individual composing his 'history' in the reign of Theodosius I for a circle of pagan friends.[23] The argument remains. Most historians, with the cautious exception of Arnaldo Momigliano and perhaps the compiler of the *Prosopography of the Later Roman Empire* (1971) accept Dessau's theory with some modifications. To Ronald Syme, the *Historia* is a work of 'historical fiction' written by a 'rogue scholar, perverse, delighting in deception',[24] who compiled his fabrication probably in the early years of the fifth century. He derived his genuine material from the *De Caesaribus* of Aurelius Victor and as yet undiscovered *Kaisergeschichte*, dating to the mid-fourth century.[25]

Baynes took a different line. His book published in 1926 and a short article in the *Classical Review* of 1928 defending it against critics concluded that the *Historia* was written at Rome in the reign of Julian (360–3) and was designed as propaganda in his favour.[26] Baynes accepted Dessau's general thesis that the *Historia* was fiction compiled originally by a single author,[27] but sought to demonstrate against Dessau and Seeck that, on the one hand, the Theodosian era was too late, while the first decade of the fourth century was too early. On the other hand, glorification of Claudian ancestors by two 'biographers' (Pollio and Vopiscus), combined with a hereditary title derived from them, and acceptance of the authority of the Senate pointed to Julian as the inspiration of the *Historia*.[28] Julian also fitted the attack in the *Historia* on unworthy sons of a ruler (*Severus*, 4). Did not Constans and Constantius II fit that bill?[29] In addition, Julian followed the example of Claudius II in his policy toward the Senate (e.g. Claudius 12.3). While the author of the *Historia* probably used Aurelius Victor's *De Caesaribus*, that would not rule out a Julianic date.[30]

Baynes worked out his case with all the skill of a trained barrister; but in the end it did not convince. As mentioned, Syme considers the *Historia* as a 'hoax'. T. D. Barnes, no less sceptical, places it nearer to Julian as 'after 337'.[31] Few today would accept the *Historia* as genuine and a worthwhile source for the history of the late third century.

It is not easy to take issue with the eminent scholars on either side of the divide. For this writer, however, the *Historia* would not only seem to be a prodigious work of imaginative fiction for one writer to undertake but also, even on a cursory reading, he appears to give a great many hostages to fortune. The frequent reference to Diocletian and to Constantius (not Constantine) as 'Scion of a family divinely appointed' (i.e. Claudius II)[32] while referring in the same breath to Maximian and 'his brother Galerius'[33] might have sounded odd to hearers in the reign of Theodosius. It was a queer mixture, for Galerius was a persecutor of the Christians, while Constantius did not enforce the murderous edicts in his dominions. Moreover, naming the Germanic chieftains 'Hariomundus, Huldagates, Hildomundus and Charioviscus' as trusted officers in Aurelian's army could not have been tactful at a time *c*.400 when Germanic commanders in the Roman army were becoming increasingly unpopular.[34] Few would want to be reminded of a pedigree of such generals extending back over a century. So far as Christianity is concerned there is a measure of agreement that Spartian's record of Severus' alleged rescript that coupled Jews and Christians and forbade conversion to either religion is likely to be genuine.[35] This is only because converts to Christianity, such as Perpetua and Felicitas at Carthage and Leonides, Origen's father, at Alexandria, were martyred, whereas their superiors in the Church were not. Moreover, Lampridius' statement that under Severus Alexander (222–35) 'Christians (as were the Jews) were allowed to be'[36] can be partially confirmed from other sources, notably Eusebius of

Caesarea.[37] It may well be that the less friendly references to Christians found in Vopiscus' *Aurelianus* or *Quadriga Tyrannorum* could have been written in the decade before the Great Persecution while the more favourable references could fit into the decade following the Edict of Milan. Then, officials were aware that Constantine was showing 'pietas' towards the Christians as these promoted imperial 'discipline' and was therefore encouraging their religion but equally had not abandoned the 'immortal gods of Rome'.[38] Until the lost *Kaisergeschichte* is found the problem of the *Historia*'s authorship and date is likely to remain unsolved.

Baynes may not have carried the day. In contrast, his Raleigh lecture on History delivered at the British Academy in 1930 remains a classic. This, as well as the two articles in volume 12 of the *Cambridge Ancient History* were and continue to be primary influences on my work.

Baynes trusted his evidence. 'For myself', he told his audience, 'have gradually come to the conclusion that the true starting point of any comprehension of the reign must be Constantine's own letters and edicts.'[39] He went on to state his belief that all the documents ascribed to Constantine were genuine, with a reservation in respect of the sermon 'To the Assemby of the Saints'.[40] And he regarded Eusebius of Caesarea as a truthful historian who published genuine documents in his *Vita Constantini*, the latter belief being fortified later by the discovery on the back of a papyrus petition from the city of Arsinoe for tax relief, a roughly contemporary official copy of part of Constantine's letter to the Eastern Provincials in 324 (*Vita Constantini* 2.24–42).[41] But Baynes in his discussion with Henri Grégoire had already provided evidence to refute the doubts of the 'forgery and interpolationist school' of continental historians.[42] The tendency of scholars was veering in the same direction. As we have seen, Duchesne had in 1890 proved the authenticity of the Donatist dossier preserved as an appendix to Optatus of Milevis' *De Schismate Donatistarum*.[43] These documents combined with Constantine's rescript to Anulinus, Proconsul of Africa, preserved in Eusebius' *Ecclesiastical History* x.5 showed that already in the winter of 312 the emperor was intervening actively in the affairs of the Church in North Africa for the benefit of Bishop Caecilian of Carthage (the Catholic party). His eventual decision in favour of Caecilian in November 316 and attempted repression of his Donatist opponents failed, and four years later he was forced to recall the Donatist leaders from exile and grant them what Augustine called 'ignominiosissima indulgentia'.[44] But they showed the emperor as a partisan for the unity of the Church, centred round the personages he regarded as legitimate.

For Baynes, Constantine was an enthusiast with a mission. He found it impossible to accept the view of Jacob Burckhardt and his followers, such as Otto Seeck, that Constantine was simply a cunning politician who used Christianity to accomplish his aim of autocratic rule or that he intended to found a new syncretist religion. Nor did he accept Henri Grégoire's attacks on the authenticity of the documents preserved in the *Vita Constantini*.[49] He found himself at one with Duchesne who commented:

> We cannot wonder too much at the artless simplicity of certain critics who approach this imperial literature (e.g. *Vita Constantini*) with the preconceived idea that it was impossible for an emperor to have religious convictions, that men like Constantine, Constantius or Julian were in reality free thinkers, who for political motives proclaimed such and such opinions. In the fourth century, if there were any, free thinkers were *rarae aves* whose existence could not be assumed or easily accepted.[50]

Baynes agreed and added, that a 'student who works with Duchesne's masterpiece in his hands the more mysterious does the condemnation of these three magnificent volumes appear'.[51] And, without a knowledge of Italian and French Roman Catholic politics of 1907–2, so it does.

Baynes's study of Constantine was also a masterpiece, though as Henry Chadwick rightly points out, he could have used the evidence of Constantine's coins from 306 onwards and the entries in the *Liber Pontificalis* under Constantine, the emperor's legislation and his building programmes to buttress his case.[52] The *Liber* shows that Constantine made and continued to make munificent gifts to the church in Rome. To the Lateran Basilica were added gifts to endow the Basilica of St Peter on the Vatican, as well as gifts of land and, in Italy, treasure to the Lateran itself.[53] The coins tell an interesting story, beginning with Constantine as a loyal supporter of the Herculians (Maximian) in 306–7, issuing *folles* as Caesar, featuring on the reverse Dea Roma seated in her temple in Rome with the inscription 'Conservatori Reipublicae' (to the Preserver of the Commonwealth) and following the tradition of Diocletian, Maximian and the Tetrarchy, 'Genio Populi Romani' (Lyons mint). A little later, 308–10, confident in his title 'Augustus', though nominally only 'filius Augusti', 'Marti Conservatori' (Trier mint) and from the London mint 'Adventus Augusti' – the emperor on horseback riding left in triumph like his third-century predecessors. The first break comes in 310 when, after the failure of Maximian's conspiracy, Constantine abandons the Herculian dynasty. His *folles* reverses now feature Claudius II facing right with radiate crown and the inscription 'Soli Invicto Comiti' (to my companion the Unconquered Sun).[54] This series, showing Sol standing with an orb in his left hand, was to remain the common type on Constantine's bronze coinage to 324, that is, the coins everyone used throughout the West. To this was added yet another, even more pagan, symbolism, the Sun's orb on an altar on the coinage of the Western mint, not least London, celebrating Constantine *vicennalia* in 324. The exception in the West is that Constantine had a cross placed on the side of his helmet, from 315 onwards, at the mint of Ticinum (Pavia). No such symbol appears, however, on the same type of helmet on other western mints.[55] Both Constantine Junior and Crispus as Caesars use the orb and altar reverse on their coins from the London mint. Sol and honour to the Claudian ancestry continued to dominate the coinage of this period.

Many explanations have been put forward for the survival of the Sun symbols on Constantine coinage from all the western mints to 324. One cannot be certain, but it would seem that down to the

defeat of Licinius (18 September 324) and the summons of the
great ecumenical Council at Nicaea (May 325), Constantine
wished to demonstrate to his subjects his loyalty and affection to
the Sun god worshipped by his divine ancestor, Claudius, and his
successors. He might have his own interpretation of the Sun god
assimilated to Christ representing the Supreme God, to whose
worship he was now devoted. As mentioned, only at Ticinum did
the Chi Rho symbol ☧ appear on his helmet, as though a private
symbol perhaps explaining his favour towards the Christians of
which, as we have seen, his officials even in North Africa were by
now (in 315) aware.[56] We do not know. Ten years later, however,
in 324 (or shortly after) both the Spanish aristocrat and Christian
poet C. Vettius Aquilinus Juventus and an anonymous Gallic
Christian poet regarded Constantine as a Christian.[57]

In his two chapters in volume 12 of the *Cambridge Ancient
History* on the Great Persecution and Constantine respectively,
published in 1939, Baynes traces the gradual decline of the pagan
cause from its position of apparent strength so long as Diocletian
ruled, to the surrender involved in the Palinode of Galerius on 30
April 311. The grudging toleration granted by the dying emperor
meant that persecution of the Christians within the empire could
no longer be successfully undertaken.[58] Constantine must have
drawn his own conclusions. The chapter on Constantine follows
the same lines as the Raleigh lecture. Some extra detail is added,
such as the Council of Arles's canon ordering abandonment of
pacifism in time of war by Christian soldiers (Canon 3) and the
date of the emperor's campaign against Licinius corrected to 324.
We are left on the death of the emperor with Christian unity
restored, except for Athanasius. He 'had but to kiss the rod and the
Emperor's triumph was complete'.[59] But he preferred to remain in
exile in Trier.

One other study which I have continued to find enormously
useful was written in 1935–6. Baynes was a stout supporter of the
Historical Association. The Southwest London Branch had
embarked on a series of lectures on Social and Political Ideas and
invited him to contribute one on the subject of St Augustine. The

result was an outstanding paper on 'The Political Ideas of St Augustine's *De Civitate Dei*'.[60] One can understand from this, he argues, why the *De Civitate* was so popular among clerics in the Middle Ages. The *Civitas Dei* is the Church and the *Civitas terrena* is the state, even *Civitas Diaboli*,[61] and the Church was the superior. This united the policies of successive popes, Gregory VII, Innocent III and Boniface VIII in their conflicts with the Holy Roman emperors. More than that, the all-pervasive dualism of Augustine's political thought shows in my opinion why in his formative years (372–83) he found the dualistic religion of the Manichees so attractive and, when he was a Catholic bishop, he turned to the dualism of the Donatist thinker, Tyconius (*fl.* 380) for long-term inspiration in his treatise on Christian doctrine.[62] No wonder, Julian of Eclanum exclaimed, that just as a leopard cannot change his spots so Augustine cannot rid himself of Manichaean dualism.[63] Though personally loyal to the Roman empire to which he attributed 'libertas Romana',[64] he also characterised 'cupiditas dominandi' (greed of domination) with love of glory as the abiding sins of the pagan empire.[65] And at a time which saw the submergence of much of the western empire beneath the invasions of the Germanic peoples he stated his preference for small states which would live together under the law like large human families.[66] But this was conditioned by obedience to the Church, the only means through which the true *Civitas Dei,* the Celestial Kingdom, could be attained. It was the duty of the state to enforce that obedience, against heretics and schismatics, by force if necessary.[67] Yet, in the last resort, all humanity, descended from a single pair, Adam and Eve, were united in common ties diverging only in their loves, that of self leading to contempt of God, that of love of God leading to contempt of self.[68] Even the peace for which all strove could be divided into 'earthly' and 'heavenly' (*De Civ. Dei* xix.14).

Such was the legacy of Augustine to the European Middle Ages on the eve of the end of Roman Africa. It was a brilliant lecture, vastly helpful to those of us who had chosen 'St Augustine' as a special subject for the Oxford Modern History School, and a useful complement today to Robert Markus's *Saeculum, History and Society in the Age of St Augustine*.[69]

Baynes was now in his sixties. He was the authority in Britain on Late Roman and Byzantine history, with a succession of outstanding contributions behind him. In 1936 he was elected a Fellow of University College. Next year he expressed the wish to resign his chair and devote himself wholly to Byzantine history. The college in appreciation relieved him of teaching duties in Ancient History and elected him Honorary Professor of Byzantine History and Institutions which he held until his final retirement in 1942 when he became Emeritus Professor. He had been elected a Fellow of the British Academy in 1930.[70]

The outbreak of war set Baynes in an entirely new role. Like other scholars studied in this book he was a patriot. As his biographer says, 'he was never a really detached scholar, and the ties of academic work were more than outweighed by what he regarded as public duty and by his strong sense of fellowship'.[71] It had been way back in 1894 at Tübingen that he had learnt German and retained his familiarity with it. For the duration, he turned his back on Byzantine research, migrated from London to Oxford and embarked on a novel project under the Press and Research Department, afterwards the Research Department of the Foreign Office. This was the translation of the entire range of Hitler's speeches from July 1922 to September 1939[72] – a huge work extending to 1,980 pages. If anyone had listened to the stark staccato gibber (as I had in March 1938, and Hitler's denunciation of Benes on 3 September 1938) that passed for a speech, they would hardly have recognised it in the clear, precise phrases of Baynes's translation, complete with footnotes and 46 pages of subject-related bibliography. Baynes told me that he thought Hitler's most effective speech was that made to German industrialists on 27 January 1932 (before the Nazi Party seized power). In this he not only showed his skill and power as an orator and an ability to use history to support his thesis, in the face of a possibly hostile audience brought together in the Industrie Klub in Düsseldorf, but also the way in which he won an audience over to his policy.[73]

Germany, Hitler claimed, was not conditioned solely by the world crisis. Its future lay with the will of the German people not only 'belonging to the Aryan race but preeminent in abilities and achievements'. Democracy, meaning decisions taken by the masses, was a failure that led to Bolshevism. If one thought that one could preserve the concepts of 'bourgeois' and 'proletariat' for all time one was mistaken. That was the way to ruin. Instead, just as industry required leadership, so also did the body politic. The hundreds of thousands of young men who had joined the National Socialist movement were showing the way forward. What if 'the whole nation possessed this idealism?' His movement was providing the leadership which would ensure German regeneration. It would not tolerate division. It would crush opposition in all its forms. The long speech – 51 pages of print – was greeted with 'long and tumultuous applause'. It marked a turning point in Hitler's fortunes.

Through the speeches of 1937–8 runs the unending thread of protest at the unfairness of the Versailles Treaty and subsequent behaviour of the victorious Allies. Germany had disarmed, they had not; Germany had imitated the democracies, but with disastrous results. The faults for successive crises lay with others, not Germany. An example of this special pleading may be taken from Hitler's successive speeches at the time of the *Anschluss*, 12–16 March 1938. For the previous five years, he claimed, on 12 March, since the 'victory of the National Socialist idea', the vast majority of the Austrian people had been oppressed 'by the most brutal methods of terrorism' by a regime that 'lacked any legal mandate' and was condemned 'by the overwhelming majority of the Austrian people'.[74] An agreement made with Schussnigg on 11 July 1936 had been broken immediately.[75] He was therefore placing the help of the Reich at the service of millions of Austrians. The world must convince itself of the 'bliss and deep joy' now being experienced by the Austrian people. Next day, announcing the *Anschluss*, he complained about the Anglo-French Note of Protest. 'These people here are Germans', he declared in an interview with G. Ward Price of the *Daily Mail* (14 March 1938) and

would have exactly the same status as the rest of Germany on the
same basis as Bavaria and Saxony.[76] At the same time, he sought to
reassure Poland; Germany had no claims on the Corridor; Poland
needed an outlet to the sea.[77] There was no mention of any claims
on the Sudetenland either. Hitler's attitude towards Great Britain
is shown to have been ambivalent. On the one hand, in a letter sent
to Lord Rothermere on 4 September 1937, Hitler looks forward
to an agreement 'between England and Germany which would
represent a weight of influence for peace and common sense of 120
million of the most valuable people in the world'.[78] On the other
hand, on 1 April 1939, Britain is blamed for the 'policy of en-
circlement' that led up to the First World War.[79] This double-talk
is revealed also in the *Documents on German Foreign Policy*. On 2
January 1938 Ribbentrop stated his view in a memorandum for
Hitler that he considered Britain as Germany's 'most dangerous
enemy' and that the sooner a showdown the better.[80] On 1
December 1941, after two and a quarter years of war, Göring
informed Fieldmarshal Pétain that Germany had gone easy on
Britain, that is, not attempted to invade after Dunkirk, in the hope
that Britain would join Germany against the Soviet Union.[81]
Hitler's speeches before the war reveal an attitude of disappointed
protest at British attitudes. Ruling a quarter of the world, the
British did not and would not understand Germany's need for
Lebensraum – and yet in the last days before the outbreak of war he
could assert to Ambassador Nevile Henderson that 'he always
wanted an Anglo-German understanding'.[82]

The *Documents on German Foreign Policy* and Baynes's translation of Hitler's speeches provide valuable original texts for
students of Hitlerite Germany to the outbreak of war. Few could
have known the enemy better than he. Hence, during the war,
Baynes did all possible to define and promote the civilised values
for which he believed this country was fighting in contrast to
Hitler. On 13 March 1942 he delivered an address entitled 'The
Custody of Tradition' to the University College Union when the
college was in its wartime residence at Bangor.[83] He appealed for
intellectual courage to meet whatever might chance after the war,

as the founders of the college more than a century before had met
the challenges of the new industrial age in the spirit of the pioneer.
Very fairly, he read from a book written by Gottfried Leske, a Nazi
flier, when a prisoner of war in Canada:

> I, for one have always found it much easier if someone tells you
> what you have got to do . . . The point is, where would we be if
> everyone in the world were to make his own life . . . I don't only
> mean that it's better for the whole nation when one man
> decides. It's also better for each one of us.[84]

As Baynes said, this expressed, simply and sincerely, what an
enemy officer thought. He rejected the *Grundrechte* or fundamental rights formulated in the Weimar Constitution. They had
proved unworkable, too burdensome and too expensive. Now
everything was settled by the Party. In reply, Baynes not only reiterated the need for freedom of research as a university teacher
must but also referred to the opening of his own University
College to students of both sexes (in 1878) and of all creeds and
faiths. But there was the need also to guard against racialism and
anti-Semitism. The spirit of the pioneer, he reiterated, must overcome that of the person who would simply fuse his spirit with that
of a leader. Finally, he spoke of what he had learnt from his study
of Hitler's speeches. He had been made aware of the complete lack
of community feeling in Germany after the end of the (First
World) War. Soldiers from the German armies had been literally
tipped on to the streets: 'nameless soldiers' like Hitler himself had
been dependent on charity. Hitler had sought to build a renewed
sense of community which would grow into a community of the
German people, a *Volksgemeinschaft*, without distinction of party
and class.[85] In Britain, while we had not fared so badly, a sense of
community was needed to be built after the war, a sense of community from which German youth would not be excluded. But
this sense would be based on the free traditions on which
University College had been founded.[86]

It was Baynes's credo. Though speaking within a month of the fall of Singapore (15 February 1942) which ended the old British Empire, and six months before its rebirth as a Commonwealth of equal partners at el Alamein (23 October 1942), Baynes showed no hint of pessimism. His generation may have failed, that represented by his hearers 'must carry into the peace the lessons it had learnt in the University during the war'. Cockney students would wish each and all 'Bon voyage'.[87]

A few months later, on 12 June, Baynes had the chance of restating his ideas in the Romanes Lectures at Oxford,[88] under the title 'Intellectual Liberty and Totalitarian Aims'. In the lecture he sought to warn his hearers of the true meaning of National Socialism and Fascism in the lives of the German and Italian people. Quoting from the writings of Nazi and Fascist writers and politicians he showed how theory and practice were a protest against the concepts that had characterised the liberal ideas of the nineteenth century. 'The Führer is always right', Hitler wrote in an open letter to von Papen on his assumption of power 30 January 1933.[89] There was too, a mystical, religious element in both movements, derived in part from the Roman Catholic background of Hitler and Mussolini. The National Socialist racial credo was not a matter of scientific demonstration but of faith (*Glaube*).[90] Ernst Krieck, head of the Information Bureau of the National Socialist Party, asserted that 'our race remains valid for us even though theory should not be able to go so far with us in all points'.[91] The enemies were objective scholarship, Liberalism and the freedom of the individual. 'Believe me,' Bernhard Rust, Minister of Education, told a student audience on 28 June 1937, 'behind the word "Freedom", [lie] the demons'.[92] By the time he had finished Baynes had given his audience as clearly as anyone could one of the basic reasons why the country was at war. No one else had tried or would try to give so convincing an account of the driving force of the Nazi and, to a lesser extent, the Fascist movement and our reasons for opposing it.

Baynes had served his country well. After the war he returned to his Byzantine studies. Two notable lectures given in November 1945 and October 1946 are published in his *Byzantine Studies and*

Other Essays (1955). These showed the scope of his specialism extending from Aristotle and Plato to the fall of Constantinople in 1453. In 'The Hellenistic Civilisation and East Rome',[93] Baynes pointed out how, while the literature and indeed many of the visible remains of the Hellenistic age, in the two centuries after the death of Alexander the Great (323 BC), had become neglected and lost,[94] this age was the seedbed of a civilisation that lasted for more than a thousand years, until destroyed in its heartlands in Asia Minor and Constantinople itself by the Muslim invaders. Baynes was able to point to the Eusebian view of the imperial Christian monarchy as a direct successor of the Hellenistic concept of divine monarchy.[95] The duty of the king had been to copy God and rule accordingly. The role of the Christian emperor was that of the imitator (*mimesis*) of the Divine Logos, itself the immanent principle of order in the universe. Both the Neoplatonist opposition and the Christian apologist drew from the same stream of Hellenistic thought. The downside of this joint legacy was the persistence of the study of rhetoric as the foundation of Byzantine education.[96] For good or evil, however, the pagan inheritance had been accepted by the Greek Fathers from Clement and Origen onwards.

In his lecture at Westfield College in October 1946 Baynes explored once more in depth the thought world of East Rome.[97] The credal statements and the Chalcedonian Definition belonged to a continuation of Greek thought and were accepted by 'the man in the street' as part of the Christian tradition that went back to the Apostles. At the same time, his religion was centred on the liturgy in which he could participate with fellow-Christians. This was tradition, unchangeable and permanent.[98] It was the liturgy of the Eucharist with its pictured symbolism, as Baynes stated, of the iconostasis and the hierarchy of Apostles, prophets, saints and finally the emperor and his family that associated the believer on earth with the heavenly host.[99] The liturgy was unchangeable and so in imitation was the Byzantine state. In contrast to mediaeval western Europe where the exploration of natural phenomena was discouraged as 'curiosity', the Byzantines, such as Agathias (late sixth century), would describe accurately the phenomenon of an earthquake, and seek to understand its meaning, but neglect to try to penetrate its cause.[100] How can anyone accurately explain things which we cannot see and which transcend our understanding, the same writer asked? There was a contrast between the genesis of enquiry among Byzantine intellectuals and the faith of the humble folk finding help and comfort in the holy man, the relic and, above all, the liturgy.

Baynes hoped that his lecture would make the study of the Byzantine Empire 'interesting', as A. C. Headlam's 'The Study of Theology' had done for Christianity.[101] He would have been encouraged today. Outside Oxbridge and London, Byzantine studies are in good heart, at Birmingham and Edinburgh to mention two centres, while the Society for the Promotion of Byzantine Studies provides continuity and links with scholarship on the Continent and throughout the English-speaking world.

In 1947 Baynes had his seventieth birthday. An address had already been presented to him on his retirement from the Chair of Byzantine History five years before.[102] Now, volume 37 (1947) of the *Journal of Roman Studies* was dedicated to him. Contributions included French (William Seston), American (Arthur Darby Nock) and Hungarian (A. Alföldi) as well as the best of contemporary British Classical scholarship. Notable, however, was a contribution of a different type, a long letter from Last to Baynes, recalling the beginnings of their friendship 25 years before, 'that evening when we met here (at Brasenose) as guests of Stuart Jones', and thanking the recipient for that friendship.[103] Then, typically, Last launched out into a long discussion of Otto Seeck's theory that a primary cause of the fall of the Roman Empire in the West was the 'Destruction of the Best' (*Die Ausrottung der Besten*), the best families that had produced the generals and administrators who had hitherto preserved the empire. Of course, comments Last, Seeck was writing in 1895 under the influence of Darwinian biology, but nonetheless the extinction of leading families in the Late Empire was striking; and he contrasts with this situation the determination (even Churchillian!) of the peoples of the eastern provinces to survive the collapse of their western counterparts. Clues were to be found perhaps in the popular literature of the East rather than 'the chronicles and official stuff'.[104]

In the next two years Baynes cooperated with H. St L. B. Moss, the author of a classic of the 1930s, *The Birth of the Middle Ages*, in a collection of essays by various scholars entitled *Byzantium: An Introduction to East Roman Civilisation*.[105] Here, in an extended Introduction, he set out eloquently what he believed to have been the achievements of Byzantium, its preservation of much of Classical literature and jurisprudence, and through its annalists the history of a succession of eras. He pointed to the Orthodox Church as a missionary church, carrying Christianity to the Slavs and providing them, in contrast to the Papacy, with a vernacular liturgy. It originated and nurtured the philosophy and life of the ascetic which the West imitated; it provided posterity with a religion-inspired art; and, finally, during the period of political instability and relative military weakness it protected central and western Europe from the onset of invading hordes from the east. Its existence willed by God, the Byzantine Empire presented an unchanging pattern of life centred round the Christian liturgy. 'The signature of their whole civilisation', wrote one of the 14 contributors (Henri Grégoire), 'was their faith.'[106]

Baynes illustrated what he meant by Byzantine devotion to popular literature by his translation with Elizabeth Dawes of *Three Byzantine Saints*.[107] Their choice was first the Stylite Daniel (d. 493) who after 33 years descended from his pillar in Constantinople to challenge the authority of the usurper Basiliscus (475–6) and vindicate the views of the emperor Zeno and his patriarch, Acacius. Theodore of Sykeon provided an illustration of how a life of purposeful squalor could be combined with a deep religious faith and administrative ability as a bishop. John the Almsgiver, the Orthodox Patriarch of Alexandria during the Persian occupation (615–30), combined a firm faith, refuting the anti-Chalcedonians, with skilful diplomacy and open-handed charity, not least in ransoming prisoners taken by the Persians. From his 'Life', one learns of trade, not without perils, between Alexandria and Cornwall. Baynes had chosen the three 'Lives' not simply as examples of different types of Byzantine holiness but because they provided illustrations of how the ordinary provincial lived and thought in the empire at the end of the sixth century. It was a world in which miracles happened, where holy men had abstained from wine and oil for 60 years and ate only uncooked vegetables with salt and vinegar,[108] and where demons afflicted the daily lives of villagers. It was a world far removed even from that of Basil of Caesarea and his contemporaries.

Baynes now felt he had said what he wanted to say, and could concentrate on reviewing the work of others and preparing his Collected Works, published as *Byzantine Studies and Other Essays*.[109] It was shortly after he sent me a copy that I saw him for the last time. By then I was settled in the Divinity Faculty at Cambridge, having decided on an academic career concentrating on early Christian history and its doctrines. Previously there had been a long flirtation with modern German studies and an engagement with Liberal politics. Baynes and Last had persuaded me that after *The Donatist Church* (1952) a full study of the persecutions against the Church was needed. Already in 1937, Last had written an extensive article on the legal aspects of Roman government policy,[110] and I should follow this up. A tea at 4b Abercorn Place was welcome, where Baynes, though far from being in good health while recovering from a broken hip, was already discussing a project on Tertullian with E. Langstadt, a German refugee from before the war, with whom he had also discussed his 'Political Ideas of St Augustine's *De Civitate Dei*', before he gave his celebrated lecture. I left him for the last time with a sense of gratitude and my mind made up.

Lectures, articles and, above all, learned reviews were always Baynes's most telling means of scholarly expression, and remain his most enduring claim to fame. He did not write many books, but the knowledge which his shorter works contained was phenomenal. His lecture on Constantine took up 30 pages of print, but the footnotes filled another 73 pages. Whether it was the precise chronology of the events immediately after Constantine's victory at the Milvian Bridge (nn. 37–42), or the emperor's policy of toleration towards pagans after the Council of Nicaea (n. 58), or the Council of Nicaea itself (n. 62), Baynes's mastery of his sources and the detail of secondary literature of every sort was complete. Reviews included among his Collected Works are full, fair and the result of intensive study of the work in hand. Thus, the long review of Ernest Stein's volume 1 of *Geschichte des spätrömischen Reichs* (History of the Late Roman Empire – 1928) includes a detailed discussion of Ammianus Marcellinus' description of Valentinian I's campaign against the Alemanni in 365. Baynes upholds Stein's reconstruction of events against those of Herrmann and Seeck.[111] Baynes's reviews were always masterly and often showed a greater knowledge of the subject in hand than the author himself. As a Classicist also, his unpublished lecture on Isocrates, the Athenian statesman who pointed the way to a union of all the Greek cities under the authority (*arche*) of Athens, shows he was not merely a specialist in Byzantine studies.[112]

Baynes suffered a long period of ill health from 1954 onwards and died on 12 February 1961. He regarded himself, as he says, as a Victorian individualist.[113] He was that, but much more. He followed in the footsteps of J. B. Bury, first, in encouraging an interest in the Late Roman Empire, but also by espousing the cause of liberty wherever possible. His inspiration might have been Bury's *History of Freedom of Thought*, published in the Home University Library of Modern Knowledge in the 1920s. His affection for him is shown by the time and effort he spent compiling a memoir and his bibliography of Bury's works.[114] Thus Baynes preserved the flow of Byzantine studies in the United Kingdom until that was taken in hand and expanded to its present status by his pupil, J. M. Hussey, and by Steven Runciman, Dmitri Obolensky and their successors. It was a pity that he was never able to complete his projected work on a social history of East Rome, or take up the editorship of a new volume on Byzantium in the *Cambridge Mediaeval History*, a new edition of Bury's original volume published in 1923.

Baynes is the historian who has influenced me most. In the professional field his advice was to be generous but not too lavish with footnotes, always to give credit where credit was due, and if one had to be severely critical in a review to try to end up on a positive note. And, personally, to remember one's students had first call on one's time and that one's research must seek to meet the needs of each new generation of scholars. 'Widening the bounds of knowledge' must not end in a mirage. Baynes's research never did.[115]

Epilogue

The six scholars whose contributions have so greatly influenced my own, all flourished in the first half of the twentieth century and mainly in its first thirty years. Apart from the great number of new discoveries they either made themselves from research on the ground, or as Duchesne and Baynes inspired others to do so, they represented a new approach to the study of the early Church. They were historians or classicists and their approach was determined by this fact. Their aim was to discover what happened in the life and mission of the Church with less interest in its specific doctrines. They were pioneers in the understanding of Christianity in terms of history. It is now time to look forward. What are the prospects for building further on their tradition today? The signals are mixed. On the one hand, important new literary discoveries have been made, while the tally of new archaeological material relating to early Christianity has been overwhelming. On the other hand, interest, especially in the United Kingdom, in the history and doctrine of the early Church has declined seriously. The extinction of the Cambridge Diploma examination in Church history despite the relatively high standard demanded and produced is a symptom; another is that no British scholar was considered well enough equipped to fill Dr Caroline Bammel's post in the Cambridge Faculty of Divinity when she died in 1995. Even more significant is the dearth of British scholars participating in writing the second volume of the *Cambridge History of Christianity* covering the prime Patristic era (325–604). And yet, there has never been more fresh material of great interest to be studied. New fields of work and new initiatives to grasp have been there for the taking.

How any of the six scholars considered here would have handled, for instance, the Divjak documents,[1] with one exception (dated to 391) throwing light on Augustine's activities between 416 and 426, must be speculative. One can hardly imagine that anything less than a bulky number of *Texte und Untersuchungen* with an emphasis on textual detective work would have stilled Harnack's curiosity. Similar treatment would have been given to Augustine's unedited sermons to be found in a manuscript compiled in *c.*1475 and retained in the Stadtsbibliothek at Mainz, dealing with an earlier period in Augustine's episcopacy (397).[2] They reveal much about the survival of Paganism in Carthage at the turn of the fifth century and Augustine's early methods of attack against them and the Donatists, as well as about Augustine's gifts as an orator.

To these outstandingly important manuscript discoveries one could add the myriad of individual archaeological discoveries that have been reported year by year, and have formed the subject of successive international congresses of Christian archaeology. The Proceedings that emerge from the lectures and papers run into three volumes of several thousand pages, covering discoveries made in every corner of the empire with the notable exception, recently, of Algeria. The Nag Hammadi documents from a mainly Gnostic library, now fully published, have attracted more than 9,800 books, articles and reviews, evidence for an academic 'industry' in early Christian history without parallel.[3]

Early Christian sites in Britain before AD 700 cannot compare in numbers with those on the Continent or in the Middle East or North Africa. But they include notable discoveries, such as the Water Newton silver,[4] the Hoxne Treasure[5] and the pagano-Christian boat burial at Sutton Hoo.[6] With these and other discoveries to report British scholarship has been well represented, not least at the Centenary Conference commemorating the death of J. B. de Rossi, held at Split (Spalato) and Poreč in 1994.

Why is it then that the subject is languishing in many of our universities, including Oxford and Cambridge? One may suggest a number of reasons. The main cause is the lack of training in Greek and Latin in schools. Without a working knowledge of both it is impossible to study early Christian writings satisfactorily, and no amount of interdisciplinary division of labour can alter this. A second reason is the decline in importance of the first four Councils and, in particular, the Council of Chalcedon with its Christological Definition, in the thinking of Anglican clergy. The Creeds and the Definition remain the title deeds of the Church, but an understanding of their meaning and why they were framed in the precise way they were would be restricted to a minority. A third factor is that the divinity faculties in Britain have not developed either a centre for the study of Antiquity and Christianity on the lines of the F. J. Dölger Institut für Antike und Christentum at Bonn University, or published a long and continuous series of translated and annotated Patristic authors, as achieved by *Sources Chrétiens* in Paris, or the much older *Corpus Scriptorum Ecclesiasticorum Latinorum* in Vienna.[7] Without these or similar outlets there is little to encourage the theological research student to embark on a career devoted to the early history and doctrine of the Church. It is not wholly accidental that during the 50 years of its existence, yearly offerings of early Christian articles to the *Journal of Ecclesiastical History* have declined from double figures to nearly nil.

Gloom, however, may be balanced by more positive developments. In Britain as in the Commonwealth, America and on the Continent many faculties of Classics have been extending their interests to Late Antiquity, which includes the history of the early Church. This has led to a more historical than theological approach to events and even-handed assessments of the arguments between orthodox and dissenters. At the moment, these faculties appear to be the true heirs of Harnack and the other scholars discussed in this volume. A further factor has been the interest of archaeologists and classicists in Late Antiquity including Byzantium. Productive excavations in Egypt, such as at Q'asr Ibrim by the Egypt Exploration Society,[8] David Phillipson at

Aksum[9] and latterly Richard Miles at Bir Massouada in Carthage[10] have shown what can be achieved by British scholars who combine Classical and archaeological disciplines when supported adequately by funding organisations. The two conferences in the summer of 2000 held at Leeds and York respectively, on early mediaeval including Late Antique themes and the conversion of northern Europe to Christianity showed that interest in the history of early Christianity was far from dead.

These are promising signs, but funding organisations, including the British Academy, need to be more aware of the opportunities for work in new areas, such as Tunisia, that lie beyond the scope of established British Schools of Archaeology. There is also need for some mutual cooperation between the mainly English-speaking and Anglican Oxford Patristic Conference and the mainly Continental- and Vatican-oriented International Congress of Christian Archaeology, both meeting at regular intervals. Time is not limitless. Year by year increasing population, particularly in the Mediterranean countries, means that more archaeological sites fall victims to urban sprawl, or are covered and destroyed on the land through the needs of greater agricultural production. It is not likely that further inscriptions as important as those from Henchir Mettich[11] or Ain el Djemala[12] are likely to be recovered from the *bled* (countryside) of Tunisia.

But one can afford to be optimistic. So long as humanity retains a desire to quest after the origins of institutions that influence its life, research into early Christian history will survive. It will take a different form, inspired by different disciplines from those familiar to the author in his research-student days. The six great scholars commemorated in this book are among those who inspired his work, and laid the foundation for a historical understanding of the complex life and progress of the early Christian Church.

Notes

Introduction

1. Berthier published his results in *Les Vestiges du Christianisme antique dans la Numidie centrale*, Algiers, 1942.

2. Recorded by myself in 'A Note on Religion and Life in a Numidian Village in the Later Roman Empire' in *Archaeology and History in the Study of Early Christianity*, London, 1988, especially pp. 265–6.

3. W. H. C. Frend, 'A Third-Century Inscription relating to *angareia* in Phrygia', *Journal of Roman Studies* 46 (1956), pp. 46–56.

4. W. H. C. Frend, 'Two Finds in Central Anatolia', *Anatolian Studies* 6 (1956), pp. 95–101.

5. A statement by the Labour Party Executive on 9 February 1940 that insisted on the overthrow of the Hitler system in Germany but recognised that 'the German claim for equality' would have to be reconciled 'with the French claim to security' carried little weight at the time. See, John Kissim, 'Bevin, Eden, and "The Old Franco-German Quarrel"', *The European Journal* (November 2001), p. 20.

6. His great work was *L'Histoire littéraire de l'Afrique chrétienne*, 7 volumes, 1901–23, to which I am much indebted.

1 Adolf von Harnack (1851–1930)

1. The key work for the study of Harnack is the biography by his daughter, Agnes von Zahn Harnack, *Adolf von Harnack*, Berlin, 1951. See also Wilhelm Pauck, *Harnack and Troeltsch: Two Historical Theologians*, New York, 1968; *Texte und Untersuchungen zur Geschichte der altchristlichen Literatur*, Leipzig, 1882– ; and extracts from Harnack's writings in M. Rundscheidt (ed.), *Adolf von Harnack: Liberal Theology at Its Height*, London, 1989.

2. Friedrich Smend, *Adolf von Harnack: Verzeichnis seiner Schriften*, Leipzig, 1927–31.

3. Translated in seven volumes as the *History of Dogma*, London, 1905.

4. Translated by T. Bailey Saunders as *What Is Christianity?*, London, 1901.

5. For von Harnack's efforts to keep the institute independent of other

Prussian and state institutes in the last year of his life, see von Zahn Harnack, *Harnack*, pp. 437–40.

6. For his relations with his father, see C. Wayne Glick, *The Reality of Christianity: A Study of A. von Harnack as Historian and Theologian*, New York, 1967, pp. 23–8.

7. Quoted in Rundscheidt, *Harnack*, pp. 10–11.

8. Von Zahn Harnack, *Harnack*, p. 46.

9. See E. P. Meijering, *Theologische Urteile über die Dogmengeschichte: Ritschls Einfluss auf von Harnack*, Leiden, 1978, ch. 1.

10. Von Zahn Harnack, *Harnack*, p. 58. Schürer was the author of the three-volume *Geschichte des jüdischen Volkes in Zeitalter Jesu Christi*, 1874, 4th edn 1909, trans. and rev. G. Vermes, F. Millar and M. Goodman, Edinburgh, 1986.

11. Von Zahn Harnack, *Harnack*, p. 56. Gebhardt published the codex in *TU* 1 (1882), pt 4.

12. Edwin Hatch (1835–89) visited Harnack at Giessen; Harnack translated two of Hatch's writings into German. Charles Bigg was also an influence.

13. Von Zahn Harnack, *Harnack*, pp. 65–75, esp. 70–1.

14. Von Zahn Harnack, *Harnack*, p. 51.

15. Von Zahn Harnack, *Harnack*, pp. 50–1. The view of his student and friend Wilhelm Bornemann, who wrote similarly in the *Christliche Welt* (1921): Pauck, *Harnack and Troeltsch*, pp. 15–16.

16. Von Zahn Harnack, *Harnack*, p. 52.

17. For the Giessen years see Von Zahn Harnack, *Harnack*, pp. 80–108.

18. The elder Harnack reproached his son for 'vanity' (Von Zahn Harnack, *Harnack*, p. 75) and for the influence he allowed Ritschl to have on him (pp. 94–5).

19. C. Schmidt, 'Gnostische Schriften in koptischer Sprache aus dem Codex Brucianus', *TU* 8/2 (1892), pt 2; and E. Amélineau, 'Notice sur le papyrus gnostique Bruce', *Notices et extraits des manuscrits de la Bibliothèque nationale et aux autres bibliothèques* 29 (1891), pp. 65–306. For the controversy between Amélineau and Schmidt, see R. S. Mead, *Pistis Sophia: A Gnostic Miscellany*, London, 1961, pp. lvii–lx.

20. A. Harnack, 'Medicinisches aus der ältesten Kirchengeschichte', *TU* 8/4 (1892), p. 66.

21. See Meijering, *Theologische Urteile*, ch. 1, on Harnack's debt, not only in the arrangement of his material, to Ritschl, and but also Harnack's admission of his debt to Ritschl's *Die Entstehung der Altkatholischen Kirche*, Bonn, 1857. Like Harnack, Ritschl began his career with a work, published in 1846, on Marcion and Luke's Gospel.

22. Cited from von Zahn Harnack, *Harnack*, p. 98 ('bleibende Dankbarkeit' to Ritschl).

23. Harnack, *History of Dogma*, English translation by Neil Buchanan London, 1905, Vol. 1, para. 1, and also p. 10.

24. Author's preface to the first edition: Harnack, *History of Dogma*, Vol. 1, p. xi.

25. 'Every historical study is an ethical task': Harnack, *History of Dogma*, Vol. i, p. viii.

26. Harnack, Prolegomena, *History of Dogma*, Vol. 1, p. 17.

27. Harnack, *History of Dogma*, Vol. 1, p. 228.

28. Harnack, *History of Dogma*, Vol. 1, p. 227.

29. Harnack, *History of Dogma*, Vol. 1, p. 277.

30. Harnack, *History of Dogma*, Vol. 2, p. 319, on Clement and Origen.

31. Augustine, *Soliloquies*, ii.7, ed. and trans. Burleigh, London, 1953, pp. 26–7.

32. Von Zahn Harnack, *Harnack*, p. 105. The elder Harnack believed that right belief in the resurrection was the touchstone of Christianity. His son had doubts about its literal character.

33. Von Zahn Harnack, *Harnack*, p. 101.

34. Von Zahn Harnack, *Harnack*, pp. 113–14. In his preface to the *History of Dogma*, written in Berlin, 1 May 1894, Harnack opens by claiming that German and English theological studies had combined to free Christian scholarship from a dependence on Latin scholarship. The *Lehrbuch der Dogmengeschichte* went through five complete editions to 1951, and smaller versions of outlines, *Grundrisse der Dogmengeschichte,* appeared in 1889, 1891, 1914 and 1921.

35. See von Zahn Harnack, *Harnack*, pp. 115–27, esp. p. 120.

36. Von Zahn Harnack, *Harnack*, pp. 129–31.

37. Described von Zahn Harnack, *Harnack*, pp. 131–44.

38. The correspondence has been edited by S. Ribenich, *Theodor Mommsen and Adolf Harnack*, Berlin, 1997. Mommsen esteemed Harnack highly, even more highly than he did his classicist son-in-law Ulrich von Wilamovitz-Möllendorf. Harnack spoke at Mommsen's funeral on 5 November 1903.

39. Von Zahn Harnack, *Harnack*, pp. 201–8. For this work, which he began in 1886, Harnack was awarded the Orden Pour le Mérite on 31 May 1902.

40. Translated by James Moffatt as *The Mission and Expansion of Christianity in the First Three Centuries*, London, 1904–5.

41. *Mission and Expansion*, p. viii.

42. *Mission und Ausbreitung*, p. 545 (Eng. trans., Vol. 2, p. 465).

43. *Mission und Ausbreitung*, p. 521 n. 1 (Eng. trans., Vol. 2, p. 424 n. 1). Anatole Toulotte, *Géographie de l'Afrique chrétienne*, Paris 1892.

44. *Mission und Ausbreitung*, p. 513 (Eng. trans., Vol. 2, p. 411).

45. See W. H. St J. Hope, *Archaeologia*, i.iii (1893), pp. 563–8.

46. *Mission und Ausbreitung*, Vol. 2, pp. 516–17 n., p. 528.

47. *Mission und Ausbreitung*, pp. 516–17 n. 1 (Eng. trans., Vol. 2, p. 417 n. 1).

48. See W. H. C. Frend, *The Archaeology of Early Christianity*, London and Minneapolis, 1996, pp. 117–18; H. Graillot and S. Gsell, *Mélanges de l'École française de Rome* 13 (1893), pp. 472–3, and, in general, 14 (1894), pp. 17–86. See over, p. 68.

49. Frend, *Archaeology*, pp. 95–8.

50. W. M. Ramsay, 'The Tale of Saint Abercius', *Journal of Hellenic Studies* 3 (1882), pp. 339–52.

51. W. M. Ramsay, *Cities and Bishopics of Phrygia*, Oxford, 1897, Vol. 2, pp. 722–9, for an account of the discovery. See over, p. 86.

52. G. Ficker, 'Der heidnische Charakter der Abercius-Inschrift', vorgelegt von Hrn. Harnack, am 11 January 1894, *Sitzungsberichte der Kgl. preussischen Akademie der Wissenschaften* (1894), pp. 87–112.

53. For instance R. de Waal, 'Die Inschrift des Abercius', *Römische Quartal-schrift* 8 (1894), pp. 329–51, and L. Duchesne, 'L'Epitaphe d'Abercius', *Mélanges de l'École française de Rome* 15 (1895), pp. 155–82.

54. A. Harnack, 'Zur Abercius-Inschrift', *TU* 12/4 (1895), pp. 1–28. Another speculation was his attribution of the psuedo-Cyprianic 'De Aleatoribus' to Pope Victor, in *TU* 5 (1889), pp. 1–135.

55. Harnack, *Mission and Expansion*, Vol. 2, p. 358.

56. See von Zahn Harnack, *Harnack*, pp. 144–60.

57. Von Zahn Harnack, *Harnack*, p. 151.

58. Von Zahn Harnack, *Harnack*, p. 157.

59. Harnack, *What Is Christianity?*, p. 8. It was not an ethical or social system.

60. Harnack, *What Is Christianity?*, pp. 11, 13.

61. Harnack, *What Is Christianity?*, pp. 24–32.

62. Harnack, *What Is Christianity?*, p. 31.

63. Harnack, *What Is Christianity?*, p. 56, cf. pp. 63ff.: 'The Lord's Prayer shows the Gospel to be the Fatherhood of God applied to the whole of life.'

64. Harnack, *What Is Christianity?*, pp. 111, 168.

65. Harnack, *What Is Christianity?*, pp. 203–5. See also Meijering, *Theolog-ische Urteile*, p. 27.

66. Harnack, *What Is Christianity?*, p. 208.

67. Harnack, *What Is Christianity?*, p. 294.

68. Harnack, *What Is Christianity?*, p. 295.

69. Von Zahn Harnack, *Harnack*, p. 228.

70. Thus, Karl Kautsky, *Der Ursprung des Christentums*, Stuttgart, 1908, translated as the *Foundations of Christianity*, London, 1925, p. 42: 'We now say of Jesus, that we are not even certain that he ever lived, and that he may have been as mythical a personage as Siegfried.' Arthur Drews (1865–1935) published his *Die Christusmythe* in 1909–11.

71. Von Zahn Harnack, *Harnack*, p. 187.

72. Adolf von Harnack, *Luke the Physician*, trans. J. R. Wilkinson, London, 1907, pp. 49–52.

73. Harnack, *Luke the Physician*, p. 166.

74. Von Zahn Harnack, *Harnack*, p. 237.

75. Von Zahn Harnack, *Harnack*, pp. 248–60. See also 'Die Benützung der königlichen Bibliothek', in *AFK*, pp. 229–61.

76. I owe this information to Professor Gerald Bonner of the University of Durham. Another example is William Bright's fine eucharist hymn, 'And now, O Father, mindful of thy love . . .'

77. Von Zahn Harnack, *Harnack*, p. 296.

78. 'Der Geist der Morgenländischen Kirche im Unterschied von der Abendländischen', repr. (without footnotes) in *AFK* at pp. 103–40.

79. Von Zahn Harnack, *Harnack*, pp. 345–6.

80. 'Ein Schreiben von elf englishen Theologen', and Harnack's answer, repr. in *AFK*, at pp. 290–9.

81. 'Was wir schon gewonnen haben und was wir noch gewinnen müssen'; speech, 29 September 1914, *AFK*, pp. 313–30; 'An der Schwelle des dritten Kriegsjahres': speech, 1 August 1916 (the third anniversary of the outbreak of war), *AFK*, pp. 333–48. He spoke as the NSDAP would of a 'national arbeitsgemeinschaft' (p. 341).

82. Speech 1 August 1916, *AFK*, p. 345.

83. Harnack to Bertha Thiersch, 31 October 1918, in von Zahn Harnack, *Harnack*, pp. 373–4.

84. See Harnack's address, 'What Has History to Offer as Certain Knowledge concerning the Meaning of World Events?', given after Barth had spoken earlier that day, repr. in Runscheidt, *Harnack*, pp. 49–63.

85. Quoted by Barth in his *Fifteen Answers*; Runscheidt, *Harnack*, pp. 97–8.

86. Set out in Barth, *Fifteen Answers*, pp. 85–106.

87. Von Zahn Harnack, *Harnack*, pp. 395–6.

88. 'The Roman Church is the most comprehensive and powerful, the most complex, yet the most uniform structure which known history has produced': Pauck, *Harnack and Troeltsch*, pp. 34–5. But he opposed Roman ecclesiasticism and the papacy's claims to infallibility.

89. Von Zahn Harnack, *Harnack*, p. 420.

90. Pauck, *Harnack and Troeltsch*, pp. 39–41.

91. Harnack had already concluded Vol. 1 of the *History of Dogma* (pp. 277ff.) with a study of Marcion, a reformer who preached redemption through Christ and the Pauline doctrine of grace.

92. See Harnack's introduction to *Marcion* where he summarises his conclusions.

93. Pauck, *Harnack and Troeltsch*, p. 37.

94. 'Die älteste Kircheninschrift': *AFK*, pp. 21–39.

95. See Frend, *Archaeology*, p. 224.

96. I owe this information to the Revd Professor Henry Chadwick.

97. Pauck, *Harnack and Troeltsch*, p. 20 n. 26.

98. A reported remark by the Revd Professor Claude Jenkins during the writer's time at Oxford 1934–40.

99. Bonhoeffer, speaking on behalf of his fellow students at Harnack's memorial service on 15 June 1930: Pauck, *Harnack and Troeltsch*, p. 17. Bonhoeffer was executed by the Nazis at Flossenburg concentration camp in April 1945.

2. Hans Lietzmann (1875–1942)

1. G. Wodke, 'Malereian der Synagogue in Dura und ihre Parallelen in der christliche Kunst', *ZNTW* 34 (1935), pp. 51–62.

2. I have taken material on Lietzmann's life from Kurt Aland's *Glanz und Niedergang der deutsche Universität*, Berlin, 1979, pp. 1–155. The subsequent selection of Lietzmann's letters are taken from this book. I have also used my Introduction to Vol. 1 of the English translation of Lietzmann's *Geschichte der Alten Kirche*, Cambridge, 1993, and Heinrich Bornkamm's memoir, 'Hans Lietzmann', *ZNTW* 41 (1942), pp. 1–12. This makes only a very brief mention of Lietzmann's career after 1933.

3. Aland, *Glanz und Niedergang der deutsche Universität*, Section 2, pp. 6–35.

4. Aland, *Glanz und Niedergang der deutsche Universität*, pp. 9–10.

5. Aland, *Glanz und Niedergang der deutsche Universität*, p. 14.

6. Aland, *Glanz und Niedergang der deutsche Universität*, p. 21.

7. 'Grundriss der evangelischen Religionskunde auf geschichtlicher Grundlage', Berlin, 1927, = No. 299, in Lietzmann's published works, Aland, *Glanz und Niedergang der deutsche Universität*, p. 1208.

8. Aland, *Glanz und Niedergang der deutsche Universität*, p. 26.

9. Aland, *Glanz und Niedergang der deutsche Universität*, p. 26.

10. Aland, *Glanz und Niedergang der deutsche Universität*, pp. 27–35, 'Der Organisator'.

11. Aland, *Glanz und Niedergang der deutsche Universität*, p. 38.

12. Lietzmann's autobiography, *Die Religionswissenschaft der Gegenwart in Selbstdarzellungen*, Leipzig, 1926, pp. 77–117, at p. 99, quoted from Aland, *Glanz und Niedergang der deutsche Universität*, p. 40.

13. Bibliography, No. 95, Aland, *Glanz und Niedergang der deutsche Universität*, p. 1199.

14. K. Holl, 'Das Fortleben der Volksprachen in Klein-Asien in der nach-Christlichen Zeit', *Hermes* 43 (1908), pp. 240–54.

15. Letter 299, Aland, *Glanz und Niedergang der deutsche Universität*, p. 340.

16. Letter 303, 11 July 1914, Aland, *Glanz und Niedergang der deutsche Universität*, p. 342.

17. Grafe to Lietzmann, Letter 310, Aland, *Glanz und Niedergang der deutsche Universität*, p. 346.

18. Thus, Dibelius to Lietzmann, Letter 309, dated 10 November 1914 (after the German failure to capture Ypres). Aland, *Glanz und Niedergang der deutsche Universität*, p. 345.

19. Bibliography, No. 144, *Petrus und Paulus in Rom. Liturgische und archaeologische Studien*, Bonn, 1915 (2nd edn, 1927), p. 245.

20. Harnack to Lietzmann, Letter 328, 7 November 1915, Aland, *Glanz und Niedergang der deutsche Universität*, p. 355.

21. Letters 329 and 331, Aland, *Glanz und Niedergang der deutsche Universität*, pp. 355, 357.

22. See, Karl Heussi, *Die römische Petrustradition in Kritischer Sicht*, Tübingen, 1955, pp. 8 and 54–5. Heussi puts Paul's letter to the Galatians after Corinthians.

23. Aland, *Glanz und Niedergang der deutsche Universität*, p. 45.

24. These were two principal manuscripts, one in the Vatican and the other at Cambrai. See Letter 320, Ratti to Lietzmann, 25 July 1915 (Aland, *Glanz und Niedergang der deutsche Universität*, pp. 350–1) and Aland's description of the work, *Glanz und Niedergang der deutsche Universität*, pp. 48–9. Lietzmann's 'Symbolestudien' continued in the early 1920s. See Nos. 205, 225, 252 and 286 of his Bibliography.

25. Cited from Aland's résumé, *Glanz und Niedergang der deutsche Universität*, pp. 69–70.

26. Letter 365, Aland, *Glanz und Niedergang der deutsche Universität*, p. 379.

27. Letter 374, Aland, *Glanz und Niedergang der deutsche Universität*, pp. 384–5.

28. Letter 384, 11 November 1917, Aland, *Glanz und Niedergang der deutsche Universität*, pp. 390–1.

29. Letter 389, 24 February 1918, Bonwetsch to Lietzmann. Aland, *Glanz und Niedergang der deutsche Universität*, pp. 394–5.

30. Thus, Letter 352 of 29 March 1916, Reitzenstein to Lietzmann. Aland, *Glanz und Niedergang der deutsche Universität*, p. 372.

31. Letter 393, 4 March 1918, Aland, *Glanz und Niedergang der deutsche Universität*, p. 396.

32. Letter 407, Aland, *Glanz und Niedergang der deutsche Universität*, pp. 405–6.

33. Letter 409, 25 October 1918, Aland, *Glanz und Niedergang der deutsche Universität*, p. 407.

34. See Aland, *Glanz und Niedergang der deutsche Universität*, pp. 74–82.

35. Aland, *Glanz und Niedergang der deutsche Universität*, p. 82.

36. Aland, *Glanz und Niedergang der deutsche Universität*, pp. 84–5.

37. Aland, *Glanz und Niedergang der deutsche Universität*, pp. 72–4.

38. See the résumé in Aland, *Glanz und Niedergang der deutsche Universität*, p. 98.

39. See, for example, Frend, 'Some Greek Liturgical Fragments from Q'asr Ibrim in Nubia', *Archaeology and History in the Study of Early Christianity*, Variorum Reprints, 1988, ch. 19.

40. Lietzmann, *Messe und Herrenmahl*, Bonn, 1926, p. 256. Hippolytus' description of the Agape, however, follows precisely acts performed at the Last Supper, i.e., a meal in the house of a private individual: *Messe und Herrenmahl*, pp. 195–7. The Last Supper itself was intended as a memorial celebration of Jesus' approaching death (251).

41. *Die Laudmauer von Constantinopel*, Abhandlungen der preussischen Akademie der Wissenschaften, Berlin (Phil. Hist. Kl.) No. 2, 1929.

42. With H. W. Beyer, *Jüdische Denkmäler*, i: *Die jüdische Katakombe der Villa Torlonia in Rom*, Studien zur spätantiken Kunstgeschichte 4, Berlin, 1930.

43. Bibliography, No. 336, under the title 'Augsburg 1530'.

44. 'Ein Beitrag zur Mandäerfrage', Bibliography, 333, Aland, *Glanz und Niedergang der deutsche Universität*, p. 101.

45. See Bibliography 352–4, with list of newspaper articles arising from Lietzmann's views. Aland, *Glanz und Niedergang der deutsche Universität*, pp. 102–5.

46. Paul Winter, 'On the Trial of Jesus', Berlin, 1961. See Aland, *Glanz und Niedergang der deutsche Universität*, p. 102 n. 27.

47. Bibliography 334, Aland, *Glanz und Niedergang der deutsche Universität*, p. 1210 and p. 95 for the quotation.

48. *Geschichte*, p. 51.

49. *Geschichte*, p. 52.

50. Letter 1096, 20 May 1939, Aland, *Glanz und Niedergang der deutsche Universität*, p. 962.

51. Letters 522, 551, 568, 606 and 782, Aland, *Glanz und Niedergang der deutsche Universität*, pp. 114–15.

52. Aland, *Glanz und Niedergang der deutsche Universität*, pp. 115–16.

53. Aland, *Glanz und Niedergang der deutsche Universität*, p. 114. The scholar in question was C. Viering, an Evangelical Privatdozent at Münster.

54. Letter 798, Lietzmann to Domke, Ortsgruppe in Wilmersdorf.

55. Letter 827.

56. Letter 828.

57. Aland, *Glanz und Niedergang der deutsche Universität*, pp. 126–7.

58. Letter 828.

59. Letter 828.

60. Letter 856 to Lyder Brun, Professor of Church History at Oslo.

61. Letter 858, 10 March 1934, 'Meine geliebte Archaeologie', Aland, *Glanz und Niedergang der deutsche Universität*, p. 762.

62. Letter 862.

63. Aland, *Glanz und Niedergang der deutsche Universität*, pp. 132–3.

64. Letter 840 to Hans von Soden which also contains the statement 'Das Neue Testament macht zwischen Juden and Heiden keinen Unterschied . . .' How volatile, however, the situation was in 1933 is shown by the invitation to Lietzmann to join the SS and his refusal only after mature consideration – Letter 849 to Karl Czapnik.

65. Aland, *Glanz und Niedergang der deutsche Universität*, p. 134.

66. Aland, *Glanz und Niedergang der deutsche Universität*, p. 135.

67. Aland, *Glanz und Niedergang der deutsche Universität*, p. 141.

68. Aland, *Glanz und Niedergang der deutsche Universität*, p. 145.

69. e.g., Letter 962 from Henri Grégoire, inviting Lietzmann to subscribe to Pirenne's Festschrift, and 1032 of Christmas 1937 from A. D. Nock.

70. Letter 1016 to Krüger, 29 July 1937.

71. Letter 965 to Grégoire, 5 October 1936; and Aland, *Glanz und Niedergang der deutsche Universität*, p. 47.

72. Bibliography, 452.

73. Schepelern, *Montanismus*, p. 162, '[The movement] did not arise out of ideas from Phrygian Mystery religions, but from the apocalyptic concepts of Judaism and Christianity' (my translation).

74. Letter 1115 to Eduard Schwartz of 31 August 1939 (para. 2). One of the delegates at this conference was Kazimierz Michalowski who a fortnight later would be a guest of Nazi Germany but as a POW!

75. Thus, to Opitz, 13 October 1939, Letter 1121.

76. Letter 1127 of 29 December 1939 to Jens Nørregaard, the Danish Church historian.

77. Letter 1128, Aland, *Glanz und Niedergang der deutsche Universität*, p. 983.

78. See my Introduction to the English translation *Geschichte*, 1993, Vol. 1.

79. Letter 1159 to Emmanuel Hirsch, 11 September 1940. In the same month (28 September) he hoped for a 'victorious peace' for Germany which would bind together all the North Germanic peoples. Letter 1163 to Söderblom. 'Heil Hitler' creeps into some of his letters to comparative strangers (e.g. 1162).

3. Stéphane Gsell and the Recovery for Scholarship of Roman-Berber North Africa

1. I owe much of the story of Gsell's life to the memoir by E. Albertini published in the *Revue Africaine* 73 (1932), pp. 20–53 (with Gsell's Bibliography). Also the *Mémoire* by Etienne Michon published in *Compte-rendus de l'Académie des Inscriptions et Belles-Lettres* (Paris, 8 June 1932), pp. 7–13 (= *CRAI*).

2. *Essai sur le règne de l'Empereur Domitien*, Paris, Thorin et Fils, 1894.

3. *Essai sur le règne*, chs 7 and 9.

4. Tacitus, *Agricola* 19 and 21. Mentioned briefly by Gsell, *Essai sur le règne*, p. 166.

5. Albertini, 'Stéphane Gsell', memoir, pp. 21–2.

6. F. Messerschmidt, Armin von Gerkan and K. Romazewski, *Nekropolen von Vulci*, Berlin, 1930, p. 10.

7. Gsell, *Essai sur le règne*, p. 311.

8. Hegesippus, cited by Eusebius, *HE* iii.19 and 20.

9. Gsell, *Essai sur le règne*, p. 315.

10. Spartian, *Vita Severi* 17.1. See Frend, 'Open Questions concerning the Christians and the Roman Empire in the Age of the Severi', *JTS* NS 25 (1974), pp. 333–51, at 345, 347.

11. Albertini, 'Stéphane Gsell', memoir, p. 24.

12. See Gsell's full account of Tipasa, 'Tipasa ville de la Maurétanie Césarienne', *Mélanges* 14 (1894), pp. 291–450, at 292.

13. Gsell, 'Tipasa', p. 298 n. 3.

14. For instance, see E. Masqueray, article in *Revue Africaine* 22 (1878) on 'Ruines anciennes de Kleuchela (Mascula)' pp. 461–67.

15. Gsell published a preliminary account of his discoveries in *Mélanges* 11 (1891), pp. 179–85, under the heading 'La basilique de Sainte Salsa'; and see 'Tipasa', pp. 385–7.

16. See Henri Grégoire, 'Sainte Salsa', *Byzantion* 12 (1937), pp. 213–24, where 'Matri sanct' was transformed into 'marturi sanct' and the dedicators 'F(ilii) et F(iliae) et n(epotes)' becomes 'F(ilii) et F(ideles) et n(autae)'!

17. *Mélanges* 11, p. 184.

18. Gsell, 'Tipasa', pp. 314 and 390–1. Possibly from AD 238: 'Tipasa', pp. 313–14.

19. 'Tipasa', pp. 357–65; and also H. Leclercq, 'Tipasa', *DACL* xv.2, pp. 2338–405.

20. A. Audollent and J. Letaille, 'Mission épigraphique en Algérie', *Mélanges* 10 (1890), pp. 397–470. Illustrated on p. 400.

21. Under the general heading 'Exploration archéologique dans le Département de Constantine (Algérie)', *Mélanges* 13 (1893), pp. 461–541; 'Ruines romaines au nord de l'Aurès', *Mélanges* 14 (1894), pp. 17–86. Followed by 'Ruines romaines au nord des monts de Batna', *Mélanges* 14, (1894), pp. 501–602. A map of Gsell's and Graillot's discoveries is published as Planche X in *Mélanges* 14.

22. See Frend, *The Archaeology of Early Christianity*, London, 1996, p. 59; and also, N. Duval and M. Janon, 'Le dossier d'églises d'Henchir Guessaria', *Mélanges* 97 (1985), pp. 1079–112.

23. Described by Gsell and Graillot, 'Exploration archéologique', *Mélanges* 13 (1893), pp. 467–71.

24. Gsell and Graillot, *Mélanges* 13 (1893), p. 470 n. 2.

25. Gsell and Graillot, *Mélanges* 13 (1893), p. 522 (Inscription 38).

26. Own observation in 1939.

27. Bath house and villa near M'chira, described briefly by André Berthier, *Les Vestiges du christianisme antique dans la Numidie centrale*, Algiers, 1942, p. 27.

28. Conveniently summarised by Berthier, *Vestiges du christianisme antique*, pp. 25–6, but evident from the pages of Gsell and Graillot. Also, see Frend, 'Religion and Life in a Numidian Village in the Later Roman Empire', *Archaeology and History in the Study of Early Christianity*, London, 1988, ch. 12.

29. See, Ch. Courtois, L. Leschi, Ch. Perrat and Ch. Saumagne, *Tablettes Albertini, actes privés de l'époque vaudale (fin de siècle)*, Paris, 1952, p. 211; and Ch. Courtois, *Les Vaudales et L'Afrique*, Algiers, 1955, p. 278.

30. Gsell and Graillot, *Mélanges* 13 (1893), p. 522.

31. Gsell and Graillot, *Mélanges* 13 (1893), p. 495.

32. Gsell and Graillot, *Mélanges* 13 (1893), Pl. vii.

33. Gsell and Graillot, *Mélanges* 13 (1893), pp. 472–3.

34. A. Berbrugger, 'Julius Caesarea: Inscriptions chrétiennes', *Revue Africaine* 1 (1856–7), pp. 114–15: Donatists 'impitoyables ennemis' of the orthodox.

35. Particularly in vol. 5 of the *Histoire littéraire de l'Afrique chrétienne*, Paris, 1920, where he discusses the Donatist leaders.

36. It was, in fact, Libyan (Berber) in southern Numidia. See Gsell and Graillot, 'Ruines romaines au nord des monts de Batna', *Mélanges* xiv (1894), p.521.

37. W. Thümmel, 'Zur Beurteilung des Donatismus', Inaugural Dissertation, Halle 1893. Thümmel was largely inspired by the work of Daniel Voelter, *Der Ursprung des Donatismus*, Freiburg, 1883.

38. Gsell, *Mélanges* 15 (1895), p. 325.

39. Albertini, 'Stéphane Gsell', memoir, p. 32.

40. S. Gsell, 'Fouilles de Benian' (1899); *CRAI* (1899), p. 277; *Monuments antiques de l'Algérie*, Vol. 2, p. 178; and P. Monceaux, *Histoire littéraire*, Vol. 4, pp. 480–4.

41. S. Gsell, *Bull. arch. du Comité* (1902), p. 527, and 'Chapelle chrétienne d'Henchir Akhrib', *Mélanges* 23 (1903), pp. 1–25.

42. Gregory, *Letters* (ed. Ewald, *MGH*), *Ep.* ii.33.

43. Gsell, 'Enquête administratif sur les travaux hydrauliques de l'Algérie', *Nouvelles archives des Missions* 10, Paris 1902, pp. 1–143.

44. M. F. G. de. Pachtère, 'Le règlement d'Irrigation de Lamasba', *Mélanges* 28 (1908), pp. 373–455.

45. S. Gsell and C. A. Joly, *Announa*, Paris, 1905, and also *Khamissa, Mdaourouch, Announa*, Services des Monuments historiques, Algiers, 1914–22.

46. S. Gsell, 'Chronique d'archéologie, *Mélanges* 22 (1902), pp. 33–45.

Curiously, Gsell also criticised time spent on 'méchantes bâtisses byzantines et berbères', though his expedition with Graillot had done most to arouse interest in these buildings!

47. Gsell, *Atlas archéologique de l'Algérie*, Paris, 1911.

48. Results were published by André Berthier and his colleagues in *Les Vestiges du Christianisme antique dans la Numidie centrale*, Algiers, 1942.

49. Above, n. 45.

50. *Hérodote*, Algiers, 1915.

51. Etienne Michon, *Mémoire* in *CRAI*, p. 11.

52. *Histoire ancienne de l'Afrique du Nord*, Paris, 1913–28, Vols 1–8.

53. *Histoire ancienne de l'Afrique du Nord*, Vol. 1, p. 99.

54. M. Doumil, 'Ou peut même trouver, que M. Gsell a exagéré la sévérité des bonnes méthodes: ou souhaitrait parfois, chez lui, un peu plus de liberté dans l'interprétation des textes, une part plus large faite à l'hypothèse.' Cited from Albertini, 'Stéphane Gsell', pp. 22–3.

55. Described by E. F. Gautier, *Le Passé de l'Afrique du Nord*, Paris, 1937, ch. 3 and published in *Memoires de l'Institut de France* (*Académie des Inscriptions*), xliii (1933), pp. 149–66.

56. 'Le Christianisme en Oranie avant la conquête arabe', *Bull. du Cinquentenaire de la Soc. de Géographie et d'Archéologie d'Oranie* (1932), pp. 17–32.

57. 'Les Martyrs d'Ammaedara', *Bull. arch. du Comité* (1934), pp. 69–82 (the Byzantine mosaic recording the martyrology of 34 Christians who 'suffered under the divine laws of Diocletian and Maximian').

58. 'Edifices chrétiens de Thelepte et d'Ammaedara', Tunis, 1933.

59. Eight volumes amounting to over 3,200 pages: see Albertini, 'Stéphane Gsell', pp. 29–30.

60. Dominique Luciani's appreciation of Gsell, published in the *Revue Africaine* 72 (1931), pp. 361–4.

61. Albertini, 'Stéphane Gsell', p. 36.

62. Reproduced opposite p. 16 of *Revue Africaine* (1932).

63. Not published until 1934. See W. Seston, 'Le monastère d'Ain Tamda', *Mélanges* 51 (1934), pp. 79–113.

64. M. Simon, 'Fouilles dans la basilique de Henchir el Ateuch', *Mélanges* 51 (1934), pp. 143–77.

65. Simon, 'Fouilles dans la basilique de Henchir el Ateuch', pp. 161 and 173; Simon also drew attention to the similarity of plan between the rural North African and rural Syrian churches (pp. 162–5).

66. P. Cayrel, 'La basilique donatiste de Ksar el Kelb', *Mélanges* 51 (1934), pp. 114–42, and Pierre Courcelle, 'Une seconde campagne de fouilles à Ksar al Kelb', *Mélanges* 53 (1936), pp. 166–97.

67. Cayrel, 'La basilique donatiste de Ksar el Kelb', pp. 125 and 134. Also Courcelle, 'Une seconde campagne de fouilles à Ksar al Kelb', p. 180, for the

importance of the eight individuals buried with honour in the church. For the martyrdom of Marculus, see Frend, *Donatist Church*, p. 179.

68. M. Labrousse, 'Basilique et reliquaire d'Henchir Tarlist', *Mélanges* 52 (1934), pp. 224–58. See also Y. Duval, *Loca Sanctorum Africae*, No. 134, pp. 281–4.

69. Jean Guey, 'Fouille à Drah Souid', *Mélanges* 56 (1939), pp. 281–4.

70. See Noel Duval, 'In Memoriam André Berthier 1907–2000', *Antiquité Tardive* 9 (2001), pp. 11–16.

71. A. Berthier, F. Logeart and M. Martin, *Les Vestiges du christianisme antique dans la Numidie centrale*, Algiers, 1942, p. 9.

72. Berthier, Logeart and Martin, *Vestiges*, map facing p. 38.

73. A. Berthier and M. Martin, 'Edifices chrétiens de Bou Takrematen', *Revue Africaine* 76 (1935), pp. 139–50, and in the *Receuil de Constantine* 63 (1935–6), pp. 221–35. Also, *Vestiges*, pp. 130–3.

74. A. Berthier and M. Martin, 'Deux basiliques chrétiens de Sila', *Receuil* 63 (1935–6) pp. 235–84. Also, *Vestiges*, pp. 40–3.

75. Duval, 'In Memoriam', p. 11.

76. Duval, 'In Memoriam', p. 13.

77. Berthier, Logeart and Martin, *Vestiges*, pp. 25–6.

78. Frend, 'A Note on Religion and Life in a Numidian Village in the Late Roman Empire', *BAC*, NS 17B (1984), pp. 263–71.

79. Augustine, *Ad Catholicos contra Donatistas*, Epistola 19.31. 'Numidia ubi praepolletis', addressing the Donatists, p. 43, col. 431, and Ep. 129.6 (*CSEL* 44.38); Frend, *Donatist Church*, ch. 4.

80. Optatus of Milevis, *De Schismate Donatistarum* (ed. C21WSA, *CSEL* 26. Vienna, 1895), iii.i (p. 68).

81. Berthier, Logeart and Martin, *Vestiges*, 48.75.

82. Duval, 'In Memoriam', pp. 14–15.

83. As suggested by Yvette Duval, *Loca Sanctorum Africae*, Appendix, pp. 419–44. In particular, the erection of 'mensae' (tables for offerings) as well as whitened altars seems to have been a frequent Donatist practice to honour dead Circumcellions (Optatus, *De Schismate Donatistarum* iii.4, p. 82).

84. See Frend, 'North African and Byzantine Saints in Byzantine North Africa', in *Orthodoxy, Paganism and Dissent*, Aldershot, 2002, ch. 17.

4. Sir William Mitchell Ramsay (1851–1939): Native and Early Christian in Asia Minor

1. W. M. Ramsay, *The Letters to the Seven Churches of Asia*, London, 1906, Preface v.

2. Ramsay, *Letters to the Seven Churches*, p. v.

3. Ramsay, *Letters to the Seven Churches*, p. vi.

4. Ramsay, *Letters to the Seven Churches*, p. v.

5. See, Henri Grégoire, Memoir written for Ramsay in the issue of *Byzantion* 6 (1931) in honour of his eightieth birthday.

6. Details from J. G. C. Anderson's biography of Ramsay in *DNB*, 1931–40, pp. 727–8. Another important influence in Ramsay's early life was H. J. Bidder, Classical Fellow of St John's College, Oxford.

7. Grégoire, Mémoire, p. vi.

8. P. Lebas and W. H. Waddington, *Voyage archéologique en Grèce et Asie Mineure pendant les années 1843–44*, especially Vol. 5.

9. See, Chapter 5, p. 112.

10. Ramsay, 'The Cities and Bishoprics of Phrygia', *JHS* 4 (1883), pp. 370–456, at p. 375. Usually, he allowed himself three and a half miles an hour on horseback. (See, *The Historical Geography of Asia Minor*, 1890, p. 103.)

11. W. M. Ramsay, 'Trois villes phrygiennes', *Bulletin de correspondance hellénique* (1882), pp. 518–19.

12. Ramsay, *Historical Geography*, Prolegomena, p. 5. Ramsay visited Waddington in December 1882. He used coins to demonstrate Oriental and Hellenistic aspects of the city of Tarsus. (See, *Cities of St Paul*, 1906, pp. 125–31, and as an aid for fixing the location of towns, such as Metropolis, see Ramsay, 'Metropolitanus Campus', *JHS* 4 (1883), pp. 53–72. Grégoire, Mémoire, p. ix.

13. Ramsay, 'The Tale of St Abercius', *JHS* 3 (1882), pp. 339–52 and *Cities and Bishoprics of Phrygia*, Oxford, 1895–7, Vol. ii, pp. 713–14.

14. Ramsay, 'The Cities and Bishoprics of Phrygia', *JHS* 4 (1883) 424–7 (No. 36), and *Cities and Bishoprics of Phrygia*, Vol. ii, pp. 722–9. For the English translation of the text, see J. Stevenson and W. H. C. Frend, *A New Eusebius*, London, 1987, pp. 111–12, Doc. 92.

15. Hegesippus, cited by Eusebius, *HE* iv.22.1. Travelling from Palestine (?) to Rome *c*.170 he found the same doctrine held by all the bishops he encountered.

16. See above, pp. 21–2.

17. Ramsay, 'The Cities and Bishoprics of Phrygia', *JHS* 4 (1883), pp. 370–451. Finding at the rate of 100 new inscriptions a month and copying 450 (p. 370).

18. Ramsay, *Cities and Bishoprics*, Vol. 2, pp. 499–502.

19. W. M. Calder, *Revue de Philologie* 1912, p. 68, and 'Philadelphia and Montanism', *BJRL* 7 (1923), p. 316.

20. Metrodorus: see Ramsay, 'The Cities and Bishoprics of Phrygia', p. 400, Inscription 18.

21. *Cities and Bishoprics*, p. 503.

22. Ramsay, *The Church in the Roman Empire before A.D. 170* (1893; dedicated to his wife), Preface, pp. xi and xv. Compare this statement with a similar one at the beginning of *St Paul the Traveller and the Roman Citizen*.

23. Ramsay, 'A Study of Phrygian Art', (part i), *JHS* 9 (1888), pp. 350–82,

and for Ramsay's 'lion theory', see Henri Grégoire, Memoir, p. xi. More likely it was derived from Hittite art.

24. 'A Study of Phrygian Art', (part ii), *JHS* 10 (1889), pp. 147–80.

25. Ramsay, 'Artemis Leto and Apollo Lairbenos', *JHS* 10 (1889), pp. 216–30.

26. Ramsay, *Church in the Roman Empire*, pp. 136–9.

27. Lebas and Waddington, *Voyage archéologique en Grèce et Asie Mineure*, above n. 8, especially no. 783.

28. Ramsay, 'The Early Christian Monuments in Phrygia: A Study of the Early History of the Church', *Expositor*, 3rd series (1888), pp. 241 and 400, and (1889), pp. 404–5

29. W. M. Calder, 'Philadelphia and Montanism', *BJRL* 7 (1923), pp. 309–55.

30. Ramsay, 'Early Christian Monuments in Phrygia' (1888), pp. 250ff.

31. J. Theodore Bent, 'Recent Discoveries in Eastern Cilicia', *JHS* 9 (1888), pp. 231–5; E. C. Hicks, 'Inscriptions from East Cilicia', *JHS* 9 (1888), pp. 236–54; and also Bent, 'Discoveries in Asia Minor', *JHS* 9 (1888), pp. 82–7.

32. Anderson, *Biography*.

33. M. G. Perrot, cited by Ramsay in *Historical Geography*, p. 9.

34. 'The Cities and Bishoprics of Phrygia', (part i), *JHS* 8 (1887), pp. 461–519, at p. 461.

35. Ramsay, *Historical Geography*, p. 23.

36. Ramsay, 'A Study of Phrygian Art', (part i), *JHS* 9 (1888), pp. 350–82, at pp. 350–1.

37. Ramsay, *Historical Geography*, p. 100.

38. Ramsay, *Historical Geography*, p. 74.

39. For example, the name Prahana succeeds Diocaesarea for the same town in Isauria (*Historical Geography*, p. 25).

40. One quizzical example of Ramsay's learning is his description of the River Halys as the frontier between the pig eaters to the west and the pig haters to the east, i.e., between European and Asiatic influences in Asia Minor. See *Historical Geography*, p. 32.

41. Ramsay, 'Early Christian Monuments in Phrygia'.

42. Ramsay, Preface, *Church in the Roman Empire*, p. xi. Ramsay describes himself as 'a student of Roman history and of Roman society who finds in the Church the cause and explanation of many problems in his subject'.

43. Ramsay, *Church in the Roman Empire*, ch. 7.

44. Canon Hick was inclined to the view that the priests should have been Paul's main opponents; as they appear to have inspired opposition to the Christians in Bithynia in 112 (Ramsay, *Church in the Roman Empire*, p. 144).

45. Ramsay, *Church in the Roman Empire*, pp. 137–9.

46. Ramsay, *Church in the Roman Empire*, pp. 9, 13–15 and 101–2.

47. Ramsay, *Church in the Roman Empire*, ch. 6. Whereas many of the North Galatians still spoke Celtic, p. 97.

48. Thus, criticising Lipsius (Ramsay, *Church in the Roman Empire*, p. 99n.) and Dr E. Schürer (Ramsay, *Church in the Roman Empire*, p. 13). 'When I read such a statement I fall into despair' (upholding the 'North Galatian' theory of Paul's missionary route).

49. Ramsay, *Church in the Roman Empire*, p. xvi, and *St Paul the Traveller*, pp. 10–14.

50. Ramsay, *St Paul the Traveller*, p. 138.

51. Ramsay, *Church in the Roman Empire*, pp. 191–2, and in *The Cities of St Paul* (1907), pp. 70–8. Ramsay believed that the Pauline opposition to autocracy and promotion of freedom of thought 'guided and stimulated the Protestant Reformation'.

52. Ramsay, *St Paul the Traveller*, p. 14, though he admits that his sense of time was bad (p. 18).

53. Ramsay, *St Paul the Traveller*, p. 11.

54. Ramsay, *Was Christ Born at Bethlehem?* 1898, ch. 2.

55. Identified by Emile Bourget in 1905. See Frend, *Archaeology*, p. 135.

56. See Ramsay's essay on Tarsus, in *Cities of St Paul*, pp. 85ff.

57. Ramsay, *Cities and Bishoprics*, pp. 743–4; Inscription 684.

58. Ramsay, *St Paul the Traveller*, p. 144.

59. Ramsay, *Cities and Bishoprics*, pp. 649–51.

60. Ramsay, *Cities and Bishoprics*, Inscription 412, dating to the end of the second century.

61. Ramsay, *Cities of St Paul*, p. 34.

62. Ramsay, *Cities of St Paul*, see ch. 1.iv, 'St Paul and Hellenism'.

63. Ramsay, 'Excavation in Asia Minor', *Proceedings of the British Academy* 1 (1903), pp. 109–111, and *Studies in the East Roman Provinces* (1906), p. viii.

64. Ramsay, *Studies in the East Roman Provinces*, p. viii.

65. Ramsay, *Studies in the East Roman Provinces*, p. ix.

66. Ramsay, 'Explorations in Lycaonia and Isauria 1904', *Studies*, p. 158. He was accompanied by Messrs. Cronin and Walter. Also, T. Callander, same title, in *Studies*, pp. 157–80.

67. See the short sketch of her life and activities at this time in Frend, *Archaeology*, pp. 132–3.

68. W. M. Ramsay and G. Bell, *The Thousand and One Churches* (1909), Preface.

69. Ramsay remarks (*Thousand and One Churches*) on the stone-robbing that had taken place between his visits to the site in 1905 and 1907. In 1954 when I visited the site, the plateau was almost bare of ruins except for the great church (Ramsay and Bell No. 1) dedicated to the Virgin.

70. Ramsay, 'The Tekmoreian Guest-friends', *JHS* 32 (1912), pp. 151–70, and *JRS* 8 (1918), pp. 107–45. Note also his discovery of an inscription from Ladik (Laodicia Combusta) commemorating the life of Bishop Eugenius, a contemporary with the persecution of the emperor Maximin in 311–12 and a sufferer

from it. Ramsay, 'The Epitaph of M. Julius Eugenius', *Expositor* (January 1910), and W. M. Calder, 'Studies in Early Christian Epigraphy', *JHS* 40 (1920), pp. 42–54, and also, 'The Epigraphy of Anatolian Heresies', *Anatolian Studies* (Manchester University Press, 1923), pp. 70–2.

71. Ramsay, *The Revolution in Constantinople and Turkey* (1909).

72. Ramsay, *Revolution in Constantinople and Turkey*, pp. 14 and 239–47.

73. Ramsay, *Revolution in Constantinople and Turkey*, p. 21.

74. Ramsay, *Revolution in Constantinople and Turkey*, pp. 34–5.

75. Ramsay, *Revolution in Constantinople and Turkey*, p. 57.

76. Ramsay, *Revolution in Constantinople and Turkey*, p. 201. Irrational fears of the Armenians (p. 259).

77. Cited from *Letters to the Seven Churches*, p. vii; also, in *Revolution in Constantinople and Turkey*, p. 260: 'The sleeping Asiatic giant has been slowly wakening'. Signs of a new time of reaction against Europe.

78. Ramsay, *Letters to the Seven Churches*, p. vii.

79. Ramsay, *Letters to the Seven Churches*, p. ix, also, 141.

80. Ramsay, *Letters to the Seven Churches*, p. 177. 'These seven representative churches stand for the Church of the Province (Asia)'.

81. Ramsay, *Letters to the Seven Churches*, p. 203.

82. Ramsay, *Letters to the Seven Churches*, pp. 205 and 256.

83. Ramsay, *Cities of St Paul*, 1903, p. 47.

84. Ramsay, *Cities of St Paul*, pp. 48ff.

85. Ramsay, *Cities of St Paul*, p. 52. 'A new God needed to save the world'.

86. Ramsay, *Cities of St Paul*, p. 57.

87. Ramsay, *Cities of St Paul*, p. 60.

88. Ramsay, *Cities of St Paul*, pp. 68–70.

89. See above, n. 36. She considered that 'Isaurian art was mainly Christian in origin' (M. Ramsay, *Studies in the History and Art of the East Roman Provinces*, p. 91).

90. J. G. Anderson, 'Paganism and Christianity in the Upper Tembris Valley', *Studies*, pp. 183–227, at p. 197.

91. W. M. Calder, 'Philadelphia and Montanism', *BJRL* 7 (1923), p. 322.

92. Ramsay, 'Excavations in Asia Minor', *Proceedings of the British Academy* (1903), p. 110.

93. Bibliography in *Anatolian Studies* (1923), p. xxxiv.

94. Ramsay, *Asianic Elements in Greek Civilisation* (1927), p. 1.

95. Ramsay, *Asianic Elements*, ch. 7.

96. Ramsay, *Historical Geography*, p. 25.

97. William H. Buckler and William Calder (eds), *Anatolian Studies* (1923), ch. 17.

98. Buckler and Calder, *Anatolian Studies*, ch. 7.

99. Buckler and Calder, *Anatolian Studies*, ch. 5.

100. Buckler and William Calder (eds), *Anatolian Studies*, ch. 3.

101. H. Grégoire (ed.), *Byzantion* 6 (1931), Preface.

102. This was written before the events of 11 September 2001 in New York and Washington. Now, Islamic fundamentalism is a direct threat.

103. Ramsay, *Cities of St Paul*, p. 22.

104. Quoted by Grégoire, *Byzantion*, Preface, p. ix.

105. Grégoire, *Byzantion*, Preface, p. viii.

5. *Mgr Louis Duchesne (1843–1922): Critical Churchman and Historian*

1. For this chapter I have relied largely on Brigitte Waché's exhaustive, but not very critical, 'Monseigneur Louis Duchesne', *Collection de l'École française de Rome* 167 (1992), 757pp (= Waché), and the collection of commemorative essays in 'Mgr. Duchesne et son Temps', *Collection de l'École française de Rome* 23 (1975), 500pp. (= *Collection*).

2. *Letters* 486 and 487 to de Rossi and de Rossi's immediate reply (3 November 1889), 488 (P. Saint-Roch, 'Correspondance de Giovanni Battista de Rossi et Louis Duchesne', *Collection* 205, 1994).

3. Mgr David commended the reprint of the *Acta Sanctorum* as a good antidote to the 'école légendaire' of French clergy. For him the truth was always to be found in the worship. See Duchesne on the Bollandists, 6 March 1911, Waché, 'Duchesne', p. 22 n. 130.

4. Duchesne, *Autobiographical Note* written 28 March 1909.

5. Cited from Waché, 'Duchesne', p. 20. His piety was characterised as 'très ordinaire'. There were hesitations before he was ordained.

6. Waché, 'Duchesne', pp. 29–30.

7. See J. M. Mayeur, 'Mgr. Duchesne et l'Université', *Collection*, pp. 317–32, at p. 319.

8. Mayeur, 'Mgr. Duchesne et l'Université', p. 321.

9. Mayeur, 'Mgr. Duchesne et l'Université', pp. 320–1.

10. Published in 1883. See *ODCC* (1957), p. 397.

11. See the author's *The Archaeology of Early Christianity* (1996), p. 86 and n. 105.

12. Cited from Mayeur, 'Mgr. Duchesne et l'Université', p. 322; Waché, 'Duchesne', p. 53. The mission to Mount Athos was designed to anticipate any 'concurrence étrangère' (Mayeur, p. 323).

13. Waché, 'Duchesne', pp. 61–5; and *BCH* 1 (1877), 361ff. Duchesne's contributions to the archaeology of early Christianity in Asia Minor are listed in F. Cabrol, 'Monseigneur Louis Duchesne son oeuvre historique', *JTS* 24 (1923), pp. 262–5.

14. *Liber Pontificalis* (ed. Duchesne), Vol. 1, pp. 177–88. See also, Charles

Pietri, *Roma Christiana*, Rome, 1976, pp. 77–96, and Cyrille Vogel, 'Le "Liber Pontificalis" dans l'edition de L. Duchesne', *Collection*, pp. 99–140.

15. See above (Harnack), p. 12.

16. Duchesne, *Études sur le Liber Pontificalis* (1877). See, Waché, 'Duchesne', pp. 66–76, and, for other unreliable statements regarding the early Popes, see Vogel, 'Le "Liber Pontificalis" dans l'édition de L. Duchesne', *Collection*, p. 104.

17. Thus, discreetly, *Letter* 19 of 3 August 1877, when Duchesne's work was under threat of the Index. Duchesne always remained on friendly terms with Renier and was visibly moved when he died. See *Letter* 337 Duchesne to de Rossi, June 1885.

18. Pitra to Duchesne: cited from Waché, 'Duchesne', p. 76. Pitra thought Duchesne too sure of himself in his criticism of others (20 February 1877).

19. De Rossi, *Letter* 18 (p. 31).

20. Waché, 'Duchesne', p. 80.

21. Duchesne, 'Les Évangiles de M. Renan', *Rev. du Monde catholique* 5 (1877), p. 314.

22. Waché, 'Duchesne', pp. 84–5.

23. Charles Bayet, 13 April 1875. Letter quoted by Florence Callu, 'Le Fonds Duchesne à la Bibliothèque nationale', *Collection*, pp. 333–43, at p. 338.

24. 'Inscription chrétienne de Bithynie', *BCH* (1878), Vol. 2, p. 289. In my *Archaeology and Early Christianity*, p. 103, I assumed mistakenly that Duchesne had found it during a second journey in Asia Minor in 1877.

25. In general, see Paul Poupard, 'Mgr. Duchesne Professeur à l'Institut catholique à Paris', *Collection*, p. 308. Emphasis on original sources.

26. Waché, 'Duchesne', pp. 109–11, Poupard, 'Mgr. Duchesne', pp. 305–6.

27. De Rossi, *Letter* 11 of 7 October 1876 (pp. 20–1). De Rossi encouraged Duchesne to include archaeology in his Church History course.

28. Described by Waché, 'Duchesne', pp. 115–19.

29. Poupard, 'Mgr. Duchesne', p. 308. In March 1880 the Faculté des lettres was suppressed by governmental decree and became the École des lettres (p. 307). Poupard is citing the opinion of Jules Lebreton.

30. Emile Poulat, 'Mgr. Duchesne et la Crise Moderniste', *Collection*, pp. 353–73, at 370, in an important letter written to Batiffol on 25 July 1882 and also, similarly, on 12 August 1882 (p. 371 n. 14).

31. Letter to von Hügel, 1 Nov 1888. See Poulat, 'Mgr. Duchesne et la Crise Moderniste', p. 359.

32. Waché, 'Duchesne', p. 155. Duchesne wanted to sustain 'the ancient edifice of the Church' but to reform it. Loisy and his friend Hébert were less interested in reform (p. 156).

33. Poulat, 'Mgr. Duchesne et la Crise Moderniste', p. 368.

34. Cited from Poulat, 'Mgr. Duchesne et la Crise Moderniste', p. 369. 'Il y a une infallibilité ecclésiastique. Elle exige un loyalisme sincère' – Batiffol to a

friend in a letter of 4 July 1898. To Duchesne he had become a 'Pharisee' and an individual devoid of sincerity.

35. See Waché's full account, 'Duchesne', pp. 164ff.

36. Waché, 'Duchesne', p. 172. Also, Poupard, 'Mgr. Duchesne', p. 309.

37. 'Le dogme va du moins clair au plus clair, non de l'erreur à la verité'. See Poupard, 'Mgr. Duchesne', p. 309.

38. Letter quoted by Waché, 'Duchesne', p. 281.

39. See the discussion of the evidence in Frend, *Archaeology and Early Christianity*, pp. 82–3.

40. Dionysius the Areopagite and Paris, cited from Waché, 'Duchesne', p. 198; Mary Magdalene and Aix-en-Provence, see *ODCC* under 'Mary Magdalene'.

41. He showed that in the sixth century there was a considerable cult of Roman martyrs in western Gaul – Waché, 'Duchesne', p. 226; De Rossi, *Letters* 253, 17 April 1884 to Duchesne. This letter indicates also his first contact with William Ramsay who had sent him a map, a card and some offprints but no address!

42. Waché, 'Duchesne', p. 199.

43. L'Affaire Bernadou is described in detail by Waché, 'Duchesne', pp. 201–30. Also, Poupard, 'Mgr. Duchesne', p. 310.

44. 'La Succéssive de Pape Fclix IV', *Mélanges* 3 (1883), pp. 239–66.

45. On Heraclias, see Augustine, p. 213.

46. 'Vigile et Pélage, Étude sur l'histoire de l'Église romaine du VIe siècle', *Rev. des Questions historiques* 36 (1884), pp. 369–440. His reply to Dom Chamard, 'Les papes du VIe siècle et le Second Concile de Constantinople', *Rev. des Questions historiques* 37 (1885), pp. 540–78. He is slightly less hostile to Vigilius in his *L'Église de VIe Siècle* (1925), pp. 154–5.

47. Waché, 'Duchesne', p. 234.

48. Waché, 'Duchesne', p. 232.

49. *Letters* 314 of 14 March 1885 (p. 399) informs him of the unfavourable impression his article had made on people in Rome, 'personnes très impartiales'.

50. *Letters* 346 (p. 447). Duchesne's 'renown in Germany' might not have gone down too well in Paris!

51. Cited from Waché, 'Duchesne', p. 243.

52. *Letters* 356 (p. 457). Waché, 'Duchesne', p. 250. Duchesne wrote to von Hügel on 30 December 1885.

53. Only the article 'L'Eglise d'Orient de Dioclétien à Mahomet', *Revue du Monde catholique* LXIV (1880), appears in Duchesne's bibliography (No. 20, in *Collection* 13, p. xxiii).

54. See Victor Saxer, 'Duchesne historien du culte chrétien', *Collection* 23, pp. 60–98.

55. For instance, *Origines du culte chrétien*, pp. 45–7.

56. *Gesta apud Zenophilum* (Appendix to Optatus, *De Schismate Donatistarum*,

ed C. Ziwsa, *CSEL* 26, pp. 186–8); Saxer, 'Duchesne historien du culte chrétien', p. 70.

57. Duchesne, *Origines*, Ch. iii. Saxer, 'Duchesne historien du culte chrétien', p. 74. He criticises Duchesne's view. 'Gallican' was only one of a number of non-Roman liturgies in use from the fourth to the sixth centuries.

58. Duchesne, *Origines*, p. 93.

59. Suggested by K. S. Painter, with reference to the inscribed 'Publianus' bowl from Water Newton, *The Water Newton Christian Silver*, British Museum Publications, 1977, pp. 15–16.

60. Duchesne, *Origines*, Preface, ii–iv; Saxer, 'Duchesne historien du culte chrétien', p. 63 (incorporated in the 5th posthumous edition, 1925).

61. Duchesne, *Origines*, Preface, p. vii.

62. Duchesne, *Bull. critique* (1890), p. 265. Also 'Sur origine de la liturgie gallicane', *RHLR* 5 (1900), pp. 31–47. (Answer to his critics, especially Dom Chambard.)

63. 'Le Dossier du Donatisme', *Mélanges* 10 (1890), pp. 590–646.

64. *Gesta apud Zenophilum*, 185ff.

65. O. Seeck, 'Die Anfänge des Donatismus', *Zeitschrift für Kirchengeschichte* 10 (1889) pp. 526ff.

66. 'Le Dossier du Donatisme', particularly valuable for Duchesne's painstaking reconstruction of missing letters and documents from the original collection.

67. 'Aeterna et religiosa'. I still have doubts whether this letter represents Constantine's own religious views at the time. See my fn. 6 on p. 152 of *The Donatist Church* (1952).

68. Mommsen's edition was the subject of a not unfavourable review by Duchesne in the *Mélanges* of the same year (pp. 381–417).

69. Listed by Cabrol, 'Monseigneur Louis Duchesne', pp. 259–62, and collected in 'Louis Duchesne Scripta Minora: Études de Topographie romaine et de géographie ecclésiastique', École française *Collection* 13 (1973).

70. See Duchesne, 'La Memoria Apostolorum de la Via Appia', *Collection* 13, pp. 361–406. See also, *Letters*, 550 of 28 June 1892, De Rossi to Duchesne, quoting a graffito from the S. Sebastiano, 'Tu quoque Petrus et Paulus conservent', which Duchesne must have known.

71. Duchesne's interest in the discovery of the tomb of St Salsa at Tipasa in 1890. *Letter* (Duchesne to de Rossi) 503 before 3 April 1890 and *CRAI* 34 (1890), p. 116, and (1892), pp. 111–14 (for the discovery, see above, pp. 62–3).

72. *Scripta Minora* xxx–xxxiii.

73. *Letters* 592–3, September 1894. The manuscript of *Jerome* had arrived! De Rossi died on 24 September. On the preparations for the edition, see Waché, 'Duchesne', pp. 299–303.

74. Waché, 'Duchesne', pp. 303–7.

75. Waché, 'Duchesne', p. 310.

76. Waché, 'Duchesne', pp. 311–26.

77. Waché, 'Duchesne', pp. 331ff. See also, Duchesne, *The Churches Separated from Rome* (Eng. trans. 1907), ch. 1. Duchesne deplored 'ecclesiastical centralisation', but saw it as inevitable for the moment (Preface, pp. vii–viii).

78. Duchesne to Portal, cited from Waché, 'Duchesne', p. 339; though he does not cite Augustine directly. For Duchesne's favour towards Anglican Orders see Lord Halifax, *Leo XIII and Anglican Orders* (1912), pp. 13–29.

79. Cited from Waché, 'Duchesne', p. 342 and see Augustine, *De Baptismo*, vii. 101, a discussion whether baptism given 'in mimo' was valid.

80. Note his insistence that 'the English Church can claim to be apostolic, only in so far as she is Roman' (*Churches Separated*, 1907 edn, p. 4).

81. See Frend, 'A Note on the Influence of Greek Immigrants on the Spread of Christianity in the West', in *Mullus* (= *Festsch. Th. Klauser, JAC Ergänzungsband* i, Münster, 1964, pp. 125–9).

82. Duchesne, 30 July 1894, cited from Waché, 'Duchesne', pp. 343–4, and *Churches Separated*, p. 3.

83. Cited from Poulat, 'Mgr. Duchesne et la Crise Moderniste', p. 361.

84. Waché, 'Duchesne', p. 428.

85. J. Carcopino, 'L'Inscription d'Ain el Djemala', *Mélanges* 26 (1906), pp. 365–481. See Frend, *Donatist Church*, pp. 40–3.

86. F. G. de Pachtère, 'Le Règlement d'Irrigation à Lamasba', *Mélanges* 28 (1908), pp. 373–435. Frend, *Donatist Church*, p. 46.

87. See René Massigli, 'Témoignage', *Collection* 348.

88. See Poulat, 'Mgr. Duchesne et la crise Moderniste'.

89. B. Neveu, 'Duchesne et Mme Bulteau', *Collection* 23, pp. 283–307.

90. Poulat, 'Mgr. Duchesne et la crise Moderniste', p. 364.

91. Also, to Loisy, 17 November 1907, Poulat 365 and Waché 533.

92. Poulat 364. Compare Harnack's views above p. 11.

93. See the long personal letter from d'Hulst on 28 August 1885 to Duchesne, quoted by Waché, 'Duchesne', pp. 219–22, and Florence Callu's review of important letters in the Bibliothèque nationale of and about Duchesne, 'Le Fonds Duchesne', *Collection* 73, pp. 333–43 at 337 (above n. 23).

94. Waché, 'Duchesne', p. 76: 'C'est plus allemand que français' (Cardinal Pitra on his thesis on the *Liber Pontificalis*, see above n. 18) and Florence Callu, 'Correspondence', p. 337, for a letter from Richard (17 September 1885).

95. Waché, 'Duchesne', pp. 80 and 101, citing Duchesne's review entitled 'Les Évangiles de M. Renan', *Revue du Monde catholique* 51 (1877), p. 314.

96. Poulat, 'Mgr. Duchesne et la crise Moderniste', pp. 357–8 and 360.

97. See Poulat, 'Mgr. Duchesne et la crise Moderniste', pp. 359–60, citing a letter of 27 April 1890 (357). He hoped in the 1880s for a 'transformation of Catholic exegesis'.

98. Poulat, 'Mgr. Duchesne et la crise Moderniste', p. 360.

99. Poulat, 'Mgr. Duchesne et la crise Moderniste', p. 367. In Batiffol's view Duchesne was not 'the father of Modernism'. His teaching 'restored religious history through his care for method and objectivity'.

100. Waché, 'Duchesne', pp. 467–8.

101. Though, to Duchesne, these contradictions did not impair the gospel message of the divinity of Christ – Duchesne to Loisy, 18 August 1881 (Waché, 'Duchesne', p. 151, n. 217).

102. Poulat, 'Mgr. Duchesne et la crise Moderniste', p. 363.

103. See the outline of his career and Bibliography concerning him in *ODCC*, p. 810.

104. To von Hügel, 17 November 1903; Poulat, 'Mgr. Duchesne et la crise Moderniste', p. 365.

105. Von Hügel's view 1895, cited from Waché, 'Duchesne', p. 530.

106. Waché, 'Duchesne', pp. 538–9.

107. See B. Neveu, 'Duchesne et Mme Bulteau 1902–1922', pp. 271–303. For Duchesne's account of the incident, *Letter* to Mme Bulteau, 21 July 1907 (Waché, 'Duchesne', p. 540, n. 62).

108. Eusebius, 'the father of ecclesiastical history' (Duchesne, *L'Histoire*, Preface (Eng. tr.) to Vol. 1, p. vii).

109. Duchesne, *L'Histoire*, Preface (Eng. tr.) to Vol. 1, p. viii.

110. Duchesne, *L'Histoire*, Preface (Eng. tr.) to Vol. 1, p. ix. Mention of the influence of his lecture notes, *L'Histoire*, Preface (Eng. tr.) to Vol. 1, n. i.

111. Duchesne, *L'Histoire*, Vol. 1, p. 41 (Eng. tr.).

112. Duchesne, *L'Histoire*, Vol. 1, p. 45.

113. Nothing apparently was set down in writing, but Duchesne got the impression that he had received an official imprimatur from the Pope, who on the whole approved his critical spirit and moderation though in places 'talvolta ma puo crudo' (Duchesne to Mme Bulteau, 23 March 1910). Discussed by M. Maccarrone, 'Mons. Duchesne e la Curia Romana', *Collection*, p. 422 and n. 78. Neveu, 'Duchesne et Madame Bulteau', p. 289.

114. Duchesne, *L'Histoire*, Vol. 2 (Eng. tr.), pp. 220–1.

115. Not apparent in the English translation, p. 489, though Duchesne mentions 'rascals in Jerusalem' and only gives a brief mention to Egeria (Etheria). He was no feminist, dismissing a suffragette demo, in Paris March 1905 as that of 'd'osselets en cage' (Duchesne to Primoli, cited from Waché, 'Duchesne', p. 489).

116. Duchesne, *L'Histoire*, Vol. 2 (Eng. tr.), p. 431. The question was discussed by Henry Chadwick, *Priscillian of Avila* (Oxford, 1976), p. 233.

117. Duchesne, *L'Histoire*, Vol. 2 (Eng. tr.), p. 225 and n. i.

118. There were also strong attacks by Père Billot, a professor at the Gregorian university in Rome, to which Duchesne replied. For the controversy and its extension into anti-Modernist polemics, see Waché, 'Duchesne', pp. 558–62.

119. See Neveu, 'Duchesne et Madame Bulteau', p. 291.

120. Waché, 'Duchesne', pp. 568–9.

121. Waché, 'Duchesne', pp. 577–80.

122. Poupard, 'Professeur de l'Institut catholique en Paris', pp. 305–17, at p. 315.

123. For the events, see Maccarrone, 'Mons. Duchesne e la Curia Romana', pp. 424ff.

124. Waché, 'Duchesne', p. 591.

125. Waché, 'Duchesne', p. 591.

126. Duchesne's defence in 'Lettre à un Ami', cited from Waché, 'Duchesne', p. 595. Pope Pius received a copy on 30 June 1911. Duchesne believed that the supernatural character of the Church could not be deduced from its origins, but its global vision as it unfolded through the centuries indicated that the Apostles had founded a more than human institution – Blondel's opinion of Duchesne's views, *Collection* 387.

127. Maccarrone, 'Mons. Duchesne e la Curia Romana', p. 433.

128. Waché, 'Duchesne', p. 603.

129. Duchesne, 'Avis aux lecteurs', in *Bulletin critique*, 15 May 1881.

130. Duchesne, *L'Histoire*, Vol. 3, Preface, p. v of English translation, though he gives Cyril credit also for showing himself a man of peace and a leader in one of the crises of the time (p. vi).

131. Maccarrone, 'Mons. Duchesne e la Curia Romana', p. 475, citing critics of *L'Histoire*.

132. Hippolyte Delehaye, *Les Passions des Martyrs*, Brussels, 1921. He dedicated his work to the President and Fellows of Magdalen College, Oxford.

133. Ernesto Buonaiuti (d. 1946), *Il Cristianesimo sull' Africa romana*, Bari, 1928. Very useful on Parmenian, Donatist Bishop of Carthage, 355–91, and Tyconius (*c*.380).

134. See above, n. 113.

135. Cited from L. Elliott Binns, *English Thought 1860–1900: The Theological Aspect*, London, 1956, p. 361.

136. Letter to Mme Bulteau (see Neveu, 'Duchesne et Mme Bulteau', pp. 276–7.

137. See above, p. 135.

138. Described by Waché, 'Duchesne', p. 626.

139. Waché, 'Duchesne', p. 627.

140. Waché, 'Duchesne', p. 673.

141. Waché, 'Duchesne', pp. 675ff.

142. Waché, 'Duchesne', pp. 640ff.

143. For unsuccessful efforts to get *L'Histoire* released from the Index, see Maccarrone, 'Mons. Duchesne e la Curia Romana', pp. 484ff.

144. 'Le Sanctuaire du saint Laurent', *Mélanges* 39 (1921–2), pp. 3–24.

145. Letter to Loisy dated 25 July 1917.

146. His chapter on 'Les Schismes romains au Vie Siecle', published in *Mélanges* (1915), pp. 221–56, still retained the charge that Pope Vigilius' clergy starved his predecessor, Silverius, 536–7, to death (p. 255). He also reiterated his account of Felix IV nominating his successor on his deathbed against canon law, made as long ago as 1883 (see fn. 4 5, above).

147. *Mélanges* (M) 84 (1972), p. 549.

148. Quentin, Introduction, p. vii.

149. Waché, 'Duchesne', Frontispiece.

150. Allocution by Pope Paul VI, *Collection* 58, p. 6.

6. Norman Hepburn Baynes (1877–1961): Byzantine Scholarship

1. I have taken the biographical information from J. M. Hussey's, 'Norman Hepburn Baynes', *Proc. of the British Academy* 49 (1963), pp. 365–73.

2. Hussey, 'Norman Hepburn Baynes', pp. 365–6.

3. 'The First Campaign of Heraclius against Persia', *EHR* 19 (1904), pp. 694–702.

4. *EHR* 25, pp. 625–43. Republished in *Byzantine Studies and Other Essays*, London, 1955, pp. 186–208.

5. On the character of Constantius, *Cambridge Mediaeval History*, Vol. 1, p. 77.

6. Ammianus Marcellinus, *Res Gestae* (Loeb ed.), xxvii.8.1.

7. See Frend, 'Pagans, Christians and the Barbarian Conspiracy', *Britannia* 23 (1992), pp. 128–30.

8. Ammianus Marcellinus, *Res Gestae*, xviii.2.3, and Julian (Loeb ed.), *Letter to the Athenians*, 279–80, cf. Zosimus, *Hist. Nova* (ed. Mendelsohn), iii.5.

9. *Cambridge Mediaeval History*, Vol. 2, Ch. 9.

10. 'Restoration of the True Cross', *EHR* (1912), pp. 287–99.

11. Hussey, 'Norman Hepburn Baynes', pp. 366–7.

12. Hussey, 'Norman Hepburn Baynes', p. 367.

13. *JRS* 12 (1922), pp. 207–29, at pp. 207–20.

14. Republished as 'Stilicho and the Barbarian Invasions', *Byzantine Studies and Other Essays*, London, 1955, Ch. 25, pp. 326–45.

15. 'Stilicho and the Barbarian Invasions', p. 330.

16. 'Stilicho and the Barbarian Invasions', p. 331.

17. 'Stilicho and the Barbarian Invasions', p. 341.

18. 'Stilicho and the Barbarian Invasions', p. 341.

19. 'Justinian and Amalasuntha', *Byzantine Studies and Other Essays*, pp. 222–6.

20. Discussed under, 'The Invasion of Radagaisus and the Revolt of Constantine', *Byzantine Studies and Other Essays*, pp. 338–42.

21. Zosimus, *Hist. Nova* (ed. Mendelsohn), vi.5; and see J. F. Drinkwater,

'The Usurper Constantine III (407–411) and Jovinus (411–413)', *Britannia* 29 (1998), pp. 269–98, at 285–6, not 'a nationalist uprising' nor 'Christian heresy' nor 'Marxist *Klassenkampf*'. Perhaps a deliberate step to weaken Constantine, by encouraging the British *civitates* to revolt from his rule. For Honorius, 'Letter to the British Cities', see Zosimus, *Hist. Nova*, vi.10.

22. I recommend Arnaldo Momigliano's chapter, 'An Unsolved Problem of Historical Forgery: The "Scriptores Historiae Augustae"', in *Studies in Historiography*, London, 1965, with Appendices and notes, Ch. 9, as a good starting point for readers' research.

23. H. Dessau, 'Über Zeit und Persönlichkeit der S.H.A.', *Hermes* 21 (1889), pp. 337–92.

24. *Historia Augusta Papers*, Oxford, 1983, p. 128: the writer was 'an imposter', and the *Historia* 'even a hoax' (p. 11).

25. Syme, *Historia Augusta Papers*, pp. 13–14.

26. Baynes, *The Historia Augusta: Its Date and Purpose* (1926), pp. 58–9.

27. 'I am convinced that from the first the S.H.A. was planned as a single work with a single aim' (Baynes, *Historia Augusta*, p. 74).

28. Baynes, *Historia Augusta*, pp. 62–3.

29. Baynes, *Historia Augusta*, p. 61.

30. Baynes, *Historia Augusta*, p. 72.

31. T. D. Barnes, 'The Lost *Kaisergeschichte* and the Latin Historical Tradition', in *Early Christianity and the Roman Empire*, Collected Papers, Variorum Reprints, 1984, ch. iv.42.

32. Baynes, *Historia Augusta*, p. 58.

33. *Claudius*, 10.7.

34. *Aurelian*, 11.4.

35. Spartian, *Septimius Severus*, 17.1.

36. Lampridius, *Severus Alexander*, 22.5.

37. Euscbius, *HE* vi.20: 'Many learned churchmen flourished at this time' (i.e., in the reign of Alexander Severus), and vi.21 for Origen's meeting with the empress Mamaea.

38. Optatus, *Acta Purgationis Felicis* (ed. C. Ziwsa), *CSEL* 26, p. 203. But 'clearly Christianity was not the main concern of the author or authors of the *Historia Augusta* taken as a whole' (so Momigliano, 'Unsolved Problem', p. 164). Hence, I am inclined to the view that the traditional view of the *SHA*'s authorship, i.e., in the West, between 293 and 325 may have something to be said for it.

39. H. Chadwick, *Constantine and the Christian Church*, 2nd edn, Oxford, 1962, p. 6.

40. *Constantine and the Christian Church*, p. 6. On the 'Speech to the Assembly of the Saints', spoken 'on the Good Friday of any year between 317 and 324', see T. D. Barnes, *Constantine and Eusebius*, 1981, pp. 73–6.

41. *Pap. London*, 878, corresponding to Eusebius, *Vita Const.*, ii.26–9. See A.

H. M. Jones, *JEH* 5 (1954), pp. 196–200; and Chadwick, *Constantine and the Christian Church*, p. vi.

42. E.g., Henri Grégoire whose series of articles attacking the veracity of the *Vita* are recorded by Chadwick, *Constantine and the Christian Church*, pp. iv–vi. The most important of these was 'L'authenticité et l'historicité de la "Vita Constantini" attribueé à Eusèbe de Césarée', *Bull. de l'Académie Royale Belge*, Classe des Lettres, Ser. 5.39 (1953), pp. 462–79.

43. See above, p. 126.

44. 'Ignominiosissima tolerantia', Augustine, *Ad Donatistas post Collationem*, 31.54. See also, H. Doerries, *Constantine and Religious Liberty*, tr. R. Bainton, New Haven, 1960, pp. 81–103.

45. Baynes, *Historia Augusta*, p.16 and n. 54, in justification.

46. Eusebius, *Vita Constantini*, ii.42; Baynes, *Historia Augusta*, p. 17.

47. Eusebius, *Vita Constantini*, ii.64–72.

48. Baynes, *Historia Augusta*, p. 21–5 (with documentation).

49. Baynes, *Historia Augusta*, pp. 4–5 and n. 5, discussing the views of some of his predecessors in the field.

50. Duchesne, *The Early History of the Christian Church* (Eng. trans. 1908), ii, p. 48 n. 2. Baynes, *Historia Augusta*, p.32, n. 8.

51. Baynes, *Historia Augusta*, p. 33.

52. Chadwick, *Constantine and the Christian Church*, p. iii.

53. *Liber Pontificalis* (Duchesne) i.172 and 176. See also, A. Alföldi, *The Conversion of Constantine and Pagan Rome*, tr. H. Mattingly, Oxford, 1969, pp. 51–2.

54. Constantinian *folles* in the writer's possession.

55. Mattingly, *Roman Coins*, London, 1928, p. 248 and Pl. lxiii.6. Alföldi, *Conversion of Constantine*, p. 43.

56. See above, pp. 125–6.

57. See Barnes, *Constantine and Eusebius*, p. 246.

58. *CAH.*, Vol. 12, pp. 671–4.

59. *CAH.*, Vol. 12, p. 698.

60. *Historical Association Pamphlet* 104, London, 1936 = Baynes, *Byzantine Studies*, ch. 21, pp. 288–306.

61. Baynes, *Political Ideas*, p. 298.

62. *De Doctrina Christiana*, Bk. iii, 30–7.

63. Cited by Augustine, *Contra Julianum* Opus Imperfectum, iv.46, compare iii.170.

64. Augustine, *Ep.* (Divjak) 10.5.3 (*CSEL* 88, p. 49). Contrasted with 'barbarica captivitate'. Christian sovereigns must, however, be subject to the law of Christ. Augustine, *Contra Cresconium* iii.51 and *Ep.* 105.7. Baynes, pp. 299–301.

65. Baynes, *Byzantine Studies*, pp. 229, 302. *De Civitate Dei* 1.30 (lust for rule) and v.12 (glory) and v.18–19. See R. A. Markus, *History and Society in the Theology of St Augustine*, 1970, p. 60.

66. Baynes, *Byzantine Studies*, p. 302.

67. Thus, Augustine, *Ep.* 93.5.17, *Contra Epist. Parmeniani* 1.10.16 and 11.17; and Markus, *Saeculum, History and Society in the Theology of St Augustine*, pp. 136ff.

68. *De Civitate Dei* xix.24.1; Baynes, *Byzantine Studies*, p. 305; Markus, *Saeculum, History and Society in the Theology of St Augustine*, p. 66.

69. Robert Markus, *Saeculum, History and Society in the Age of St Augustine*, Cambridge, 1970.

70. See Hussey, 'Norman Hepburn Baynes', p. 367.

71. Hussey, 'Norman Hepburn Baynes', pp. 367–8.

72. Hussey, 'Norman Hepburn Baynes', p. 68.

73. Baynes, *The Speeches of Adolf Hitler, August 1922–August 1939*, Royal Institute of International Affairs, 1942, Vol. 1, pp. 777–829. Baynes was impressed with its content and importance and translated it in its entirety. His long-standing interest in things German, shown by the long quotations in German in his *Historia Augusta*, would be worth a study.

74. *Speeches*, Vol. 2, p. 1416.

75. *Speeches*, Vol. 2, p. 1418.

76. *Speeches*, Vol. 2, p. 1423.

77. *Speeches*, Vol. 2, pp. 1424–5.

78. *Speeches*, Vol. 2, p. 1356.

79. *Speeches*, Vol. 2, p. 1591.

80. Ribbentrop, 'Memorandum for the Führer', dated 2 January 1938. *Documents on German Foreign Policy*, HMSO, Vol. 1, p. 168. The writer was a member of the Editorial Board 1947–51.

81. *Documents on German Foreign Policy*, Vol. 13, p. 920: 'Germany had spared England too long because she believed the English would still possibly join up'.

82. *Speeches*, Vol. 2, p. 1687.

83. Reprinted as an Appendix to *Byzantine Studies*. Even in this dark hour it never crossed the mind of Baynes that we might lose the war. I can testify to the same spirit in the Cabinet Offices.

84. *Byzantine Studies*, p. 377.

85. *Byzantine Studies*, p. 387.

86. *Byzantine Studies*, p. 388.

87. *Byzantine Studies*, p. 388. Compare p. 373 for Baynes's enthusiasm for the cockney origins of the college.

88. Published by Oxford University Press, 1942.

89. Romanes Lecture, p. 20.

90. Romanes Lecture, p. 11, quoting Hitler's views.

91. Romanes Lecture, p.12.

92. Romanes Lecture, p. 27.

93. *Byzantine Studies and Other Essays*, ch. 1. The James Bryce Memorial

Lecture delivered at Somerville College, Oxford, on 17 November 1945.

94. *Byzantine Studies and Other Essays*, p. 2.

95. *Byzantine Studies and Other Essays*, p.10. Baynes quotes Eusebius, *Demonstratio Evang.* iii.7.140. Unification of the (eastern) Mediterranean under the single government of Rome had greatly facilitated the spread of the early Christian mission.

96. *Byzantine Studies and Other Essays*, p. 13.

97. 'The Thought-World of East Rome' (1947) = *Byzantine Studies and Other Essays*, ch. 2.

98. *Byzantine Studies and Other Essays*, pp. 44–5.

99. *Byzantine Studies and Other Essays*, p. 29.

100. *Byzantine Studies and Other Essays*, p. 36.

101. *Byzantine Studies and Other Essays*, p. 46.

102. Hussey, 'Norman Hepburn Baynes', pp. 368–9.

103. 'Letter to N. H. Baynes from Hugh Last', *JRS* 37 (1947), pp. 152–6.

104. 'Letter to N. H. Baynes from Hugh Last', p. 155.

105. Baynes and Moss, *Byzantium: An Introduction to East Roman Civilisation*, Oxford, 1948.

106. H. Grégoire, 'The Byzantine Church', in Baynes and Moss, *Byzantium*, p. 132.

107. Elizabeth Dawes and N. H. Baynes, *Three Byzantine Saints: Daniel the Stylite, Theodore of Sykeon, John the Almsgiver*, Oxford, 1948.

108. Dawes and Baynes, *Three Byzantine Saints*, p. 73.

109. *Byzantine Studies and Other Essays*, London, 1955.

110. H. Last, 'The Study of the Persecutions', *JRS* 27 (1937), pp. 80–92.

111. *Byzantine Studies and Other Essays*, pp. 317–21.

112. *Byzantine Studies and Other Essays*, pp. 144–68. It seems incredible that this essay was never previously published.

113. Baynes, *The Custody of a Tradition*, pp. 376–7.

114. Published by Cambridge University Press, 1929, 184pp.

115. In reply to my enthusiasm following the publication of *The Donatist Church* in 1952, Baynes reminded me that 'if I succeeded in placing one extra block on the pyramid of knowledge in my lifetime, I had done well!'

Epilogue

1. Published by Divjak in *CSEL* 88 (1981), and see for commentary, various contributors, *Les Lettres de Saint Augustin découvertes par Johannes Divjak*, Études Augustiniennes, Paris, 1983.

2. Published by F. Dolbeau as 'Sermons inédites de Saint Augustin prêchés en 397', *Revue Bénédictine* 101 (1991), pp. 240–56, and subsequent numbers, and in the *Revue des Études Augustiniennes* (1991) and following years.

3. Cited from R. McL. Wilson in Colin Sherbok and J. M. Court (eds), *Religious Diversity in the Roman World: A Survey of Recent Scholarship*, Sheffield, 2001, p. 171.

4. Kenneth Painter, *The Water Newton Early Christian Silver*, British Museum Publications, 1977.

5. Catherine Johns and Roger Bland, 'The Hoxne Later Roman Treasure', *Britannia* 25 (1994), pp. 165–73.

6. See M. O. H. Carver, *The Age of Sutton Hoo*, London, 1992, and, for the 1939 excavations, C. W. Phillips and others, 'The Sutton Hoo Ship Burial', *Antiquity* 14 (1940).

7. Oxford Early Christian Studies, published by Oxford University Press, are a welcome sign of activity, but more needs to be done before we achieve the bulk and continuity characteristic of similar Continental series such as *Sources chrétiens*.

8. Reports published in the *Journal of Egyptian Archaeology* (1964) and following.

9. See Phillipson's lecture published in the *Proc. of the British Academy* III (with earlier bibliography)(2001), pp. 23–59.

10. Report by Richard Miles, the excavator, forthcoming.

11. *CIL*, viii.10576, 25902.

12. J. Carcopino, 'L'Inscription d'Ain el Djemala', *Mélanges de l'École française de Rome*, 26 (1906), pp. 365–461.

Select Bibliography

While I do not intend to add to the text of this book, there are a number of useful books on early Christian history recently published in the English-speaking world, to which the attention of readers is drawn.

Barnes, T. D., *Constantine and Eusebius*, Cambridge, Mass., 1981.

Berardino, Angelo (ed.), *Encyclopedia of the Early Church*, English translation, Cambridge, 1991.

Bowersock, G. W., *Hellenism in Late Antiquity*, Ann Arbor, 1990.

Brown, Peter, *Power and Persuasion in Late Antiquity*, London, 1992.

—— *The Body and Society: Men, Women and Sexual Renunciation in Early Christianity*, New York, 1988.

Chadwick, Henry, *Heresy and Orthodoxy in the Early Church*, Aldershot, 1991.

—— *The Church and Ancient Society*, Oxford, 2001.

Drake, H. A., *Constantine and the Bishops*, Baltimore, 1990.

Esler, Philip F. (ed.), *The Early Christian World*, 2 vols, London, 2000 (essays on many aspects of early Christian life and thought).

Fowden, G., *Empire to Commonwealth*, Princeton, 1993.

Frend, W. H. C., *The Archaeology of Early Christianity*, London and Minneapolis, 1996

—— *Orthodoxy, Paganism and Dissent in the Early Christian Centuries*, Aldershot, 2002.

Garnsey, P., and C. Humphress, *The Evolution of the Late Antique World*, Cambridge, 2001.

Hall, Stuart G., *Doctrine and Practice in the Early Church*, London, 1991.

Hanson, R. P. C., *The Search for the Christian Doctrine of God*, Edinburgh, 1988.

Horbury, W., *Jews and Christians in Contact and Controversy*, Edinburgh, 1998.

Kelly, J. N. D., *Golden Mouth: The Story of John Chrysostom*, London, 1995.

Lane Fox, R., *Pagans and Christians*, Harmondsworth, 1986.

Lieu, S. N. C., *Manichaeism*, 2nd edn, Tübingen, 1992.

—— *Manichaeism in Mesopotamia and the Roman East*, London, 1994.

McKechnie, Paul, *The First Christian Centuries*, Leicester, 2001.

McLynn, N. B., *Ambrose of Milan: Church and Court in a Christian Capital*, Berkeley, 1994.

Markus, R. A., *The End of Ancient Christianity*, Cambridge, 1990.

——*Sacred and Secular*, 2nd edn, Cambridge, 1990 (important for the study of St Augustine).

Minns, D., *Irenaeus*, Washington, D.C., 1994.

Palmer, A. M., *Prudentius on the Martyrs*, Oxford, 1989.

Pelikan, J., *Christianity and Classical Culture*, New Haven, 1993.

Robinson, J. M., *The Nag Hammadi Documents in English*, 3rd edn, Leiden, 1988.

Ross, B. A., *Synesius of Cyrene*, Lund, 1991.

Rousseau, P., *Basil of Caesarea*, Berkeley, 1994.

Russell, N., *Cyril of Alexandria*, London, 2000.

Shahid, I., *Byzantium and the Arabs in the Fifth Century*, Dumbarton Oaks, 1989.

Stead, C. C., *Doctrine and Philosophy in Early Christianity*, Aldershot, 2002.

Thomas, C., *Christianity in Roman Britain to A.D. 500*, London, 1981.

Wickham, L. R., *Conflicts of Conscience and Law in the Fourth Century Church*, Liverpool, 1997.

Wilken, R. C., *The Land Called Holy*, New Haven, 1992.

Williams, Rowan D., *Arius*, 2nd edn, London, 2001.

Young, F., *From Nicea to Chalcedon*, London, 1983.

Index